Aesthetics:
The Key Thinkers

Continuum *Key Thinkers*

The *Key Thinkers* series is aimed at undergraduate students and offers clear, concise and accessible edited guides to the key thinkers in each of the central topics in philosophy. Each book offers a comprehensive overview of the major thinkers who have contributed to the historical development of a key area of philosophy, providing a survey of their major works and the evolution of the central ideas in that area.

Key Thinkers in Philosophy available now from Continuum:

Epistemology, edited by Stephen Hetherington
Ethics, edited by Tom Angier
Philosophy of Language, edited by Barry Lee
Philosophy of Religion, edited by Jeffrey J. Jordan
Philosophy of Science, edited by James Robert Brown

Aesthetics:
The Key Thinkers

Edited by
Alessandro Giovannelli

continuum

Continuum International Publishing Group

The Tower Building
11 York Road
London SE1 7NX

80 Maiden Lane
Suite 704
New York NY 10038

www.continuumbooks.com

British Library Cataloguing-in-Publication Data
A catalogue record for this book is available from the British Library.

ISBN: HB: 978-1-4411-9878-5
       PB: 978-1-4411-8777-2

Library of Congress Cataloging-in-Publication Data
Aesthetics : the key thinkers / [edited by] Alessandro Giovannelli.
       p. cm. – (Key thinkers)
Includes bibliographical references and index.
       ISBN 978-1-4411-9878-5 (hardcover) – ISBN 978-1-4411-8777-2 (pbk.) – ISBN 978-1-4411-4154-5 (ePub) – ISBN 978-1-4411-8027-8 (PDF) 1. Aesthetics–History–Sources. I. Giovannelli, Alessandro. II. Title. III. Series.

BH81.A39 2011
111′.8509–dc23

2011028614

Typeset by Newgen Imaging Systems Pvt Ltd, Chennai, India
Printed and bound in India

Contents

Notes on Contributors

Sondra Bacharach is Senior Lecturer of Philosophy at Victoria University of Wellington (New Zealand). She has published articles and book chapters on collaborative artistic authorship, the role of historical context in art interpretation and individuation, and philosophy in film.

Malcolm Budd is Emeritus Grote Professor of Philosophy of Mind and Logic at University College London (UK), Fellow of the British Academy, and President of the British Society of Aesthetics. His most recent books are *The Aesthetic Appreciation of Nature* and *Aesthetic Essays*.

Noël Carroll is Distinguished Professor of Philosophy at the Graduate Center of the City University of New York (USA), and past President of the American Society for Aesthetics. His long list of books and articles includes his most recent *Art in Three Dimensions*.

Angela Curran is Assistant Professor of Philosophy at Carleton College (USA). She has coedited *The Philosophy of Film: Introductory Text and Readings* and is currently working on *the Routledge Guidebook to Aristotle and the Poetics*.

David Davies is Professor of Philosophy at McGill University (Canada). He has published widely in aesthetics, especially on issues in philosophy of film, photography, literature, and the visual arts. He is the author of *Art as Performance*, *Aesthetics and Literature*, and *Philosophy of the Performing Arts*.

Richard Eldridge is Charles and Harriett Cox McDowell Professor of Philosophy at Swarthmore College (USA). His most recent books are *Literature, Life, and Modernity* and the coedited collection *Stanley Cavell and Literary Criticism: Consequences of Skepticism* (Continuum).

Susan Feagin is Research Professor of Philosophy at Temple University (USA) and Editor of the *Journal of Aesthetics and Art Criticism*. She has published many journal articles and book chapters, and is the author of *Reading with Feeling: The Aesthetics of Appreciation*.

Gian Carlo Garfagnini is Professor of Medieval Philosophy at the University of Florence (Italy) and Vice-President of the Italian Dante Society. He has authored numerous articles, focusing especially on the relationship between ethics and politics between the thirteenth and the fifteenth centuries.

Alessandro Giovannelli is Assistant Professor of Philosophy at Lafayette College (USA). He has published articles and book chapters on the imaginative engagement with characters, art and ethics, and the philosophy of film and literature.

Alan H. Goldman is William R. Kenan, Jr. Professor of Humanities and Professor of Philosophy at the College of William and Mary (USA). His most recent books are: *Aesthetic Value*; *Practical Rules: When We Need Them and When We Don't*; and *Reasons from Within: Desires and Values*.

Scott Jenkins is Assistant Professor of Philosophy at the University of Kansas (USA). His major research interests are Kant, German Idealism, and Nietzsche, on all of which he has published several articles.

Gary Kemp is Senior Lecturer of Philosophy at the University of Glasgow (UK). He mainly works in philosophy of logic and language but has a serious interest in aesthetics. His latest book is the forthcoming *Quine versus Davidson: Truth, Reference and Meaning*.

Thomas Leddy is Professor of Philosophy at San José State University (USA). He is the author of many articles and contributions, focusing on art interpretation, creativity, the aesthetics of architecture, pragmatist aesthetics, and the aesthetics of the everyday.

Gerhard Richter is Professor of German and Comparative Literature at Brown University (USA). His most recent book, titled *Afterness: Figures of Following in Modern Thought and Aesthetics*, is forthcoming.

Elisabeth Schellekens is Senior Lecturer at the University of Durham (UK) and Associate Editor of the *British Journal of Aesthetics*. She has published her *Aesthetics and Morality* with Continuum and is coauthor (with Peter Goldie) of *Who's Afraid of Conceptual Art*.

Joseph Shieber is Associate Professor of Philosophy at Lafayette College (USA). He has published articles and book chapters in epistemology, philosophy of language, the history of modern philosophy, and the history of twentieth-century analytic philosophy.

Robert Stecker is Professor of Philosophy at Central Michigan University (USA). His numerous publications include the books: *Artworks: Definition, Meaning, Value*; *Interpretation and Construction: Art, Speech, and the Law*; and *Aesthetics and Philosophy of Art*.

INTRODUCTION

Alessandro Giovannelli

Aesthetics, the discipline aimed at the study of beauty and art, is flourishing within anglophone, analytic philosophy.[1] In the past 30 years or so, there has been a boom in publications, an expansion in the scope of the discipline's interests, and a widening of the range of questions it addresses. Some of the reasons for this rapid growth have to do with the evolution of philosophy as an academic discipline within the English-speaking world. Most notably, analytic philosophy has expanded into all areas of investigation, well beyond its original focus on language and the sciences, and beyond its more traditional subfields of logic, metaphysics, epistemology, and ethics. In addition, aesthetics has benefited from contemporary philosophy's opening up to the idea that language is only one of the loci of meaning, and that truth and knowledge need not be found only in literal descriptions of the world. Hence, aesthetics has become a privileged place for investigations of the conveyance of meaning and truth by means of metaphor, fiction, or expression, brought about by both linguistic and nonlinguistic means. Further, like analytic philosophy in general, analytic aesthetics has become eclectic, open to the ideas and methods of other disciplines and programs, especially scientific ones: psychology and anthropology, as well as cognitive science and evolutionary biology for example.

Other reasons for the good health of contemporary analytic aesthetics are more specific. First of all, some of the developments of contemporary art call for theoretical reflection. Whether it is through environmental or urban art, experimental theater or conceptual architecture, contemporary art continues to prompt philosophical thinking on such concepts as "art," "art form," and "medium." There is also increasing attention, within the academic circles and society at large, for more broadly construed artistic phenomena—including those that belong to the *popular* or *mass* arts—and for their possible impact on society (TV shows, music videos, graphic novels, fashion design, and even commercial advertising, for example, are considered art forms by many—and debates on their various effects on audiences are quite frequent). Further, the invention of new media, especially the various digital technologies, has brought with itself great potential for changing traditional art forms, introducing new forms of art, and expanding access to artistic phenomena. In sum, as the world of art has changed and expanded, contemporary aesthetics has become more and more inclusive, with a consequent proliferation of the questions it addresses.

Finally, it should be mentioned how changes within other disciplines that target the arts, especially literary and film theory, have also contributed to the flourishing of analytic aesthetics. As many scholars working in those disciplines directed themselves toward a cultural studies approach, they left room for philosophers to address issues regarding the nature, value, and experience of art in its different forms. Hence, today it is mostly within aesthetics that such questions as, say, the role of narrators in literary works or the importance of the medium in art cinema are asked.

Whatever else could be said about aesthetics today, an approach to the discipline should closely look at its historical development. This collection aims at providing an overview of philosophical aesthetics by looking at the main thinkers who shaped the discipline throughout its history. As the essays here collected prove, the philosophical interest for matters regarding the arts and aesthetic experience has accompanied the history of Western philosophy since its origins. That should not be surprising, given the existence of artistic practices throughout human history and of a natural propensity, in humans, toward the aesthetic appreciation of objects as found in nature, art, or ordinary experience.

As a unitary philosophical discipline, however, aesthetics is a fairly recent product. The contemporary use of the term "aesthetics" (from the Greek *aisthētikos* for "of sense perception") is due to Alexander Baumgarten (1714–1762), who adopted it in his 1735 dissertation on poetry (1954), to designate the science of knowledge acquired through the senses. It was Kant who in 1790, in the Preface to his *Critique of the Power of Judgment*, called "aesthetic" those judgments that "concern the beautiful and the sublime in nature or art" (2001, 57). Prior to finding unitary treatment within an identifiable discipline—in the eight-eenth and indeed more fully in the nineteenth century (see Chapter 6, on Hegel)—aesthetic questions were addressed either as part of broader philosophical projects devoted to metaphysical, epistemologi-cal, or political issues or in treatises dedicated to the individual arts.[2]

It should be noted that nowadays "aesthetics" is most often used interchangeably with "philosophy of art" (a use that dates back to Hegel). The term "aesthetics" in its etymological sense is both broader and narrower than "philosophy of art." The scope of aesthetic issues exceeds that of questions having to do with art, in so far as beauty and other aesthetic qualities can be found outside the realm of art, in natural objects and environments as well as nonartistic human prod-ucts. On the other hand, so many issues regarding the arts have noth-ing to do with aesthetic properties or experiences, not even when the latter are understood most broadly (on the aesthetic, see Chapter 18, section 1). What is art, what is the essence of the different art forms, which values can artworks have, what does the interpretation of an artwork entail, which roles can art play in society or in an individual's personal moral growth, and so on and so forth, are all philosophy of art questions, which do not appear to be immediately aesthetic. Indeed, attempts to reduce the philosophy of art to aesthetics (see, for exam-ple, Chapter 13, on Monroe Beardsley) or the aesthetic appreciation of nature to art (see Chapter 15, on Richard Wollheim, and Chapter 18, section 1) presuppose a distinction between aesthetics and philosophy of art in the first place.

These important qualifications notwithstanding, and keeping in mind the divergence from the etymology of "aesthetics" and the exist-ence of aesthetic questions beyond the realm of art, the identification of aesthetics with the philosophy of art is harmless enough not to raise worries in the following.

Going through the history of aesthetics also means encounter-ing different conceptions of art: as not distinguished, for the ancient Greeks, from other technical activities (say, carpentry) or from what we now refer to as "crafts" (weaving or pottery, for example); or as mostly bound to religious institutions and rituals in medieval times. It is only in the first half of the eighteenth century that the notion of the "fine arts" emerges, thanks to thinkers as Jean-Baptiste Dubos (1670–1742) and that Charles Batteux who, in his 1746 *Les beaux arts réduits à un même principe* (*The Fine Arts Reduced to a Single Principle*) offered the first unified system of the fine arts.[3] And, as mentioned, the notion of the popular or mass arts has become quite crucial in the twentieth and twenty-first centuries.

The eighteen essays that make this book cover twenty-one key thinkers, to which a chapter or portion thereof is dedicated, and also comprise two broad surveys, one on medieval aesthetics (Chapter 3) and one on contemporary developments (Chapter 18). Seeking comprehensiveness would have been unrealistic and hence the list of thinkers covered is necessarily selective. Some sacrifices were imposed by the achievement of two worthwhile goals. On the one hand, room was made for some notable twentieth-century figures who are rarely on the radar of analytic philosophers, being within the province of what is called "continental philosophy": Martin Heidegger, Walter Benjamin, and Theodor W. Adorno. On the other hand, the collection dedicates substantial space to contemporary aesthetics, through six chapters devoted to post-1950 aesthetics: on Monroe Beardsley, Nelson Goodman, Richard Wollheim, Arthur Danto, and Kendall Walton, complemented by the chapter on contemporary developments. It should be noted that the final essay also addresses, in limited detail, the views of key figures who do not have a dedicated chapter, notably Frank Sibley (1923–1996) and George Dickie (b. 1926). Yet, the essay mostly expands on the views of some leading thinkers in today's aesthetics. It is especially exciting, of course, that several of the contributors to this collection figure among them.

The authors of the chapters were asked to combine clarity to rigor and sophistication, hence allowing readers with different degrees of acquaintance with the norms of philosophical scholarship to have access to the main ideas of the thinkers covered. The essays they produced prove that this was not just desirable but also achievable. Hence, the audience for this book can reasonably range from the beginner who wants to learn about the field of aesthetics to the reader who is better versed in the discipline and seeks insightful perspectives on these key thinkers. Naturally, the book can also be used as a companion to the primary literature. Accordingly, the bibliographies appended to each chapter list the primary sources and suggest opportunities for further reading.

Each chapter is self-contained and can be read independently of the others. Of course, the most natural way of approaching the essays is by following the chronological order. The traditional historical division would be as follows: ancient aesthetics (Chapters 1–2, on Plato and Aristotle); medieval aesthetics (Chapter 3); the modern period (Chapters 4–5, on Hume and Kant); the eighteenth-nineteenth century (Chapters 6–7, covering Hegel, Schopenhauer, and Nietzsche); the contemporary period, divided between the early part of the twentieth century (Chapters 8–12, from Croce through Adorno) and the second half of the twentieth century through our times (Chapters 13–18).

The chapters and parts thereof can also be looked at in clusters, according to one's specific interests, with informative connections, comparisons, and contrasts thereby emerging. Perhaps the most obvious of such clusters is one that concentrates on the role of representation in art, the notion of realism, and more generally art's symbolic relation to reality. To that effect, the reader might want to look at the chapters on Plato and Aristotle, at the medieval discussion on iconoclasm (Chapter 3, section 2), and—for the contemporary approaches—at the essays on Goodman, Wollheim, Danto, and Walton especially. A nice contrast could be achieved by adding the essay on Fry and Bell. Naturally, all the above-mentioned authors are particularly relevant to addressing the relationship between art and knowledge, although in that respect it is also significant to look at Schopenhauer, Nietzsche, Benjamin, and Adorno.

For the relation between art and emotion, an equally ambitious route as the one just presented could be followed. It would comprise Plato, Aristotle, Hume, Kant, Croce, Collingwood, Fry, Bell, Dewey (who, with the chapter on Croce and Collingwood, also constitutes a small cluster on art as expression), and section 5 of Chapter 18. For the more specific interest in tragedy and the emotions it elicits, it would be pertinent to combine Aristotle to Hume (section 6) and to Nietzsche (and, again, to section 5 of Chapter 18).

The place and role of art in society can be addressed by concentrating on Plato, Aristotle, Nietzsche, Dewey, Benjamin, and Adorno. The intertwining between art and culture and the importance of art history are instead central to Hegel's system of philosophy, but also to Danto's approach and the institutional and historical definitions discussed in section 2 of Chapter 18.

The theme of beauty is dominant in medieval aesthetics and in Kant. Yet, the relevant chapters would be best referred back to the essay on

Plato. A broader cluster on the notion of aesthetic experience could comprise the relevant parts in the essays on medieval aesthetics, Kant, Fry, Bell, Dewey, Beardsley, and in Chapter 18 (section 1).

The role and nature of interpretation and art criticism are emphasized in the essays on Hume, Dewey, Benjamin, and, in different ways, in all the chapters on contemporary analytic aesthetics from Beardsley onwards.

Additional smaller clusters can be identified. For instance, the reader interested in music will find Schopenhauer, Nietzsche, Dewey, and Adorno especially relevant. The issue of creativity in art is differently addressed by Plato, on the one hand, and Dewey, on the other. Finally, intriguing connections can be established between Heidegger and Goodman, for the view that art can construct worlds, and perhaps the medieval conception of the world as God's work of art.

* * *

I am thankful to Sarah Campbell and her staff at Continuum for their ongoing assistance. Many thanks to Pam Bodenhorn for her assistance in compiling the index. I am also thankful to Lafayette College for supporting the project through a publishing grant and its Excel Program, which allows students to assist with scholarly projects. Indeed, the cooperation of Jonathan Cohn, Cara Cordeaux, and especially Eric Henney has been invaluable. I am in debt to Jerrold Levinson for his advice and careful comments. Most of all, I am thankful to the sixteen philosophers and friends who have accepted to lend their expertise and time to this project. I am honored to have had the opportunity of gathering a group of scholars from five different countries.

Notes

1 Analytic philosophy is no longer exclusively anglophone. Yet, it remains dominant only within the English-speaking countries and Scandinavia.
2 Paradigmatic of the inclusion of aesthetic questions within broader frameworks are the examples of Plato and Aristotle, and of the medieval thinkers (Chapters 1–3). The approach to single art forms is somewhat exemplified by, again, Aristotle and by Hume in his essay on tragedy (Chapter 4, section 6). More paradigmatic examples would be, however, such works as Vitruvius's first century BCE *Ten Books on Architecture* (2001) or Leon Battista Alberti's 1436 *On Painting* (1966).

3 The classical account of the emergence of the notion of "fine arts" and of a system of the arts is Kristeller (1951/1952).

References

Alberti, Leon Battista. 1966. *On Painting*. John R. Spencer (ed.). New Haven, CT: Yale University Press.

Baumgarten, Alexander Gottlieb. 1954. *Reflections on Poetry, Alexander Gottlieb Baumgarten's Meditationes philosophicae de nonnullis ad poema pertinenibus*. Karl Aschenbrennen and William Holter (trans.). Berkeley, CA: University of California Press.

Kant, Immanuel. 2001. *Critique of the Power of Judgment*. Paul Guyer and Eric Matthews (trans.). Cambridge: Cambridge University Press.

Kristeller, Paul Oskar. 1951/1952. "The Modern System of the Arts: A Study in the History of Aesthetics," parts I and II. *Journal of the History of Ideas*, 12, 496–527 (1951), and 13, 17–46 (1952).

Vitruvius. 2001. *Ten Books on Architecture*. Ingrid Rowland and Thomas Howe (eds.). Cambridge: Cambridge University Press.

CHAPTER 1

PLATO
(c. 427–347 BCE)

Robert Stecker

With respect to the arts, Plato is most famous for purportedly banning one particular art form—poetry—from the Republic, his ideal state. Another very common attribution is that he defines art as representation. Often enough, overviews of the history of aesthetics leave matters there.

So we should start by clearing the decks. Plato never did these two things for which he is most famous. First, there is no total ban on poetry. He did give several important criticisms of poetry that people still grapple with today, and did exclude poetry from many of the functions it had in the Athens of his day, and that the representational arts still have for us today. He advocated the censorship of much poetry but at the same time gave poetry a crucial role in the early education of the leaders of the state. Second, Plato never defines art as representation nor in any other terms. *Mimēsis*, a Greek word that is sometimes appropriately translated "representation," but at other times should be translated as "imitation" or "image-making," plays a crucial organizing role in his thinking about the several art forms, but the issue of defining what we now call the fine arts was not one Plato took up. He never asks, "what is art?" in the way he does ask, "what is justice?" or "what is piety?" His interest with respect to the arts lay elsewhere.

Plato's main interest in the arts concerns the closely related issues of their effect on people, their value, and, in the light of these, the role they should play in society. In Plato's Athens, poetry was thought to be a repository of both knowledge and wisdom. Plato questions not only whether this reputation is deserved, but also whether poetry in particular, and art in general, might in fact create a barrier to the acquisition of these goods. Second, Plato recognizes that poetry and other arts are both expressive of states of mind and have a powerful emotional effect on their audience. But he wonders whether this is a good or bad thing. Finally, a theme that runs well beyond Plato's thinking about the arts is whether we should count all pleasures as goods. Included in this thinking are the pleasures of sights and sounds—what we might today call aesthetic pleasure. Plato recognizes that "lovers of sights and sounds" truly enjoy those things but he questions whether this pleasure is always something of positive value (*Republic*, Book V, 476b). Plato's thinking on these matters—what one might call his critique of artistic value—will occupy the bulk of this chapter, but we should first become clear about the concept of art he brings to the table.

1. Plato and the concept of art

Plato wrote about individual art forms such as poetry, music, and painting, but there is some controversy as to whether he had a concept under which he could think of these forms as *art* forms. Part of this controversy derives from the now widely held view that the concept of fine art, which groups together poetry, music, painting, sculpture, and architecture, only arose in the eighteenth century and hence before that there was just no concept that closely enough corresponds to our concept of art or the fine arts. The Greek word that is the best candidate for translation as "art" is *technē*, which covers all sorts of activities and their products that can be practiced or produced skillfully by learning a set of rules or procedures. Hence, such human activities as navigation and saddle making are both instances of *technē*. On the other hand, in the dialogue *Ion*, Plato has the character Socrates question whether poetry is really produced by skill or knowledge, or instead by inspiration. If the only concept available to Plato when thinking about the arts were derived from the meaning of *technē*, he would be in a poor position to think about art in the relevant sense.

But there is no reason to think Plato in particular or the ancient Greeks in general had such limited conceptual resources. In Book III of the *Republic*, Plato links together poetry and music with painting, sculpture, architecture, embroidery, weaving, and furniture making—arts and crafts that produce items all capable of grace, rhythm, and harmony, or of course their opposites (401a). It is true that there is no sharp line here between art and craft; yet it is at least as important that the principle organizing the items mentioned in this part of the *Republic* is not that of item produced by skill or according to rules but rather item capable of expressing or exemplifying states of the psyche or (what we would call) aesthetic properties of outer reality.

Even before Plato, there is a tradition of grouping together a collection of "both musicopoetic and visual arts which . . . had come to be considered mimetic" (Halliwell 2002, 43). It is this concept, which Plato adapts for his own purposes, that approximates to our own concept of the arts. In its breadth, it is probably closer to our twenty-first-century concept of art than is the eighteenth-century concept of fine art. It is plausible that conceptions of art or the arts vary over time with respect to the range of things they cover and the crucial properties the conceptions ascribe to those things. This does not prevent us from seeing these varying conceptions as conceptions of art that carve off roughly equivalent practices and forms—poetry, painting, music, and so on—from others.

2. Art and education

Plato discusses poetry and other arts in many dialogues, but the richest source of his aesthetics is the *Republic*, which contains two extended discussions of the arts. The first is found in Books II and III, and the second and most famous of all of Plato's writings on this topic is in the final chapter, Book X.

The relevant stretches of Books II and III are concerned with the early education of the guardians, the ruling class of the state. (The guardians will eventually occupy two different tiers—the actual rulers of that state and the soldiers who protect it—but at this stage they all receive the same education.) The discussion begins with the role of poetic stories in this education and eventually goes on to address music and the other arts and crafts mentioned above. The import of this discussion goes well beyond the role of art in the education of children, but it is a good place to begin.

Regarding poetic stories, the question is never whether they have a role in education, but which stories ought to play this role and which should be excluded. So issues of censorship are definitely in the foreground, but equally important is the power of stories to shape character and the way we perceive and emotionally react to the world. Some stories do this in a harmful way, but others are beneficial.

Stories can be harmful in several different ways. First, they can express falsehoods about important matters such as about the nature of the gods, the behavior of heroes, and the kinds of lives that can achieve happiness or well-being. That stories can do this is not merely a theoretical possibility. The preeminent literature of ancient Greece— the *Iliad* and the *Odyssey* of Homer, the stories of gods and heroes in the poetry of Hesiod, or the tragedies of Aeschylus—are rife with passages that need be eliminated if their works are to be read at all. Second, stories can be harmful in the attitudes and dispositions that they instill. For example, in the works just mentioned, death—both of those one loves and one's own—is portrayed as a great misfortune, and grief is often expressed with wailings, lamentations, and even more excessive behavior, at least as Plato would see it. This is precisely the wrong attitude toward death, according to Plato, if one is to live courageously and put the fact that we die in proper perspective. There is more than one way in which poetry can instill such attitudes. It does so by representing role models such as heroes who possess just such attitudes and who exhibit such behavior. But even more insidious is the kind of dramatic representation where the characters in a story express such attitudes for themselves, and where, in reciting a poem or performing in a play that tells the story, one will naturally be prompted to take on those roles and identify with the characters. In taking on such roles one adopts the attitudes, and this leads to actually acquiring them. This brings us to the last way that stories harm: in allowing us to adopt the character and personality of all types of humanity in acting out dramatic representations, it hinders the formation of the right character and disposition for guardians.

Plato's remedy for avoiding such harm is not to eliminate poetic stories from early education, but to limit stories to those that are beneficial: those that express truths rather than falsehoods about the gods, the heroes, and the type of life that leads to happiness; those that express appropriate attitudes toward life and death, or at least that put misguided attitudes in the mouths of characters who are not role models—that is, men and women of "low character." What can and cannot be dramatically represented is even more strictly limited. Here only the representation of people of high character is permitted, lest one identify with vicious characters or, just as bad, become facile at adopting the attitude of almost anyone. The more one does this, the more one tends to become a person of bad character or of no particular character at all. (A person of bad character acquires dispositions to feel emotions, desires things, and act in ways that are harmful to himself and others. A person of no character does not have firm dispositions one way or the other but is ruled by external circumstances such as the expectation of others or the role one happens to occupy.)

The same goes for music, which in ancient Greece accompanies the recitation of poetry, and even for painting, weaving, embroidery, architecture, and so on. Some of these items may not have an obvious representational content as poetry (and painting) do, but for Plato they all have an expressive character. In virtue of this, they fall under the concept of *mimēsis*, at least as Plato sometimes uses the term. There were a variety of modes of music in ancient Greece, and each mode has a characteristic expressive content. Music expressive of lamentation and grief is as undesirable as poetry and tragic drama that is expressive of those emotions, especially since they would accompany each other. Equally bad are compositions that have a great variety of expressive content, just as the dramatic representation of a great variety of characters is bad. The appropriate kind of music possesses a rhythm and grace of form expressive of the good moral character represented in appropriate poetry. The artifacts that make up the visual environment created by painting, architecture, sculpture, and other arts and crafts are capable of having similar expressive qualities. At their best, they are expressive of a grace and harmony that, as we discover in Book IV, is characteristic of the soul of a just person.

We can learn a good deal about the nature of the arts as Plato conceives them from this discussion of their role in early education. First, although he characterizes the poetic stories he mentions as *pseudeis logoi*, which might be translated either as "false discourses" or as "fictional stories," he believes that they are capable of expressing both truths and falsehoods about important matters, just as we think that fictional literature can tell us something important, or instead mislead us, about the actual world. Second, these stories can express attitudes—some harmful, some beneficial—toward significant aspects of life, and children can easily be influenced to adopt those attitudes. (When we turn to Book X, we will see that adults can be so influenced as well.) Third, the very form of a work can be expressive of a character or a state of mind—some admirable, some contemptible—and this can affect the character and states of mind of those who encounter the works, for good or ill. This permits art forms like music and architecture, and even crafts like embroidery and weaving, to have an expressive character. Even when such works lack what we would regard as representational content, their expressiveness counts as a kind of *mimēsis*.

Most of us would agree that the three characteristics just outlined are important, if not universal, features of artworks. They imply that artworks can be both beneficial or harmful, which seems to be precisely the message of Books II and III. (What I leave out for now is our likely disagreement with Plato about which works are beneficial, which harmful.) Given this implication, it is surprising that Book X gives a much harsher assessment of the value of poetry and painting. We should then try to understand such a critique and why it is so harsh.

3. Art and knowledge

Book X criticizes poetry and, more generally, representational art on two fronts: as a source of illusion and false belief and as a powerful force capable of corrupting the psyche with harmful emotions and attitudes. These criticisms should not surprise the reader of Books II and III, since something similar was already said there. The difference is that in those earlier parts of the *Republic*, these charges were directed at *some* works of art and poetry, and *some* parts of a given work, while allowing for *other* works and passages that not only escape the criticism but also are positively beneficial. This is not so in Book X. Most poetry, with the exception of that which praises the gods and good men, is banished. Representational art more generally is not banished, but, again unlike what occurs in the earlier books, only its failings are under discussion.

Let us focus first on art's failure as a source of knowledge. Plato's conclusion is that art is incapable of being such a source. In fact, he seems to go further and argue that art is incapable of even expressing truths or of representing reality. This radical conclusion again is in tension with his earlier discussion in Books II and III. Plato famously reaches this conclusion about poetry by way of an argument based on an analogy with painting.

The reasoning regarding painting begins with another analogy: that of the images produced by a mirror. Socrates asks Glaucon, his interlocutor, to imagine a craftsman who can make anything, and suggests that the simplest way to do this is to imagine someone who takes a mirror and turns it around in all directions. "With it you can quickly make the sun, the things in the heavens, the earth, yourself, the other animals, manufactured items, plants, and everything else mentioned just now." "I could make them appear, but I couldn't make the things themselves as they truly are" is the correct reply given by Glaucon (596e). Paintings, like mirror images, give the visual appearance of things. Plato develops this idea further with a discourse on the "three beds." The bed with which we are most familiar is the material artifact made by a craftsman. But there is also, according to Plato, the form of the bed—that in which all material beds participate and in virtue of which they are beds. According to the metaphysics Plato develops in the middle books of the *Republic* (Books V, VI, and VII), the forms are what are most real; they have the highest degree of reality. Compared with the form of the bed, even the bed made by a carpenter is a "shadowy" thing. But literal shadows, images, and other "appearances" are even less real, and the first moral of the discourse on the three beds is that paintings are to be put in this category. "Then imitation," Socrates says at this point referring to painting, "is far removed from the truth" (598b). This is a metaphysical conclusion. It is one that can certainly be disputed. Paintings are material artifacts; it can be argued, just as beds are. Representing is a property of the painting—which, if it is a painting of a certain type, shows us how things look. It's a mistake to think of the painting itself as a look or an appearance.

The discourse on the beds also has epistemic implications, which for our purposes are more important. The middle books of the *Republic* develop an epistemological doctrine that claims genuine knowledge is knowledge of the forms. To understand the nature of justice, one may start with examples of just actions, people, or states, but until one knows what makes these instances just, one's understanding falls short of knowledge. What makes them just is their participating in the form of justice; so to know what justice is, one must have knowledge of the form. Once one has that, one may even reject some of the initial examples as things that appeared to be just but in fact were not. Now go back to paintings. Whatever their metaphysical status, they represent appearances and hence grasp "only a small part of each thing and a part that is itself only an image" (598b). Paintings do not even give us true beliefs about the material objects they represent; much less do they give us knowledge of the form that makes the object an instance of its kind. So it is not just that many paintings give us false beliefs, but that they are constitutionally incapable of giving us knowledge.

What is true of painting is true of poetry. It too represents appearances. To do that one needs neither knowledge nor true belief. We may conclude—Socrates suggests—"that all poetic imitators, beginning with Homer, imitate images of virtue and all the other things they write about and have no grasp of the truth" (600e). Poetry too, on this account, is constitutionally incapable of being a source of knowledge.

4. Art and emotion

Both painting and poetry represent the way things appear, and this renders both incapable of providing knowledge or even, by good luck, representing things as they really are. However, poetry has a subject matter that potentially makes it far more dangerous than painting. It represents what human beings do, as well as their beliefs that "as a result of these actions, they are doing either well or badly and . . . experience either pleasure or pain" (603c). In short, drama in particular, but other kinds of poetry as well, represent people acting and reacting in the face of what life throws their way, their motives, the emotions they feel, and their often emotion-driven assessment of their behavior and its outcome. Painting, at least in Book X, represents the surface of things, while poetry represents human beings with inner lives and human actions as components of psychological chain reactions. Poetry does so, however, without real knowledge of human excellence, and furthermore with the aim of pleasing its audience. The behavior of excellent human beings—the behavior recommended by reason, which consists in moderation and restraint, "unvarying calm" in the face of misfortune (or good fortune for that matter)—is highly recalcitrant to effective dramatic representation. If it were represented, it would not be appreciated by the majority of the audience to whose experience such reactions are quite foreign. Rather it is the reactions suggested by the unreasonable part of the soul that are dramatic and easily appreciated by the majority. Hence it is action and emotion antithetical to a life of virtue and happiness that dramatists and other poets naturally tend to represent and that audiences desire. But it is often the protagonists, such as tragic heroes, who are represented as so acting.

So poetry will nearly always express an attitude toward life, a conception of how human beings should live, which is in fact incompatible with living an excellent life. This provides a basis for, but is not in itself, the gravest charge against poetry. That charge is that the work has a tremendous power to transmit precisely the emotions it expresses, and the attitudes to life implicit in them, to its audience: "with a few rare exceptions, it is able to corrupt even decent people, [and] that's surely an altogether terrible thing" (605c). That poetry has the power to infect its audience with the emotions it expresses is not new to Book X. We saw something like this discussed in Books II and III. It goes further back to the early dialogue, the *Ion*. What is new to Book X is the idea that poetry is not merely sometimes harmful, but that (with the exception of poetry that praises the gods and good men) it is always and inevitably harmful. This is why *most* poetry is banished from the *Republic*.

5. Art and pleasure

The arts may be valued or condemned on many grounds, some of which we have discussed above, but perhaps the most common standard of value for an artwork is that it is aesthetically pleasing or, more simply, it is enjoyable. Plato was keenly aware that the arts are a source of pleasure, and often an intense one. He was also aware that many people took this capacity to please as a standard of artistic value. In Book V of the *Republic*, he refers to lovers of sights and sounds who "like beautiful sounds, colors, shapes, and everything fashioned out of them" (476b). Plato himself, through the character Socrates, confesses to the great enjoyment he finds in the very poetry he banishes in Book X. "When even the best of us hear Homer or some other tragedian imitating one of the heroes sorrowing and making a long lamenting speech . . . we enjoy it, give ourselves up to following it, [and] sympathize with the hero" (605c–d). And "there is a definite gain in doing so, namely pleasure" (606b).

However, Plato rejects this as the right standard for evaluating artworks, even though he might admit that it is the right *internal* standard. That is, he understands that many artworks are made with the aim of giving pleasure, and that those lovers of sight and sounds are doing no more than employing criteria implicit in artistic practice. But there are more important external standards that we should bring to objects we find pleasing, and this is as true for aesthetic pleasure as any other. He finds two problems in the stance of the lovers of sights and sounds. One is that, in being wholly focused on sensory experience, they are incapable of achieving genuine knowledge, which, according to Plato, requires reasoning to a nonsensory realm of the forms. Second they are equally incapable of an encounter with the best and truest kind of beauty, which is beauty itself—the form of beauty. The two deficiencies are clearly closely connected.

In Book X as well as elsewhere in his writing, Plato brings forward another external standard by which to judge pleasing things, namely, whether they are beneficial or harmful. He has no objection to harmless pleasures, which early in Book II are counted among things good in themselves. In *Republic*, Book IX, Plato mentions pleasures of smell that are sometimes "very intense" (584b). He commends these, but they do not carry the baggage created by the mimetic nature of poetry. When a pleasure brings about serious harm, such as the corruption of character, that takes precedence over whatever intrinsic value it has in virtue of being enjoyable. That is also the conclusion of the Book IX discussion, which asserts that the actual worth of some pleasure should be determined by reason. We don't disagree with Plato in believing that one should forgo harmful pleasures. If we find Plato's use of this standard surprising in connection with the arts, it is either because we disagree with his assessment of the harmfulness of pleasures derived from art, or because of complex attitudes regarding artistic autonomy. Plato would not buy into any version of the latter idea, and it is a nice question whether he is wrong to reject it.

The previous paragraph raises the question of whether, like harmless pleasures, all pleasures are intrinsically good or whether there are pleasures that simply are not good at all. Consider the pleasure of the torturer as a possible example of the latter. Whether or not Plato thought that the pleasures of poetry have intrinsic value (albeit outweighed by the harm it does), it is interesting that the Book X discussion of poetry ends with an invitation to dramatic poetry to give a defense of itself by answering the question why it should exist in a well-governed society. Perhaps Plato's own regret at banishing something so enjoyable motivates him to give it a chance to show its worth.

6. Reconsidering art

There are several important discussions of *mimēsis* and art in Plato's later works. The most extensive is the discussions of art in the *Laws*, which revisits issues of political philosophy covered in the *Republic*. In the *Laws*, dance and poetry sung to musical accompaniment are again keystones in education, and again it is important to choose the right kind of dance and poetry and exclude the wrong kind. In society at large, poetry and drama are performed. Comedy is explicitly permitted, where it was banned in the *Republic*, because, it is said, without the comic one cannot understand the serious. The role of performers in comedy is restricted to slaves and other noncitizens, suggesting that there is something dangerous about actually adopting the role of ludicrous people, a danger that does not equally carry over to the audience. Unlike comedy, tragedy is still banned. What is also forbidden is any innovation in the arts. There are certain forms that are expressive of good character or that, like comedy, are in some way useful, and artistic activity is to stick with those.

Poetry has a somewhat more extensive role in the society represented in the *Laws* than it does in the *Republic*, and that raises the question whether later in life Plato changed his view about it and the other arts. If there is change of view, it might concern the possibility that *mimēsis* in some instances is a source of knowledge or at least of some value in the acquisition of knowledge. This is suggested by the comment on comedy mentioned above (without it one cannot understand the serious) and an extensive discussion of *mimēsis* in the *Sophist*, in which different kinds of the latter are distinguished. However, part of the reason why poetry is given more leeway in the *Laws* is that, unlike the *Republic*, it does not represent an ideal state. The presence of more poetry in the society of *Laws* may in part be a recognition that, in actual society, it will have a greater presence than is ideal.

The discussion in the *Laws* is also valuable because it helps bring into focus some abiding views about poetry and other arts that may be obscured by the more sweeping condemnation of *Republic*, Book X. Of all types of poetry, Plato thinks tragedy, which includes the epics of Homer just as much as the plays of Aeschylus, is the most dangerous. In tragedy, one's happiness is a matter of fate, out of one's control. Emotions are portrayed as quite appropriately overwhelming reason in the face of misfortune. Death is among the greatest of evils. These attitudes about life and death—virtually an alternative philosophy to Plato's—are so seductive when represented in tragic poetry, yet so wrongheaded, that they must not even get a hearing. Tragedy is not only unable to convey knowledge about serious matters, it undermines the possibility of acquiring such knowledge. What is equally dangerous is variety and innovation in all the arts because Plato thinks that this invites the imaginative adoption of many different points of view, something that, by Plato's lights, can only confuse one who pursues the truth.

7. Plato and us

Plato has a conception of the arts as a collection of activities and media that, in its explicit extension as well as its open-endedness, bears much similarity to our own. He saw that the arts have a great capacity to provide what we would call aesthetic pleasure. He recognized not only the representational, but also the expressive properties of the arts. Plato also understands that those who participate in the arts, even simply as its audience, tend to imaginatively adopt the emotions and attitudes individual works express. The main difference between Plato and us is in our evaluation of these capacities. We tend to think that aesthetic pleasure is for the most part morally unproblematic. It fulfills a human need for the stimulation of our senses and imagination. Plato would question both whether this is really a human need and whether, given the representational and expressive capacities of art forms, it is ever morally innocent. We may agree that there are some artworks, especially narrative or dramatic ones, that ask us to identify or sympathize with morally flawed or positively evil characters. Some of us have qualms about this, but many among us think this is actually a good thing. Just as one needs comedy to understand the serious, imaginatively occupying the perspective of morally flawed beings might help us to understand the good. In fact, we tend to think that one of the great things about art is the many alternative conceptions of things and points of view that it offers. This is precisely the variety and innovation that Plato thinks is harmful. One could say with some justice that he fears almost patholog-ically such variety of perspective. Alternatively one could say he offers arguments for the epistemological incapacity and the corrupting power of the arts, arguments that we as defenders of a more accepting view of the arts must answer.[1]

Note

1 I thank Alessandro Giovannelli, Nick Smith, Nickolas Pappas, and David Worldsdorf for helpful comments.

Primary sources

Plato:
1997. *Plato: Complete Works*. J. M. Cooper (ed.). Indianapolis, IN: Hackett.

(Other Platonic dialogues besides *The Republic* that discuss art and poetry include *Ion*, *Apology*, *Gorgias*, *Phaedrus*, and *The Laws*.)

References and further reading

Janaway, Christopher. 1995. *Images of Excellence: Plato's Critique of the Arts*. Oxford: Clarendon Press.
Halliwell, Stephen. 2002. *The Aesthetics of Mimesis: Ancient Texts and Modern Problems*. Princeton, NJ: Princeton University Press.
Moravcsik, J. M. E., and P. Temko, eds. 1982. *Plato on Beauty, Wisdom and the Arts*. Totowa, NJ: Rowman and Allenheld.
Nehamas, Alexander. 1999. *Virtues of Authenticity: Essays on Plato and Socrates*. Princeton, NJ: Princeton University Press, Part III, "Plato: Questions of Beauty and the Arts," 252–299.
Stecker, Robert. 1992. "Plato's Expression Theory of Art." *Journal of Aesthetic Education*, 26, 47–52.

CHAPTER 2

ARISTOTLE
(384–322 BCE)

Angela Curran

The *Poetics* by Aristotle is the first and most important work of a philosophical account of an art form ever written. In the Greek, the title means, "On the poetic [craft]" (*Peri poētikēs*), but much of the *Poetics* focuses on a specific genre of poetry: ancient Greek tragedy, specifically Greek tragedy performed in the fifth and fourth century BCE. The meaning of its key ideas—especially the concept of *katharsis*—has been hotly disputed. The recommendations for plot and character in the *Poetics* has been both widely influential on playwrights—and, more recently, screenwriters—and chastised by others for its rigid prescriptions for tragic plots and characters. But whether embraced or criticized, Aristotle's views on tragedy still hold sway today and they are often taken to have implications for other forms of narrative fiction, such as the novel or film. The *Poetics* is currently receiving renewed interest from philosophers of art, who find in Aristotle's work insightful suggestions as to how a narrative art form like tragedy engages the audience's emotions and prompts learning.

Many scholars think the works of Aristotle that have survived are in fact notes he made for himself or his students, not polished works prepared for public distribution. Aristotle's writing style is often cryptic, compressed, and difficult to follow, with many terms in need of clarification. The *Poetics* is especially challenging in this respect due to its poor state of preservation. Internal and external evidence (specifically *Politics* 1341b 38–40) suggests that there was a lost second book of the *Poetics* that discussed comedy and the concept central to the work, *katharsis*. What remains is the first book, and there is a great deal of scholarly disagreement both at the level of details of the text and at the broader level of what overall arguments this book contains.

What is clear is that the work is not an instructional manual aimed at advising playwrights. For Aristotle, poetry, like speech making, is a "productive" science. As such, it involves a *technē* (translated as "art" or "craft"), a practical skill that embodies an underlying knowledge put to the service of some goal. The poet need not know what the principles of good poetry making are to make good poems and plays, but the student of philosophy can study these works to uncover the knowledge that is implicit in the successful production of the poetic craft. This is what Aristotle does in the *Poetics*. To be sure, the work has implications for the practice of poetry. However, Aristotle's goal is not practical, but philosophical, and he draws on the views he has developed in other areas of his philosophy, especially metaphysics, psychology, and ethics.

What is the philosophical framework that Aristotle is operating with, then, in the *Poetics*? His account of the genre of poetry and related arts like painting and music is broadly teleological: poetry came into existence to establish a certain end or goal (*telos*) and the features we find in poetry are there in the service of this larger end. But to what purpose or end does Aristotle think poetry and tragedy aims? Aristotle never directly tells us his answer (cf. Shields 2007). All is not hopeless, however, for he offers some clues as to how to answer the central question of the aim of poetry and the subgenre of tragedy. To better understand Aristotle's answer, we need to investigate closely two notions central to his work: *mimēsis* and *katharsis*.

The reader of the *Poetics* will find it structured roughly as follows: (1) chapters 1–2 analyze the grounding concept of *mimēsis*; (2) chapter 4 deals with the origins of poetry; (3) chapter 6 presents Aristotle's definition of tragedy, and chapters 7–19 discuss tragedy's various component parts, especially the elements of the plot; (4) chapters 23–26 address epic poetry and the poet's use of wonder, surprise, and the impossible.

1. Mimēsis

1.1. The meaning of "mimēsis"

Aristotle says that some arts use the medium of color and shape, others use the medium of the voice, but poetry uses the medium of language, and more specifically the combination of rhythm, language, and melody in order to produce a *"mimēsis"* (1447a 13); he also says that painting, music, and poetry create *"mimēsis* of character, emotions, and action" (1447a 25). Some scholars translate *"mimēsis"* as "imitation," "representation," or "depiction," but none of these terms is a perfect rendering of Aristotle's meaning.

Using "imitation" suggests that poetry is a copy of some preexisting thing. Yet, Aristotle makes clear that the subjective matter of poetic *mimēsis* is not limited to things that have actually occurred. Certainly there was no Antigone who defied her uncle, King Creon. The subject matter of poetic *mimēsis* is either the actual (1451b 29–32) or the possible (1451b 5): that is, the objects of *mimēsis* can include those the poet makes up. Nor does the poet need to adhere to historical or scientific fact, provided that the *mimēsis* he produces is still plausible and true to life (1460b 30–32; see also 1460b 15–20). So Aristotle's *mimēsis* is not that of a copy or imitation of some preexisting reality.

"Representation" or "depiction," might be better translations, since a representation need not be of some existing object. However, a representation—say, a depiction of a subway stop on a map—might bear no likeness to the thing it represents. Yet, in one context Aristotle uses "likeness" (*homoiōma*) as a synonym for *"mimēsis."* He says that music can be a likeness or *mimēsis* of a character trait or emotion in that it can have the same effect on one's soul, as would experiencing the emotion or developing the character trait in real life (*Politics* 1340a 20–25 and 38–39; see also Belfiore 1985). A *mimēsis* might then be a likeness of some object or set of events—either possible or actual—one that is made with the goal of producing some of the same effects as those that would be produced were these things witnessed in real life.

1.2. The origins of mimēsis
In *Poetics* 4 and 5 Aristotle gives two related causes for poetry: (1) it is a distinctive feature of humans that they, more than any other animal, learn by engaging in *mimēsis*: for example, a child might learn how to speak by imitating the words of her parent; (2) all human beings take delight in exactly executed imitations, since they can learn from these imitations and learning is naturally delightful (1148b 4–24). The pleasure we take in contemplating a portrait is not due to its craftsmanship, aesthetic qualities, or even subject matter, for we can even enjoy contemplating precise

images of repulsive and vile corpses and animal forms (1448b 8–10): it is grounded in the fact that we understand (*manthanein*) and infer what each element is, for instance, that "this is so-and-so" (1448b 15–17).

Just what we do when we "understand and infer" what each element in the portrait means is not exactly clear, though Aristotle's example suggests some kind of process of assigning meaning to the elements in the portrait and deducing the corresponding features in the subject. But Aristotle's discussion here has a strong connection to the account of knowledge acquisition offered in *Metaphysics* 1, 1. All humans desire to know, and knowledge (*epistēmē*) and inquiry begin with the natural delight we take in sense perception, an ability we share with animals, and proceed to the grasp of universals (e.g., "Human Being" or "Cat") that are implicit in sense perception and to an understanding of the sort of thing a cat or a human being is. Since human beings are by their essential nature inquisitive, it is natural that they would seek out and take pleasure in any activity that exercises their nature, and Aristotle implies that our central pleasure in *mimēsis* relates to the way in which poetry exercises and satisfies our natural capacity for knowledge. But there is considerable debate, which we will return to below, about Aristotle's view of the extent and nature of this knowledge.

2. Tragedy

As the instinct to make mimetic works developed, Aristotle says, more complex forms emerged, branching into a more serious side of poetry—tragedy and epic poetry—and a less serious branch of poetry, comedy (1448b 20–25).

Comedy imitates the actions of people who are socially and morally inferior to the average human being, while tragedy and epic poetry imitate superior people (leading some to speculate that in the lost Book II of the *Poetics* Aristotle espoused a "superiority" theory of comic pleasure). Epic poetry differs from tragedy because the latter typically proceeds in a more limited time frame, allowing for a greater concentration of pleasure (1462a 18–1462b 1). Tragedy also employs different methods of making verse: in epic the events are told from the point of view of a narrator, while in tragedy the story is enacted from the perspective of characters in the play. In addition, tragedy, but not epic poetry, makes use of tune and rhythm (1449a 5–1449b 12).

Aristotle's general practice throughout his investigations is to offer a definition of a thing, since a sound definition helps us understand what a thing is in its essential nature. So, in *Poetics* 6, he pulls together his earlier remarks and offers us the following definition of tragedy:

> Tragedy, then, is a *mimēsis* of an action that is elevated, complete, and of magnitude; in language embellished in distinct forms in its sections; employing the mode of enactment and not narrative; and through pity and fear accomplishing the katharsis of such emotions. (1449b 24–28)

The most central aspects of the definition are:

1. tragedy is a *mimēsis* of an action that is serious or admirable (*spoudaios*);
2. the action must be complete and whole and have magnitude;
3. tragedy brings about a *katharsis* (root meaning "purification" or "purgation") by means of pity and fear.

Tragedy is a *mimēsis* of action and life (1450a 19), but especially of action that is serious or admirable. This requirement on tragic action refers back to chapter 2, where he contrasts the admirable characters of tragedy with the inferior characters in comedy (1448a 2). Tragedy features larger than life characters who are "better than most," both in terms of their moral standing and their social status (1448a 3; also 1458a 15–20). But tragedy often shows good people going from good fortune to bad, a circumstance that, if the plot was not executed properly, could provoke moral confusion or outrage, rather than pity and fear, which are the proper responses to a tragedy.

To evoke pity and fear, the plot must have a certain sort of structure: it must imitate an action that is "complete and whole." That is, a plot must have a beginning, middle, and end (1450b 22–23). The beginning gives the audience all it needs to know about how the action of the play gets started. The middle is that which follows from the preceding events in a way that conforms to the audience's expectation of probability and truthfulness as to how such a series of events might unfold; and the ending must not occur at an arbitrary point but bring the action to some kind of narrative closure (1450b 25).

Tragic action must not only have well-ordered parts: it must have a sufficient magnitude or length. This is what, Aristotle thinks, gives the plot its beauty (1450b 35). A plot must be long enough for one to be able to allow for the change of fortune to occur and be explicable, but short enough to hold all the events in memory. In the ideally preferable "complex" tragedy, the plot encompasses both a reversal of fortune (*peripeteia*) and a recognition on the part of the tragic character, that is, a shift from ignorance to knowledge (*anagnorisis*) (1452a 12–15).

Now, it should be stressed that an essential aspect of a well-ordered plot is that it does not simply thread one event after the other; rather, it should proceed as a "probable or necessary sequence of events" (1451a 14–15 and 1460b 12). In fact the success of the emotional impact of tragedy depends on the audience seeing the plot as unfolding in a way that conforms to their expectations of what a plausible and true-to-life sequence of events would look like. The point, then, of having a well-ordered plot is that this is the best means of evoking pity and fear in the audience. The question remains, however, of what the poet's goal is in evoking this emotional response.

3. Katharsis

An answer to the above question has often been sought in Aristotle's notion of *katharsis*. This is because the idea that tragedy offers a *katharsis* of pity and fear occurs at the end of the definition, the place Aristotle often reserved for the goal or final end of the thing defined. But just what Aristotle means by *katharsis* is hotly contested. The term "*katharsis*" is used in just two places in the *Poetics*: once in Chapter 6, at the end of the definition of tragedy, and once in Chapter 17, where Aristotle makes an incidental reference to a ritual of purification or *katharsis* in a play by Euripides. In *Politics* 8 Aristotle discusses *katharsis* in the context of ritual purification ceremonies and refers to a clearer discussion of the concept in his work on poetry (1341b 38–39), something that the extant text of the *Poetics* does not provide. Although we cannot be sure what Aristotle means by *katharsis*, this has not stopped commentators from offering numerous interpretations of this central notion. Of the many interpretations offered, some emerge as leading contenders (cf. Halliwell 1998, Appendix 5, for a helpful survey). The most influential accounts have followed the two main root meanings of *katharsis*, as either purgation or cleansing and purification.

The *purgation* theory, proposed by Jacob Bernays in the mid-nineteenth century, argues that *katharsis* is a purgation or removal of the emotions of pity and fear analogous to a medical purgation of some noxious substance from the body. Tragedy is therapeutic, for it helps the spectator rid herself of unhealthy pent-up emotions and, in doing so, provides her with a sense of enjoyable relief. The evidence for this reading comes from *Politics* 8, where Aristotle says the spectator's tendency to experience emotional excess is relieved by listening to certain kinds of music that first excite and then release the excess emotions, thereby helping the soul "settle down" by producing a calm that helps keep one's emotions to a manageable level (1342a 7–15). The point of tragic *katharsis* is then the purgation of noxious emotions that threaten physical and psychological well-being.

The purgation theory, however, is open to a persuasive objection. Aristotle would agree that emotions could be felt excessively or improperly. But he does not think of emotions as unhealthy items in need of discharge. Emotions on Aristotle's view are an essential part of a fully human life, and they should not be discharged or purged, but retained and refined, so that—as Aristotle explains in his *Nicomachean Ethics*—we feel the right emotion at the right time.

Looking at Aristotle's theory of tragedy in light of his ethics prompts, then, the other main trend in the interpretation of *katharsis*, the clarification theory (see, for example, Nussbaum 1986, 388–390). To feel pity and fear for tragic characters, the audience must believe that the events that befall the tragic characters could be the sort of thing that could happen to them. Fear is felt for someone "like us" (*Poetics* 1453a 5–6), and we feel pity for someone when we believe that the misfortune that has befallen him or her can happen to us (*Rhetoric* 1386a 24–27). By responding to worthy tragic characters and their predicaments, the spectator can then "clarify" for herself when it is appropriate to feel these emotions in real life, as well as improve her "understanding" of what sorts of things she might expect to possibly occur in her own life and how she should respond to them (cf. Martha Nussbaum's essay in Rorty 1992; for the view that Aristotelian *katharsis* is an *intellectual* rather than *emotional* clarification, see Golden 1976).

One advantage of the clarification account is that it can explain Aristotle's remark that the definition of tragedy in *Poetics* VI is a summing up of his earlier discussion in *Poetics* 1–5. *Katharsis* appears to be the one item that does not correspond to anything in the previous discussion. On the clarification account offered by Nussbaum (and also propounded by Stephen Halliwell) *katharsis* picks up the discussion in *Poetics* 4 about the pleasure of learning that poetry offers. But others remain unconvinced that *katharsis* involves the pleasure of learning (see, for example, Jonathan Lear's essay in Rorty 1992). How can tragic *katharsis* provide an ethical education for those who already understand how to experience pity and fear in the right way at the right time? In numerous places (especially *Poetics* 26) Aristotle suggests that tragedy should appeal to just such an audience. The clarification theorist replies that there is always room for improvement, even in the virtuous person.

Even if this is true, it is not clear how exactly tragedy could provide ethical training. This problem can be put in the form of a dilemma that seems to apply to all spectators of tragedy, virtuous or otherwise. Either the spectator has the appropriate response of pity and fear to the characters or she does not. If she does, this shows that she is already able to recognize when feeling pity and fear is appropriate. Tragedy does not then teach her something new that she does not already grasp. It just provides an opportunity for her to exercise her (antecedently held) grasp on virtue. If instead she fails to respond appropriately with pity and fear to the characters' situations, then tragedy has not taught her anything. Either way, it is hard to see how tragedy issues in some kind of new understanding of when pity and fear are required.

Because of the problem in understanding the broad emotional benefits of tragedy, others argue that, in the katharsis clause—"the *katharsis* of such passions (*toiauta pathēmata*)"—*pathēmata* refers not to the emotions of pity and fear, but to the events in the plot. This interpretation finds support in Aristotle's claim in *Poetics* 6 that the events and the plot are the goals of tragedy (1450a 20–23). As Alexander Nehamas maintains (in Rorty 1992), a coherent plot that resolves all the narrative questions raised earlier in the play is the goal of tragedy and the point of *katharsis*. It is drastic to take the emotions out of the experience of tragedy, especially since later chapters make clear that the well-ordered plot is there to facilitate a feeling of pity and fear (see especially *Poetics* 13 and 14). Yet, an even more radical interpretation proposes that the *katharsis* language was not Aristotle's own, but a later addition, and so concludes that it is advisable to drop talk about *katharsis* altogether (Scott 2003).

Even if we decide that no definitive interpretation of *katharsis* can be given, we should try to understand why Aristotle thinks it is beneficial for everyone—the virtuous and ordinary folk alike—to experience the emotions in the context of tragedy. There are two key aspects of Aristotle's answer to this question: (1) the experience of emotions in the setting of theater makes these emotions more manageable in real life; and (2) pity and fear facilitate a grasp on the universal truths embodied in the particulars of the plot.

Normally pity and fear are experienced as painful emotions, according to the account of them Aristotle offers in the *Rhetoric*. Yet experiencing these emotions in response to the characters' predicaments clearly gives rise, he claims, to some sort of pleasurable relief. These observations—that in the context of tragedy the painful feelings of pity and fear can give rise to a feeling of pleasure—lead to what has become known as the paradox of tragedy: how can viewers of tragedy take pleasure in that which would in everyday contexts be unpleasant and painful to experience?

Aristotle gives no indication that he thinks that the normally painful emotions of pity and fear somehow get "converted" by tragic *mimēsis* into pleasant feelings, as David Hume proposed when he considered the paradox of tragedy. But a skillful plot puts the pitiful and fearful events of everyday life into some kind of a coherent whole, and thereby gives the spectator a pleasurable understanding of these incidents that is not available when we experience these emotions in ordinary life. Pity and fear are not discharged or necessarily clarified or refined in a virtuous person who experiences these emotions in the right way, at the right time. For such a person, the pain felt in experiencing pity and fear in response to the character's suffering remains, but her emotional engagement with them calls forth a pleasurable understanding that helps to make the experience of pity and fear in real life easier to bear. What is transformed or altered, then, is the overall experience of pity and fear in the context of tragedy, and not the feeling of pain associated with pity and fear, as Hume proposed. This association of pleasurable understanding and painful emotions helps a person regard pity and fear and the real-life incidents that call them forth differently.

4. The philosophical nature of
poetry and the goal of tragedy

The pleasures of tragedy, for Aristotle, are diverse: they involve both a practical component, that of helping to make our experience of painful emotions in everyday life more manageable, and an intellectual or philosophical one, that of offering an understanding of the wreckage and rubble of the incidents from our everyday lives. In *Poetics* 9, Aristotle expands further on the quasi-philosophical nature of poetry, helping us better understand how emotional engagement with tragic characters facilitates some kind of intellectual insight.

Poets write stories about what happens to particular individuals in specific circumstances. Yet, in grasping the plot, the audience grasps a universal truth, embedded in the particulars of the narrative, that explains how the character comes to suffer the fate she does. To the extent that we recognize that the character's fate could be our own, we obtain self-knowledge and possibly some greater understanding that may approximate philosophical knowledge, insofar as philosophy is concerned with universals—what happens to a certain type of person in certain types of situations—and not particulars—what happened to the character of Oedipus when unbeknownst to him he encountered his father at the crossroads (1451b 5–10).

While this "cognitive" interpretation of Aristotle is a minority view, some critics strongly disagree with it. For Aristotle says in *Poetics* 13 and 14 that tragedy must conform to the audience's expectations of what is plausible and likely, otherwise the response of pity and fear is not possible. Aristotle acknowledges that what is likely or plausible to believe need not be necessary or truthful (1460b 30–32 and 15–20). This might call into question his view that tragedy provides any genuine understanding of the truth.

On the other hand, the text of *Poetics* 9 makes no reference to the audience's expectations. Aristotle suggests that if the plot of a play such as *Oedipus the King* is true, then it shows what a person like Oedipus would necessarily or likely do in the circumstances of finding that he is the cause of the plague on his kingdom. Aristotle does say later, in *Poetics* 24, that it is important to maintain the impression of a necessary or likely sequence of events, for otherwise the emotional impact of the tragedy would be spoiled, and that the likely but impossible is to be preferred to the unlikely but possible (1460a 25–27). This does not show that the poet's concern is not with understanding; it just shows that the emotional impact of tragedy—and the grasp on the universal truth in the plot—cannot be achieved if the plot fails to conform to the audience's expectations of what is likely.

Combining *Poetics* 4 and 9, we might then conclude that artistic activity is on a par with other knowledge seeking activities such as scientific inquiry (cf. Shields 2007). But here we should be cautious in what we conclude Aristotle is saying. He says that poetry is "more philosophical and more elevated" than history (1451b 3–5), but this does not mean that the poet is doing the work of the philosopher. A good tragic plot, Aristotle suggests, organizes the pitiful and fearful events of everyday life into some kind of coherent whole, and this has implications for how an audience member can come to understand things better in her own life. But to do so, the poet need not impart philosophical knowledge, which for Aristotle is knowledge of essences, of the necessary and defining features of kinds (e.g., "God," "human being," "lion"). What the spectator grasps in making sense of the tragic plot may be some empirical generalization regarding how certain types of human beings respond in certain types of situations, say, "Virtuous people have a noble response to misfortune." Such a generalization may be new to the spectator or be a truth that she grasped previously; yet, by her emotional response to the characters, this generalization comes emotionally alive as it was not before. What the audience takes away from tragedy, then, need not be an understanding akin to the study of essences that the philosopher examines, but some more modest insight about human behavior, one that nonetheless has practical implications for how everyone—ordinary people as well as virtuous persons—manages their emotions in real-life circumstances.

5. The *Poetics* and aesthetics

The *Poetics* has inspired significant developments in aesthetics. One trend concerns the relationship between the ethical and the aesthetic. Aristotle recommends plot patterns that are based on the likely ethical regard the audience will take toward the characters. Audiences feel pity and fear for good and decent characters who err, but are not morally vicious; they feel moral confusion when an exceptionally good person suffers due to no fault of her own; and they feel repulsed when a vicious person triumphs.

Wayne Booth (1988) has developed Aristotle's suggestions by arguing that, with literature, the reader's ability to emotionally engage with the characters in a fiction is based on the ethical esteem they hold for them. Nussbaum (1986, among other works) has developed her "clarification" account of *katharsis* into a more general argument that literature is an important adjunct to philosophy, for it provides the opportunity to refine our "moral perception" regarding ethical concepts like justice and virtue. And recently philosophers have debated the "puzzle of imaginative resistance"—one aspect of which is the idea that readers imaginatively "resist" characters whose moral viewpoints strongly differ from their own. These discussions are indebted to Aristotle's psychological observation that ethical regard forms an important basis for the reader's reaction to dramatic characters.

Another Aristotelian tendency in aesthetics concerns the identification of certain literary and film genres—suspense, mystery, comedy, melodrama, and horror— by reference to the intended emotional effects on the audience. Noël Carroll, for example, has developed an account of the horror genre in terms of its production of the emotions of fear and disgust in the audience (see Chapter 18, section 5). He identifies mystery as the genre intended to produce suspense in the audience, and melodrama as intended to invite pity for the melodramatic protagonist.

Following Aristotle, philosophers of film and literature argue that sympathy plays an important role in our affective engagement with characters in film, and they have sought to understand the nature of this engagement, how it differs from empathy (or "shared feeling") with characters, and whether or not "identification" is the best way to explain Aristotle's requirement that the tragic characters must be "like ourselves" in order to feel pity and fear for them (1453a 5–6).

We can see, then, that the *Poetics* has inspired a number of important trends in aesthetics and promises to continue to do so. Perhaps the most significant debates the work has engendered focus on what role tragedy plays in ethical improvement, and on whether it is the essential goal of art that we learn from it. Regardless of the answers to these questions, Aristotle makes clear to us that artistic activity and aesthetic appreciation are an essential part of a fully human life. For this reason aestheticians will continue to turn to the *Poetics* for a valuable defense of the relevance of art today.[1]

Note

1 I thank Alessandro Giovannelli for his many very helpful comments and editorial advice on this chapter.

Primary sources

Aristotle:
1995. *Poetics*. S. Halliwell (ed.). Cambridge, MA: Harvard University Press.
1932. *Politics*. H. Rackham (trans.). Cambridge, MA: Harvard University Press.
1926. *Rhetoric*. J. H. Freese (trans.). Cambridge, MA: Harvard University Press.

References and further reading

Belfiore, Elizabeth. 1985. "Pleasure, Tragedy, and Aristotelian Psychology." *Classical Quarterly*, 35, 349–361.
Booth, Wayne. 1988. *The Company We Keep*. Berkeley, CA: University of California Press.
Golden, Leon. 1976. "The Clarification Theory of Catharsis." *Hermes*, 104, 437–452.
Halliwell, Stephen. 1998. *Aristotle's Poetics*. London: University of Chicago Press.
Heath, Malcolm. 1996. *Aristotle's Poetics*. London: Penguin Books.
Nussbaum, Martha. 1986. *The Fragility of Goodness*. Cambridge: Cambridge University Press.
Rorty, Amélie, ed. 1992. *Essays on Aristotle's Poetics*. Princeton, NJ: Princeton University Press.
Scott, Greg. 2003. "Purging the *Poetics*." *Oxford Studies in Ancient Philosophy*, 25, 233–263.
Shields, Christopher. 2007. "Rhetoric and the Arts." In *Aristotle*. New York: Routledge, 375–397.

CHAPTER 3

MEDIEVAL AESTHETICS

Gian Carlo Garfagnini

During the Middle Ages aesthetics never was an autonomous discipline. Treatises that specifically address matters regarding the arts and beauty are rare and, when they exist, are framed within a theological and metaphysical investigation. Indeed, the medieval aesthetic discussion occurs all within the context of a rational investigation of the Bible, aimed at one's eternal salvation and at the acquisition, from the pagan tradition, of any conceptual tool that could help achieve that ultimate goal. Views on the beautiful were first developed by the so-called Fathers of the Church (from which the term "patristic") as they sought a synthesis between biblical texts and Greek philosophy. Their ideas were to be passed on to subsequent medieval thinkers, but always informed by the same fundamental concerns.

Despite their differences, medieval authors ultimately agree on the connection between the beautiful and the good and on the claim that beautiful is what arouses pleasure. Such pleasure derives from contemplation, in Latin a *visio*, which can be either of sensory, worldly beauty or, more fundamentally, of a nonsensory, moral and divine, beauty. Worldly beauty is nothing but a reflection of the solely true beauty, eternal and immutable: that of God. And the attempt to access such a beauty within the created world is meaningful only within man's ampler project—by means of a rational understanding of the laws governing the universe—of getting closer to God.

1. From sacred scriptures to patristic school

The Old Testament appears to have a dual attitude toward the issue of beauty. On the one hand, according to the Vulgate, that is, the Latin translation of the Bible accepted by the Church, "beautiful" is the term God uses to comment on His own creation (Genesis 1.31). Further, the Book of Wisdom describes the divine creation as ordered according to "measure, number, and weight" (Wisdom XI: 21). On the other hand, the transience and vanity of material beauty is emphasized. The New Testament, too, lends itself to different interpretations: while it insists on sensory beauty being just a manifestation of spiritual beauty, it also suggests the possibility that the autonomous value of the beautiful be grasped as a feature intrinsic to a created thing as such. These are different but not contradictory claims; contrasts between them will arise only later, because of biblical interpretations emphasizing one claim at the expense of the other. The interpretations emerging from the Jewish tradition concentrate on the derived nature of the sensory beautiful and the importance of a subjective appreciation of it. The interpretations that were more open to Greek and Roman culture underline the immediate and objective value of beauty, considering it first and foremost as proportion and harmony between the parts.

The Greek Father Basil of Caesarea (329–379), in his *Homilies of the Hexaemeron*, defines the beauty of the created world as *pankalìa*, that is, as (1) beauty deriving from the arrangements of the parts that constitute the universe; (2) simplicity, insofar as such parts comprise a harmonic whole; and (3) light, propagating directly and making everything it reaches shine. To these concepts, which had Stoic and Neoplatonic origins, Basil adds the idea of beauty as (4) a relation, emphasizing the importance of its reception by the subject and of the correspondence between the object and its intrinsic goal. Hence, the world is beautiful because of the harmony between its parts, of humans' capacity to enjoy its overall arrangement as a way to get to the Creator, and, finally, of its perfect correspondence to the goal for which God created it. Just as an artist manipulates the existing matter to realize the idea he has in mind, so God is an artist, one whose raw material is nothingness.

The same conception reappears in the *Dionysian Corpus*, the set of writings medieval thinkers attributed to a disciple of Saint Paul, Dionysius the Areopagite, but that are actually by a fifth-century anonymous writer, now known as the pseudo-Dionysius. One of such writings, the *De divinis nominibus* (*On the Divine Names*), affirms a spiritualistic and theocentric aesthetics that is more abstract than Basil's. It combines characteristics of the biblical God with those of the first being of Neoplatonic philosophy; that is, it equates the beautiful to the good, which at an absolute level is Being as such, the One. Another Neoplatonic theme found in the work of the pseudo-Dionysius is the theory of emanation, which identifies the beautiful with the light that propagates from the One and that, shining on all things, brings them into existence. There is here, then, a transition from Basil's somewhat empirical conception of the beautiful to a metaphysical conception that inevitably devalues the sensory dimension.

Within Latin patristic thought, the foundations for a reflection on aesthetics are laid by Augustine (354–430). He expresses his views on the subject in *De pulchro et apto* (*Of the Beautiful and the Fitting*), now lost, in *De vera religione* (*Of True Religion*), in *De ordine* (*Of Order*), and in the three treatises on *Genesis*. After asking "whether things are beautiful because they please or whether they please because they are beautiful," Augustine responds that "they please because they are beautiful" (*De vera religione*, XXXII, 59), hence affirming the objective, autonomous character of sensory beauty, despite its nondivine nature. In defining such beauty, Augustine appeals to the criterion of proportion: the beautiful (*pulchrum*), which is distinguished from both what is appropriate or fitting (*aptum*) and what is merely enjoyable (*suave*), is an objective quality of things, insofar as their makeup results from a harmony between the parts, governed by measure and number. Such an aesthetic objectivism is nonetheless accompanied by an emphasis placed on the role of the subject who "sees" the beautiful and defines it, through an understanding that is possible only when the encounter of the subject with the object is characterized by disinterestedness and tranquility of mind. These novel elements notwithstanding, Augustine's aesthetics is still inspired by a theocentric vision, since the properties that make things beautiful ultimately exist only as traces of the divine beauty.

2. From Boethius to the twelfth century

Boethius's (c. 480–526) aesthetic reflections, found in *De consolatione philosophiae* (*The Consolation of Philosophy*) and *De institutione musica* (*Fundamentals of Music*), are part of his program for spreading Greek thought in the West and codifying a new philosophical-theological vocabulary. Inspired by the Pythagorean conception of the beautiful as form, proportion, and number, Boethius ends up emphasizing, in accordance with a spiritualism that had its origin in the East, the nature of worldly beauty as just an "appearance," a remote trace of the true Beautiful and true Good. Worldly beauty is inescapably bound to the senses and hence to the human inability of going beyond a thing's surface, to the thing's essence: "It is not your nature, but the weakness of the eyes of the onlookers that makes you appear beautiful" (*De consolatione philosophiae*, III, 8). Art is approached more theoretically than practically, for its capacity of facilitating understanding and transmitting knowledge. Boethius introduces a distinction, which would last throughout the Middle Ages, between two kinds of activities: those that depend on a set of rules, principles, and skills, which belong to art (*ars*), and the *artificia*, the products of manual labor, which instead belong to the sphere of technology. Boethius's aesthetics, which is almost exclusively dedicated to music, can be described as mathematical in its foundation, intellectual in its consequences, and metaphysical in its perspective. Music, which for him comprises poetry, can be seen as deriving from the cosmic music that stems from the universe's perfection.

The so-called Carolingian Renaissance,[1] that is, the intellectual rebirth that grounded the attempt to construct a Christian identity that would be capable of culturally unifying the West, had an impact on aesthetics, too. Alcuin of York (735–804), especially, with his strong interest for the classics, tried to combine the scripture-based religious point of view with the ideas articulated by the ancient thinkers. For him, beautiful things reflect that divine plan—beautiful by definition—that was at the basis of the creation. Accordingly, the value of a work of art amounts to the work's being a representation of the truth. For this reason, literature, which among the arts is best able to express the concepts needed to reach the truth, has for Alcuin a privileged position. Regarding the relationship between object and subject, Alcuin strengthens the distinction between the exterior form (*dulcedo*) of a work and the expression of an interior harmony (*ordo*), giving primacy to the latter of the two.

The question of the aesthetic is explicitly addressed by John Scotus Eriugena (c. 810–877). Eriugena's deep knowledge of Greek had allowed him to introduce Neoplatonism to the West, through his commentaries on the *Corpus Dionysianum*. Eriugena advances a philosophical view that centers around a unitary conception of the cosmic process, from the creation of the universe to its final resolution in God. The universe is the manifestation of the Divine (*teofania*) and must be understood as a complex symphonic unity, within which matter and sensory beauty play a role comparable to that of spiritual entities. The fundamental characteristic of beauty, which must be enjoyed in a completely disinterested way and out of neither material nor spiritual need, is that of being essentially ineffable: "God realizes Himself in the creation, manifesting Himself in wondrous and ineffable manner; though invisible, He becomes visible, and though incomprehensible, He becomes comprehensible" (*De divisione naturae* [*The Division of Nature*], III, 17). Indeed, since all things derive from prototypes within the inscrutable divine reason, the higher we get in considering them, the more beautiful they are for being closer to their creator, and the harder it is for human reason to understand them and for our limited vocabulary to express them.

Between the eighth and the ninth century, the only moment when an aesthetic issue takes the center stage in medieval philosophy occurs; it is regarding the value of sacred images. The dispute on their value started within the Eastern Empire of Byzantium but it resonated strongly in the West, too. At stake, besides some rather concrete political motivations, were two of the most fundamental theological positions, affecting the entire contemporary understanding of reality. On the one hand, the iconoclasts firmly denied the possibility of representing the Divine; on the other, the iconophiles were persuaded that as man can perceive the truth only by means of the senses, so sensory representations are a necessary means to unite with God. Charlemagne himself took a middle-ground position, sympathetic to the iconoclasts' position, but opposed to the destruction of the sacred images.

The other period of major intellectual flourishing prior to the full Middle Ages is the twelfth century "renaissance." Together with a growth in population and trades, and the rebirth of the city, this century saw the establishment of cultural centers aimed at the study of the sacred scriptures as well as the liberal arts, law, and medicine: most notably, the centers at the Saint Victor Abbey in Paris, the Abbey of Clairvaux, and the Cathedral of Chartres.

One of the protagonists of this period is Hugh of Saint Victor (1096–1141), who dedicated the seventh book of his *Didascalicon* to an analysis of both divine, invisible beauty and sensory beauty. Hugh emphasizes the importance of the latter, describing its fundamental characteristics and declaring its relative autonomy. Although defending a sort of panaestheticism of all created reality, he does not embrace the traditional *pankalia*; rather, he insists on the possibility for earthly things to be beautiful, and on such beauty to be a means for humans to overcome their limits. Hugh distinguishes the products of mental activity between things that are appropriate, convenient, and liked, pointing to a process that has at its apex the production of what is beautiful. He pays great attention, then, to the human capacity to create things, albeit always within the limits of a reality that has itself been created and in strict agreement with nature. Hugh's descriptive approach to aesthetics, however, was to be abandoned by his successor at Saint Victor, Richard (d. 1173), who reverted to a mystic approach centered on the aesthetic contemplation a subject could have of the invisible, divine beauty.

Bernard of Clairvaux (1091–1153) holds a view that is quite close to the theses of Hugh's school. His *Sermones in Cantica Canticorum* (*Sermons on the Song of Songs*) represent the canonical view for the order of the Cistercian Fathers with respect to beauty. The beauty Bernard is interested in is moral beauty, which derives from the harmony of a soul and its accordance with the word of God. Aesthetics, then, is for him a sort of philosophy of spirit, within which the dialectic between spiritual and sensory beauty is resolved all in favor of the former. Given his view that what is beautiful is simple—so as to match the essential uniqueness of the Creator—among the arts Bernard favors architecture and music, for which he proposes an aesthetic model characterized by harmony and precision.

Architecture occupies an equally central place within another great cultural center of the twelfth century—that of the school of the Cathedral of Chartres. The Chartres masters claimed that the divine revealed word of God ought to be consistent with the fruits of logical reasoning as found in the works of the ancient thinkers. Accordingly, they conducted their investigations by reading the Bible together with the first part of Plato's *Timaeus*, in the translation and commentary by Calcidius. They considered beauty an attribute of the world itself and God an artist who had acted according to unchanging rules and categories, such as form, figure, number, relation, and accordance between the parts. God gave the initial creative impulse (*creatio*) to a living work that was then capable of developing autonomously according to its own structure (*exornatio*). To understand the beauty of the cosmos, then, one must adopt a mathematical approach, so as to consider the things of the world for what they are in themselves, not as symbols of realities beyond them. Architecture—the most significant art form because image, however imperfect, of the divine creative activity—ought to be evaluated, then, not according to moral or ascetic criteria but according to aesthetic considerations.

3. The thirteenth century: Franciscan and Dominican thought

The thirteenth century is the apex of medieval philosophy. It is the century during which the best-known figures are active, the most major institutional and religious transformations happen, and the national states become self-aware, bringing the universalism of the Empire and of the Church to an end. Most important, it is the century of the return of the Aristotelian corpus into the West, bearer as it was of a global vision of the world and of a new vocabulary to express it. It is the century during which the first universities and the scholastic way of elaborating and transmitting knowledge are born. It is also the century of the mendicant orders.

The scholastic masters raised new questions with respect to aesthetics, addressing the essence of the beautiful and aesthetics' relation to art and other disciplines. They abandoned a theocentric and mystic approach as well as a merely descriptive one, and attempted a conceptual approach, starting from such questions as "What is beautiful?" and "How do you define its essence?"

The Franciscan school is especially interested in the beauty of the world, according to the view of the school's founder, Saint Francis of Assisi (c. 1181–1226), that the universe shines of the divine beauty in each of its parts, even the lowest. The first relevant philosophical for-mulations, yet still ones that follow the tradition preceding them, are found in the work of William of Auvergne (d. 1249) and in the *Summa fratris Alexandri* attributed to Alexander of Hales (c. 1180–1245). Robert Grosseteste (1175–1253) also addresses the aesthetic question within his metaphysics of light. The novelty in Grosseteste's approach lies in considering the beautiful as harmony between the parts not qualita-tively but quantitatively, so as to open the discourse to mathematical and geometrical proportions. To such a view Grosseteste adds a con-ception of light as a primary element within which proportions are per-fect because they are grounded in identity: light is indivisible and hence always identical to itself. Combining his views on the mathematical-geometrical proportions to the thesis that light is the primary condition for the existence of things, Grosseteste claims that the world can be described as beautiful because it is the work of its creator, because of its perfect form, and because of the accordance between the parts, which are governed by the linear precision of light. Finally, this math-ematical understanding of aesthetics is combined to a characteriza-tion of human action as not just aimed at knowing but also at doing. Hence, all arts are conditioned by logic, music, and mathematics, and have a practical outcome.

In a similar way, Bonaventure of Bagnoregio (1221–1274) begins with the assumption that beauty derives from light, which is pro-portion, congruity, and perfect identity; yet, he adds to this met-aphysical approach an interest for the empirical and psychological dimension, concentrating on a subject's capacity to be in harmony with the object he or she perceives thanks to the senses and the intellect. Such a state does not reflect just a universal harmony but the subject's own sensibility—that of someone who is capable of recognizing in things that same divine spark that is also within him or herself. Because of the emphasis he places on the importance of the subject, Bonaventure can attribute the artist a certain degree of crea-tivity, conceiving the artwork not just as a representation of some-thing external to its creator, but rather as a projection of the artist's inner states. It is no coincidence, then, that Bonaventure develops an understanding of formal beauty within a more general reflection on what is beautiful, and grants an important role to the imagination in the creation of a work of art. Bonaventure's reflections on aesthetics, albeit framed within his attempt to explain the dependence of the created world on the Creator, refer back to the distinctive feature of Franciscan thought, of attributing value to the intrinsic beauty creatures have and to the capacity of an individual—religious believer or artist—to express it.

The issue of beauty is also addressed by the major representatives of the Dominican order. Albert the Great (1193–1280), in the lectures he held in Cologne on the *De divinis nominibus*, defends his position by first explaining the views that preceded it. He begins with the distinction between absolute and sensory beauty, defining the latter according to the criteria of proportion, measure, and color. Then, he goes back to the issue of sensory beauty's participation in divine beauty and presents a rather original theory of light. He likens the Neoplatonic notion of light to the Aristotelian notion of form (that for which anything is what it is): as form gives individual existence to matter, so the light emanating from the first Being realizes a possibility for being, which all sensory things have; as form indicates the essence of something, so an object hit by light is more or less beautiful according to how much of its essence can be seen in the shape through which the object is perceived. This leads Albert to maintain two theses: (1) relativism regarding beauty, which becomes a sort of shared background from which the individuality of a beautiful thing emerges, insofar as each form is distinct from every other form and hence its full realization implies a perfection that must be different from that of every other form; (2) the distinction between substantial beauty, which relates to the essence of things, and accidental beauty, which results from the simultaneous presence of different contingent features.

Ulrich of Strasbourg (d. 1287), a pupil of Albert, is one of the few authors who dedicates a treatise to the topic of beauty and ugliness. In *De pulchro*, Ulrich uses a synthesis of Neoplatonic and pseudo-Dionysian ideas, of Aristotelianism, and of Albert's theory of light to defend a mystical *aesthetic transcendentalism*: God is not just supreme beauty but also efficient, formal, and final cause of every beautiful thing.

The peak of scholastic thought is reached with Thomas Aquinas (1225–1274). Like the other medieval thinkers, he never addresses aesthetics explicitly. Nevertheless, he shows awareness of the views prior and contemporary to him: Albert's thesis of light as form; the distinction between sensory and spiritual beauty; the thought that imperfect beauty is the reflection of perfect beauty, and that the former naturally tends to become one with the latter; the conceptual, but not actual, difference between the beautiful and the good; and the definition of beauty as proportion and clarity. Though he embraces all these notions, Aquinas is primarily interested in those that have to do with sensory beauty, and stays away from any form of mysticism.

Aquinas defines the beautiful as what a subject perceives with pleasure: that "the very perception of which pleases" (*Summa Theologica*, I-a IIae, q. 27). The two statements are compatible, since seeing, linked to the most important and noble organ, subsumes any other perceptual capacity. According to such a definition, then, the cause of pleasure produced by beauty does not trace to an absolute ideal; rather, in Aristotelian fashion, it is found in the dialectic between subject and object, that is, in the subjective recognition of the objectively beautiful and good qualities of an object when observed. Among other things, that allows him to state that the object—once perceived—can be known by the subject through a combination of senses and intellect: man, by his sensory capacities, captures the external object and assimilates it, scrutinizing through the senses the object's inherent qualities, forming a precise image of it, and expressing a judgment about it.

Regarding the relationship between the good and the beautiful, Aquinas maintains that good is that which we desire, while beautiful is that which we contemplate. While conceptually distinct, the two values nonetheless coincide in things, for everything that is good is beautiful and vice versa. Elaborating on Augustine's view, Aquinas claims that the aesthetic sentiment must be disinterested. Yet, Aquinas's interest in concrete cases brings him to acknowledge that not all aesthetic pleasures can be fully disconnected from what is necessary or helpful to the satisfaction of human needs. The aesthetic sentiment has nonetheless its own individuality, between the pleasures that are primarily sensory and biological, on the one hand, and those that are purely intellectual and moral, on the other.

To define the beautiful, Aquinas appeals to the notions of proportion—in a broad sense, which includes qualitative and quantitative relations—and of transparency (*claritas*). To these, he adds the criterion of the *integritas*; yet, since that is nothing but the perfection of an object according to its nature, it in fact reduces to the concept of proportion.

Much space is dedicated to the definition of art and to distinguishing it from science and morality. Aquinas concludes that: (1) art is the capacity of producing according to the commands of reason; (2) the making of the artistic product is the true criterion for evaluation of an artwork; (3) the aesthetic pleasure is legitimate to have, provided that it is within the limits of rational moderation.

4. From the thirteenth to the fourteenth century

As the beginning of the thirteenth century had seen the emergence of the universities and the progressive introduction in their curriculum of the works of Aristotle and of his Greek and Arab commentators, the last years of the century marked, not so much a decadence of scholastic thought but a change in the theological and philosophical approach and the beginning of a new cultural era. At the end of 1200, Church authorities started reacting against a mode of philosophical investigation that had progressively become reluctant to comply with the limitations imposed by religious orthodoxy. On the other hand, those interested in rational investigation began to reconsider the results of adapting Aristotelian thought to the values of Christianity. Paradigmatic of the Church's reaction were the condemnations, by the Bishop of Paris, Étienne Tempier, of the teachers of the Faculty of Arts, who had demanded more autonomy for their disciplines. The results of the rational consideration were instead the strong contrasts that emerged, between the Franciscan and the Dominican teachers, on the authority that the thought of Aquinas ought to be given.

Starting with the end of the thirteenth century, the attention to the role of the subject in perceiving, recognizing, and defining what is beautiful—which Bonaventure, Albert, and Aquinas had emphasized—received a sharp acceleration. Significant in this respect is the view of Witelo, a Polish scholar contemporary of Aquinas who wrote a book on optics and perspective (*Perspectivorum libri decem seu Optica*). Such a work is evidence of an increasing interest in empirical observation regarding perceptual knowledge, rather than in formulating views grounded in metaphysical or theological assumptions. Witelo aims at analyzing vision in terms of its real, physical data, turning its investigation into a psychological one. And it is this empirical foundation that allows him to list the most common errors in visual and aesthetic perception.

John Duns Scotus (c. 1265–1308)—a Franciscan teacher who is one of the most prominent figures within philosophical investigation subsequent to Aquinas—writes in his *Opus Oxoniense* that "beauty is not an absolute quality of a beautiful body but the combination of all of its properties, that is, size, shape, and color, as well as the combination of all the relations between these properties and the body, and of such relations with each other" (*Opus Oxoniense*, I, d. 17, q. 3, n. 13). Going back to the traditional definition of beauty, he defends a view of beauty in which the concept of relation has a primary role.

Scotus makes a similar shift to tradition regarding the concept of form, which he understood both in Aristotelian fashion and as figure, "external arrangement of a thing." Form also becomes that part of an artwork that, once realized, resembles the idea the artist had in his or her mind while producing the work. In that perspective, Scotus is open to an approach that emphasizes the role of subjective creativity, and presents an idea of art as not merely aimed at understanding but also at making: art, he writes, amounts to "the right concept of what must be done" and in one's being able to realize it with appropriate techniques and materials.

William of Ockham (c. 1287–1347), while rethinking the philosophical foundations of the previous century, takes distance from aesthetic objectivism even more than Scotus does. Indeed, to Ockham, terms of form and figure stand only for the disposition of actual objects, and hence ought to be compared to actually existing substances. The idea of an entity exists only in the mind of the artist, not in reality, and it is only from reality that anything real can be produced. As for the union between the good and the beautiful, Ockham maintains that what is good/beautiful is an object of desire that must be disciplined according to justice, that is, by moderation and the application of the rules of reason. Finally, Ockham analyzes the concepts relevant to art and nature, claiming that the former is characterized by the freedom of the artist while the latter is governed by necessary laws. Even the term *imago*, used to refer to art, must then be connected to what we could call the freedom of the artist's fantasy, independently of any objective model. In sum, although neither what Scotus nor Ockham say ever amounts to an explicit and comprehensive treatment of aesthetics, their efforts in defining the relevant concepts and the value they both place on the subjectivity of the artist undoubtedly represent a break from tradition and the beginning of a modern approach to aesthetics.

The last contribution to aesthetics that is here worth considering is that of Dante Alighieri (1265–1321), who, without being either a teacher or a clergyman, wrote some of the most significant literary works ever written. For quite some time, philosophically, Dante has been considered simply a follower of Aquinas. Yet, more recent studies have brought to light his curiosity for and acquaintance with the intellectual debates of his time, "within the religious schools and regarding the discussions between philosophers" (*Convivium* II, XII, 7). In his *Divine Comedy*, in *Vita nova* (*The New Life*), and in the *Convivium* (*The Banquet*) alike, he presents a view of love that, as a sentiment of an individual human being, is source of both natural and artistic beauty. Dante reaches this conclusion by merging the Neoplatonic view of love as cosmic energy with the spiritualization of the loving sentiment typical of the troubador poems and the Italian *Dolce Stil Novo* (literally "sweet new style"). For Dante, poetry, because of its deriving from the inner sphere—from the ideas, emotions, and inspirations springing from the poet's soul—needs no external justification. That is all the more true considering that the poet, with his art, does not aim at producing mere delight or at being useful, but rather at explaining the highest human values: truth, goodness, and beauty. Poetry, which finds justification in its beauty, is then a vehicle for truth: it is, accordingly, theology—discourse about God and anything that from God derives.

5. Conclusion

Although marginal to the great theological and philosophical questions that were at the core of the scholars' intellectual work, the medieval investigation of aesthetics left a noteworthy legacy to modern thought. It preserved and passed on to subsequent inquiry philosophical views from the antiquity that would have otherwise been lost. Yet, that is not its most significant accomplishment. The modern era is rooted in the Middle Ages, and it is during that period of time that some of the questions that still inform our way of reflecting upon the world emerged.[2]

Notes

1 So-called because it occurred under the reign of Charlemagne (742–814).
2 Many thanks to Serena Masolini for her invaluable assistance in editing this chapter. Translated from the Italian by Alessandro Giovannelli. Translator's note: whenever possible, for quotations from the original texts, the translations found in Tatarkiewicz (2005) have been used.

Primary sources

Alighieri, Dante. 1909. *Dante's Convivio*. W. W. Jackson (trans.). Oxford: Clarendon Press.

Aquinas. 1981. *Summa Theologica*. Fathers of the English Dominican Province (trans.). New York: Benziger Bros.

Augustine. 1953. *Augustine: Earlier Writings*. J. H. S. Burleigh (trans.). Philadelphia, PA: Westminster.

Boethius. 2008. *The Consolation of Philosophy*. P. G. Walsh (trans.). Oxford: Oxford University Press.

Eriugena, John Scotus. 1987. *The Division of Nature*. Montreal: Bellarmin/Dumbarton Oaks.

References and further reading

Benson, R. L., and Giles Constable, eds. 1982. *Renaissance and Renewal in the Twelfth Century*. Cambridge, MA: Harvard University Press.

Eco, Umberto. 2002. *Art and Beauty in the Middle Ages*. H. Bredin (trans.). New Haven, CT: Yale University Press.

Jaeger, C. S. 2010. *Magnificence and the Sublime in Medieval Aesthetics*. Basingstoke, UK: Palgrave Macmillan.

Tatarkiewicz, W. 2005. *History of Aesthetics*, Vol. 3: *Medieval Aesthetics*. R. M. Montgomery (trans.). London: Continuum.

CHAPTER 4

DAVID HUME
(1711–1776)

Alan H. Goldman

David Hume never wrote a book on aesthetics, yet the nature of aesthetic judgment was a subject that he addressed intermittently throughout his philosophical career. His writings on the subject are scattered throughout several books and essays, concluding with the late essay, "Of the Standard of Taste," published in 1757 (Hume 1987d). This mature piece is a classic in the field, culminating the eighteenth-century British tradition in aesthetics and setting the tone for the future history of the subject in its focus on the central question of the subjectivity or objectivity of aesthetic evaluations.

1. Early writings

From his earliest writing in *A Treatise of Human Nature* (orig. publ. 1740), Hume tried to steer a middle course between radical subjectivism or relativism and objectivism in regard to judgments of beauty or aesthetic value. He writes there that subjective pleasure constitutes the essence of beauty, aesthetic pleasure being a particular kind of pleasure (Hume 1961, 426). Reiterating the subjectivist stance in an early, 1742 essay, "The Skeptic," he writes: "beauty and worth are merely of a relative nature, and consist in an agreeable sentiment, produced by an object in a particular mind, according to the peculiar structure of that mind" (Hume 1987c, 163). The sentiment in which beauty consists is calm as opposed to a violent passion according to Hume, which is why it is easily confused for a property of the object itself (1987c, 165). This view is endorsed again ten years later in *An Inquiry Concerning the Principles of Morals* (orig. publ. 1751), where he repeats that beauty lies in the sentiment produced by an object in a mind of a particular fabric or structure, and not in the form of the object itself (Hume 1957, 110).

Yet, in the *Treatise* he also says that beauty is an order of parts fitted to give one pleasure because of one's nature or customs (Hume 1961, 271). Here, then, beauty is like a secondary quality in John Locke's sense: a power an object has in virtue of its form to produce a pleasurable response in us (as, for example, the color red is the power to produce a red sensation in appropriate responders). Certain forms naturally produce this response and, therefore, may be considered themselves beautiful. In this account, as opposed to elsewhere in the *Treatise*, where he writes of beauty as simply a sentiment, the focus is on the object and its properties, which cause the response. A beautiful object is one that causes a pleasurable response in a viewer in favorable circumstances in virtue of its form. To be beautiful is to be such as to cause such a response. Here beauty lies not just in a sentiment, but rather in the relation of an object or a form to the sentiment, its disposition to produce a particular response. Certain forms are "fitted" to produce pleasurable responses, although presumably they will do so only in someone endowed with the properly functioning sensibility and in favorable conditions. In the *Treatise* these two descriptions of beauty—one focused on the subjective sentiment and the other on the object and the formal properties that cause the sentiment—simply coexist in different places. At this stage, Hume seems unaware of this shift in focus between the subjective and the objective, though he will attempt its resolution in his later essay.

In these early writings on the nature of beauty, Hume also makes an initial and partial attempt to spell out which formal properties in an object cause the pleasurable response that leads us to call it beautiful. Francis Hutcheson (1694–1746), Hume's most prominent predecessor in the British tradition in aesthetics, described such form as "unity amidst variety" (Hutcheson 1971). While following Hutcheson in seeing beauty as a relation between an object's form and a subjective response, Hume nowhere endorses this description of the objective side of the relation. And he seems right not to. While some objects and artworks may be beautiful in virtue of their combined unity and complexity, there are also countless counterexamples. Instead Hume in the early works gives only a partial account of beauty, one that is very much in tune with his account of moral properties.

Moral properties or virtuous character traits for Hume are those that are such as to prompt moral approval in normal and unbiased judges. And this "being such as," the objective side of the relation, is analyzed in terms of utility, or usefulness, and immediate agreeableness. Benevolence, for example, is socially useful or beneficial, while good humor and modesty are immediately agreeable. Hume suggests that some ascriptions of beauty rest on these same criteria, as applied to formal appearances. Beauty in the bodies of people and animals, for example, derives from the appearance of utility, suggestions of strength and agility (Hume 1957, 69). The appearance of utility is central to beauty in architecture as well. Square windows and doors, for example, would not appear beautiful because they would not be conducive to use by us. The base of pillars should be broader than the top so as to suggest the idea of stability or security. This appearance of utility as a criterion of beauty applies even to paintings: imbalance is not beautiful in a picture because it suggests danger or falling. The idea of utility produces pleasure in us, as it also does in the realm of morals, because we are sympathetic to the interests of our fellow humans. Other features are beautiful not because they give rise to the idea of utility, but simply because they are immediately agreeable. These include the regularity of facial features in people, as opposed to bodily features suggesting strength or agility.

But the parallel between aesthetic and moral properties even in the early writings is only partial. The properties are distinct for Hume, first, because the sentiments produced, while pleasing in the case of both goodness and beauty, are distinct. Second, while genuine utility is the source of moral approval, it is the appearance of utility that gives rise to the sentiment of beauty. These differences allow for a strong analogy between moral and aesthetic properties, but other disanalogies are more telling. While social utility is the basis for ascribing all the virtues that we recognize as specifically moral, Hume nowhere suggests that this is even close to an exhaustive ground of aesthetic value or beauty. Even more significant is the fact that reference to utility disappears entirely from the mature essay, "Of the Standard of Taste." This may be explicable in part by the fact that his examples are literary rather than visual. But the point remains that, unlike Hutcheson, Hume never attempts a complete specification of those objective formal properties that give rise to the pleasing sentiment of beauty, and the initial partial attempts become even more partial and less specific later on.

2. The need for a standard: Aesthetic rules

What we find at the beginning of the mature essay is a more explicit and self-conscious focus on the tension between the subjective and objective sources of ascriptions of beauty. Hume starts by attributing both views to commonsense thinking about aesthetics. Yet, while previously he was content to simply describe the aesthetic property of beauty in both ways, now he sees them in opposition. The subjective view in common sense is reflected in the ancient proverb, "There is no disputing about matters of taste." People recognize wide differences in tastes in art and literature both within cultures and, even more so, across them. And some apparent agreements mask what are in fact disagreements. People might agree that elegance in writing is always good, but this is because elegance is already an evaluatively loaded term. People agree that elegance is good, but they will disagree about which objects or artworks are elegant. (Here Hume may already be conceding too much to the objectivist in assuming that elegance is always good in an artwork. An elegant performance of Stravinsky's *Rite of Spring* might not be better for that; it might be too elegant so as to detract from its raw power.)

Hume follows this observation of widespread disagreement in tastes and its recognition in common sense with a repetition of his original philosophical claim that responding to objects with ascriptions of beauty is a matter of sentiment and of feelings of pleasure. He now expands on this claim by pointing out that while factual judgments refer to states of affairs in the world and are, therefore, true or false, sentiments do not refer at all. They are self-contained, therefore, neither true nor false. Thus it appears that tastes constituted by such sentiments are all on a par. As in tastes in foods, we like what we like, and that is the end of the matter.

On the other side from these disagreements in tastes are widespread agreements in certain aesthetic judgments. Milton is better than Ogilby, Hume notes (which is why you have not heard of Ogilby), and he might have noted of his contemporaries that Mozart is better than Salieri. Those few who might prefer Ogilby to Milton (or Salieri to Mozart) have worse taste than their counterparts, and it certainly follows that some tastes are better than others. Hence, there must be a standard that distinguishes worse taste from better. Hume takes his task in this essay to be that of making this standard explicit. While sentiments cannot be true or false, they can be appropriate or not, and Hume's standard will distinguish the appropriate or fit reactions from the inappropriate ones. In the remainder of the essay, what we find are several, progressive attempts to specify such a standard.

His first suggestion along this line is that, if there are standards, there must be aesthetic rules or principles that link objective properties of artworks or other objects to aesthetic properties like beauty. This point echoes in different terms his earlier claim that certain forms are naturally suited to cause pleasurable responses in viewers. Since causal relations require perfectly regular connections between causes and effects according to Hume, there must be rules linking these objective forms to the responses constitutive of beauty, if the forms cause the responses. We discover these rules as we discover any causal relations: through observation.

But now the first real complication sets in. Hume claims that there are aesthetic principles and that these could comprise standards of taste, but he has great difficulty identifying any. The examples he offers are either easily counterexemplified or once more contain evaluative terms. We saw in earlier writings that he took the appearance of utility to connect to judgments of beauty, yet there is no mention of that here (perhaps again because his examples are from literature). Instead he first mentions the poet Ariosto and implies that we can abstract rules indicating good- and bad-making properties in his writing. On the negative side are his "monstrous and improbable fictions," his mixture of comic and serious styles, his lack of coherence, and interruptions of narration. On the positive side are his natural pictures of "gay and amorous" passions (Hume 1987d, 232).

None of these is remotely plausible as a suggestion of an aesthetic rule. *Alice in Wonderland* and *Frankenstein* both contain monstrous and improbable fictions; Shakespeare mixes comic and serious styles; many absurdist plays lack coherence; and George Eliot and Herman Melville constantly interrupt their narrations. Of course, these works (except for those of Shakespeare) could not be known to Hume, but all of them provide clear counterexamples to his suggestions of aesthetic rules. His positive rule is even more ridiculous, since any piece of pornography will present natural pictures of gay and amorous passions without having aesthetic merit on that score. Later in the essay Hume again appeals to coherence, to the actions of fictional agents being in keeping with their characters, and to artworks achieving their intended ends as aesthetically good-making properties. The first criterion, as seen, fails to account for the value of absurdist plays. The second of these criteria is violated by Joseph Conrad's Nostromo, one of the great fictional characters. The third is not an appeal to utility in the earlier usual sense, but refers to aesthetic goals or ends. But these themselves can be evaluated, and not every intended end is worth achieving. Not every such achievement is aesthetically worthy.

3. Paradigm works and critics

Hume himself seems to doubt his initial appeal to aesthetic rules, for he quickly changes the subject, first pointing out that such rules are not generally readily apparent and then suggesting another possible standard, those paradigm works in the canons of art and literature that have withstood the test of time. Once more, however, we cannot appeal directly to these works as our standard of taste since it is not clear how or even whether newer works must resemble them in their objective properties in order to have aesthetic value. Yet, Hume suggests that we can abstract the rules of art from these paradigm works. We need such an indirect method of identifying rules because, as noted, they will not be apparent to the average reader or viewer.

According to Hume, we must seek to locate the rules of art in the properties of paradigm works, where these good- and bad-making properties are found "singly and in a high degree" (1987d, 235). Once we have located the rules by reference to paradigm works, we can dismiss as inadequate critics those who fail to appreciate the positive or negative value of these properties when these are present but not so intense or readily apparent. Once more his suggestion here is problematic. The problem is that properties of artworks are never isolated, even in canonical works. They always occur in combination with other properties that can affect their aesthetic values in the contexts of the works in question.

It is clear at this point, however, that Hume has changed the subject again, at last approaching his final proposal for a standard of taste. What he discusses in the central part of the essay are the features that adequate or ideal critics must possess. These critics are the relatively few on whom the rules of art regularly operate. They are those in whom aesthetically valuable objective properties regularly cause pleasurable responses. Their judgments constitute, therefore, Hume tells us, the true standard of taste. Those aesthetic judgments or tastes that disagree with theirs can be dismissed.

Some of the features of these critics are straightforward and unproblematic. Since fine works of art and literature contain many elements in complex relations, competent critics require first of all experience and sometimes training in how to appreciate them. They must be, as Hume puts it, practiced. They require multiple encounters with particular works and others of their kind. As pointed out, in earlier writings he noted that some objects immediately please and give rise to immediate judgments of beauty. But other aesthetic evaluations, similar to moral judgments based on social utility, require much reasoning to precede. The literary examples fall into the latter class. Thus, competent critics must also, second, be adept at making comparisons. They must place the works being judged in the proper comparison classes in order to judge them accurately. Great works are excellent of their kind or style.

Third, competent critics must be free from prejudice. For Hume this means more than not having a personal relation to the authors they judge. When judging works from other times and cultures, critics must be able to place themselves in the contexts of the originally intended audiences. They must disregard or correct for differences in cultural outlooks that might otherwise stand in the way of appreciating the works. The one exception noted by Hume is that of alien moral outlooks. Critics, he thinks, cannot be positively engaged by works that endorse objectionable moral views; nor should they.

These features of ideal critics, as noted, seem relatively unproblematic, although there may be some inconsistency—not noted by Hume—between his requirements to place works in proper comparison classes and to place oneself in the historical contexts of original intended audiences. Adhering to the latter requirement would rule out comparisons with later works, which might nevertheless be relevant to aesthetic evaluation. But perhaps Hume would have denied this last claim. Or, he might have said that placing oneself in the intended audience's position is essential to interpret a work, while a complete evaluation of the work might require comparisons that the original audience could not make.

All these features of ideal critics are required in order to allow their central feature to operate properly: what Hume calls "delicacy of taste." In an earlier essay, "Of the Delicacy of Taste and Passion," published in 1741, Hume describes fine taste as both an ability to finely discriminate all parts of a picture or poem and as the disposition to be emotionally moved by them (1987a, 4). In the mature essay he once more initially combines these abilities under the terms "delicacy of imagination" and "delicacy of taste" (Hume 1987d, 234–235). Later in the essay he distinguishes "strong sense" from "delicate sentiment" (Hume 1987d, 241). The ability to perceive all relevant parts of a work and their relations to each other is clearly required of competent critics. In fact, the articulation of such complex structures is the way we identify such critics. But the ability to react in the right way or with the right sentiments is more problematic as a means of identifying ideal critics. Here is where Hume is sometimes accused of circularity in his reasoning. Great works are those to which all competent critics react positively as the standard of taste, yet here competent critics seem to be the ones who react positively to the best works.

4. Questions regarding Hume's critics

In fact three questions arise in regard to Hume's final standard: (1) How do we identify the ideal critics? (2) Why are the judgments of such critics normative for us? (3) Will these critics agree in their judgments so as to settle aesthetic disagreements among us? Hume is aware of the first question and responds. The problem of identifying proper aesthetic judges is more severe than in the case of other response dependent properties like colors, since most of us are not competent judges of artworks as opposed to colors. Aesthetic rules, according to Hume, are subtle and operate only on a small minority in special circumstances. We have seen that he holds that certain forms are naturally suited for pleasurable responses, yet the features of ideal critics are not natural, but the result of extensive experience or training. They are natural, if at all, only in the sense that such experience removes obstacles to their proper functioning. So how does Hume respond to this problem of identification?

He can escape the charge of circularity if he can identify either ideal critics or great artworks and their properties independently of one another. He could identify the critics independently if he dropped the requirement that they be properly emotionally sensitive to works and maintained only the other requirements, including the ability to discriminate and relate all the parts of complex works. I suggested above that this latter ability is how we in fact identify competent critics (perhaps requiring also that they be otherwise emotionally normal). Yet Hume never considers this suggestion. He instead claims again that we can identify great artworks as those which stand the test of time, which are appreciated across different ages and cultures. We then identify competent critics by the way in which "they receive [such] productions of genius" (Hume 1987d, 243). We must use this circuitous route because, as noted above, we cannot specify the ways in which newer works must resemble older ones in order to have aesthetic value. We cannot specify rules of art despite Hume's abstract claim to the contrary. (Earlier in the essay he claims that we can identify the rules by reference to the paradigm works and competent critics by their grasp of the rules [Hume 1987, 237]. But if paradigms could teach us the rules, we would not need the critics.)

As to our second question, why the judgments of ideal critics should take precedence over our more mundane tastes, the simplest answer is that these critics perceive complex works more accurately than we do. If such works are themselves of great aesthetic value, it must be their real properties that cause deep pleasurable responses, and ideal critics are better able to perceive these properties. Only if one is responding to correctly perceived properties of works can one expect or demand similar responses from others. Thus, if we are to assert our judgments at all, we must seek to perceive the works we judge as those with developed powers of discrimination do. Perhaps this is why Hume simply claims in the "Standard of Taste" that superior taste is universally acknowledged to be preferable (1987d, 242).

But this last claim is questionable. While superior critics may get more pleasure than we do from complex works, they may get less pleasure from simpler and more obvious works. And finer discrimination and a larger comparison base do not always enhance appreciation. Those with perfect pitch may hear an orchestra as slightly off-key, spoiling the performance, and comparing Karl Stamitz to Mozart only makes Stamitz sound worse. Hume could still claim (although he does not do so explicitly) that paradigm works in the canon offer deeper satisfactions than more superficial works, so that those who can appreciate these canonical works can best advise us how to derive such deeper pleasure from more recent creations.

It is in earlier essays that Hume expands upon the benefits of superior taste. In "Of Eloquence" (orig. publ. 1742) he simply says that bad taste is due to ignorance, echoing what Plato said about morality and foreshadowing John Stuart Mill's claim that those who experience both sorts of pleasure always prefer the higher (doubtful). In "Of the Delicacy of Taste and Passion," Hume argues that superior taste, first, better enables us to control the pleasures available to us (1987a, 5), presumably by broadening the possible sources of pleasure. Second, it allows us to escape "the hurries of business." Along these lines it can be claimed that more complex works occupy us more fully, offering a more complete escape from the messy affairs of our everyday pursuits. Third, people with superior tastes tend to associate with one another, forming close-knit minorities. Such groups tend to be strongly united by common feelings, and such social bonds are another benefit of good taste (Hume 1987a, 7).

Finally, in his moral writing Hume suggests that serious attention to the arts develops finer emotions, softens one's temperament, and so leads to virtue (1957, 170). This claim is far more subject to doubt: for every Verdi (good character), there seems to be a Wagner (bad character). Thus not only good taste, but also artistic genius, seems to be independent of moral goodness. Deleting such hyperbole, Hume has still provided adequate indication of why we should prefer to have sophisticated tastes in art, of why the judgments of critics with such tastes should be normative for us.

5. Ultimate relativity and standards

Turning finally to our third question, at the end of his mature essay Hume allows for "blameless diversity" in aesthetic evaluations, that is, disagreement even among fully competent critics. He is clear about the sources of such disagreements, but not so clear about their degree. The sources according to Hume are two: temperament that changes with age on the one hand, and cultural setting on the other. Young people might prefer romantic art; older people might prefer more reflective works (Hume 1987d, 244). Likewise, the preferences of Italians might differ from those of the English.

At one point Hume says that these differences do not "confound all the boundaries of beauty," but affect only the degrees of approval or disapproval of various works (1987d, 243). This implies that the same works should be judged good by competent critics, who should disagree only about how good they are. But later Hume notes that, unlike Italians, French and English critics might disapprove of a play by Machiavelli (Hume 1987d, 245). This implies deeper disagreements than those about degrees of positive response.

In either case Hume must admit at the end that there are no absolute standards of taste, no single right evaluations of artworks or objective degrees of value that works possess. This means that, despite his explicit claims to the contrary, there are no strict rules of art either, no principles or laws that link objective properties of works with degrees of aesthetic value. In fact, despite these contrary claims, Hume himself indicates the two reasons why there are no such rules. The first lies in the ultimate differences in taste even among fully competent critics, which we have just seen Hume recognize. If evaluations are ultimately relative to different tastes, then there cannot be rules that objectively determine them.

Second, in noting earlier that rules should be apparent only when objective aesthetic properties are found "singly and in high degree" (as they never are), Hume indirectly recognizes that combining properties in different contexts alters their aesthetic values. An objective feature of a particular work that makes it aesthetically better will not have positive value in the context of another work with different other features. A beautiful musical phrase in a Mozart symphony would sound awful in a piece by Stravinsky. This is another reason why there are no rules linking objective features with aesthetic values.

Despite his admitted failure to provide an absolute standard of taste, Hume not only succeeds in providing standards or normative requirements on sound aesthetic judgments, but his account is also as plausible as any we have. If we are unfamiliar with the kind of work we are judging, if we lack knowledge of other works with which to compare it, if we are inattentive and so fail to discriminate the aesthetically relevant elements or relate them in a way that could best reveal their value, or if we are biased by idiosyncratic personal associations, then our aesthetic judgments will be unreliable. Certain judgments can, therefore, be dismissed even if there is no single correct one. We do in fact find disagreements even among our best critics, even different reactions to works in the canon. But the features exemplified by such critics are, as Hume claims, standards of taste. We must only seek out the judgments and explanations of competent critics whose tastes we generally share.

6. Postscript: Hume on tragedy

In one other essay not yet mentioned here, his "Of Tragedy" (orig. publ. 1757) Hume addresses another question in aesthetics that dates back to Plato and Aristotle. The question is why we feel positively, indeed seek out, works that express and seemingly cause in us negative emotions such as sadness or fear. The answers that aestheticians have given are numerous, ranging from catharsis or release of negative feelings, to educating ourselves about our emotions, to learning to cope with negative emotions, to feeling good when in control of them, to the emotions themselves not being negative when they lack actual objects. Hume's answer is unique if not the most plausible of the set.

He theorizes that when emotions combine, the stronger of the two dominates the weaker and transforms it. A negative emotion such as sadness turns positive when combined with a stronger positive feeling we derive from the perception of great beauty. Conversely, the positive feeling we get from beauty makes the emotion of sadness even stronger when it dominates the feeling of pleasure, as when a funeral speech is eloquent. Great tragic works of art are able to be experienced positively, while lesser such works are not.

The problem with this theory is the lack of psychological evidence that emotions in fact combine in this way. Furthermore, the theory fails to explain why people seek out suspense novels and horror movies that frighten them without being very beautiful. Perhaps for these reasons this essay is not nearly so much discussed or so well received in contemporary aesthetics as is "Of the Standard of Taste." That essay has clearly withstood the test of time and taken its place in the canon of seminal works in aesthetics.

Primary sources

Hume:
1957. *An Inquiry Concerning the Principles of Morals.* Indianapolis, IN: Bobbs-Merrill. Originally published 1751.
1961. *A Treatise of Human Nature.* Garden City, NY: Dolphin. Originally published 1740.
1987a. "Of the Delicacy of Taste and Passion." In *Essays: Moral, Political, and Literary.* Indianapolis, IN: Liberty Fund. Originally published 1741.
1987b. "Of Eloquence." In *Essays.* Originally published 1742.
1987c. "The Skeptic." In *Essays.* Originally published 1742.
1987d. "Of the Standard of Taste." In *Essays.* Originally published 1757.
1987e. "Of Tragedy." In *Essays.* Originally published 1757.

References and further reading

Carroll, Noël. 1984. "Hume's Standard of Taste." *Journal of Aesthetics and Art Criticism*, 4, 181–194.
Gracyk, Theodore. 1994. "Rethinking Hume's Standard of Taste." *Journal of Aesthetics and Art Criticism*, 52, 169–182.
Hutcheson, Francis. 1971. *An Inquiry into the Original of Our Ideas of Beauty and Virtue.* New York: Garland. Originally published 1729.
Korsmeyer, Carolyn. 1976. "Hume and the Foundations of Taste." *Journal of Aesthetics and Art Criticism*, 35, 201–215.
Levinson, Jerrold. 2002. "Hume's Standard of Taste: The Real Problem." *Journal of Aesthetics and Art Criticism*, 60, 227–238.
Mothersill, Mary. 1989. "Hume and the Paradox of Taste." In G. Dickie, R. Sclafani, and R. Roblin (eds.), *Aesthetics.* New York: St. Martin's, 269–286.
Shelley, James. 1998. "Hume and the Nature of Taste." *Journal of Aesthetics and Art Criticism*, 56, 29–38.

CHAPTER 5

IMMANUEL KANT
(1724–1804)

Elisabeth Schellekens

Kant's aesthetic theory has a firm place within his critical philosophical project as a whole. In this respect, his account of aesthetic experience harbors explanatory ambitions far more extensive than any analyses of beauty and taste alone would appear to afford. Kant's wider legacy is, in truth, an attempt to formulate a comprehensive *system* targeting not only the objects and subjects of experience in general, but also the relation between them. This project, which includes examinations of the conceptual schemes at our disposal, the manner in which those schemes are applied to various aspects of the world, and how the subjective and objective features of reality influence one another, is developed mainly in three *Critiques*. The *Critique of the Power of Judgment* (Kant 2001) is the last work in this series, and contains an elaborate study of a kind of judgment or, more specifically, of a psychological process that leads to a reflective act of judging. According to Kant, aesthetic judgment, conceived as one instance of "reflective judgment,"[1] is to be understood in terms of a highly structured and sophisticated inquiry into a certain kind of perception, contemplation, and assessment.[2]

A distinctive feature of Kant's theory is that the notion of the aesthetic employed is both broader *and* narrower than the concept we are familiar with today. On the one hand, it is narrower because Kant is exclusively concerned with beauty and the sublime. By "aesthetic," Kant has a certain kind of experience in mind: an experience primarily linked to our awareness of the beautiful and the sublime as a matter of definition. His attention is, therefore, not directed at any of the other aesthetic qualities that contemporary philosophers tend to include in their investigations, such as being stylish, garish, dumpy, dainty, or even ugly.[3] On the other hand, Kant's use of the aesthetic is also broader than our current one, for it is derived from the ancient Greek *aesthesis* and, as such, primarily refers to the "sensory" or that which is experienced through the senses. For Kant, aesthetic judgment centers around the pleasurable *sensation* that beauty gives rise to; and that subjective experience in turn reveals something important about the role of the sensory in our attempts to understand the world and our place in it.

1. Kant's project and philosophical aims

While Kant is certainly not the first to examine beauty or aesthetic experience from a philosophical perspective, the approach adopted in the *Critique of the Power of Judgment* carves out a new area of conceptual analysis by introducing terms that raise the investigation's philosophical stakes significantly. Aesthetics, on the Kantian account, is first and foremost an investigation into the workings of our mind, and their epistemological reach into the external world. Aesthetic judgments are judgments of taste, where taste is defined as the "faculty for judging an object or a kind of representation through a satisfaction or dissatisfaction" where "[t]he object of such a satisfaction is called beautiful" (2001, 5, 5:211).

Now, for Kant, there are three general mental faculties, each with their own "faculty of cognition," "a priori principles," and "applications." Whereas the understanding (*Verstand*) contains the constitutive a priori principles for the faculty of cognition as applied to nature, and reason (*Vernunft*) contains the principles for the faculty of desire as applied to freedom, the power of judgment (*Urteil*) contains the principles of the feeling of aesthetic pleasure and displeasure. One of the main aims of the *Critique of the Power of Judgment* is to isolate those a priori principles— this, as we shall see, is no mean feat, especially in light of the claim that "[n]o objective principle of taste is possible" (2001, 34, 5:285).

Generally speaking, Kant thus sets out to establish what we can have knowledge of or what there is "out there" for us to know: to what extent, if any, do the subjective aspects of experience delimit what we can legitimately say about the objective world? It is perhaps surprising, then, that Kant opens his third *Critique* by drawing a clear distinction between aesthetic and cognitive judgments, emphasizing that judgments of beauty do not share the cognitive aims of ordinary judgments and cannot yield knowledge in that way. This is not to say that aesthetic judgment, already classified by Kant as a kind of reflective judgment in its own right, cannot exhibit some of the marks of cognitive judgments, as we shall soon see. Nor does it imply that aesthetic judgments, despite being judgments of taste, share all their features with other kinds of judgments based on sensation. As Kant writes:

> With regard to the agreeable, everyone is content that his judgment, which he grounds on a private feeling . . . be restricted merely to his own person . . . It would be folly to dispute the judgment of another that is different from our own in such a matter, with the aim of condemning it as incorrect . . . [T]hus with regard to the agreeable, the principle Everyone has his own taste (of the senses) is valid. (2001, 7, 5:212)

However,

> [w]ith the beautiful it is entirely different. It would be ridiculous if . . . someone who prided himself on his taste thought to justify himself thus: "This object . . . is beautiful for me." For he must not call it beautiful if it pleases merely him . . . if he pronounces that something is beautiful, then he expects the very same satisfaction of others: he judges not merely for himself, but for everyone. (2001, 7, 5:212–213)

Aesthetic judgments are thus to be conceived as occupying some kind of middle ground between entirely objective cognitive judgments and purely subjective sensory ones—although they are not straightforwardly objective ascriptions, they are not limited to individual reports of subjective states either. Rather, aesthetic judgments capture something about the *relation* between the subjective and the objective that reaches beyond the restricted boundaries of either sphere. Tackled from this angle, the *Critique of the Power of Judgment* can thus be seen as an attempt to examine a very unique kind of judgment, one that by its very nature bridges the gap between mind and world.

2. Key concepts

2.1. Aesthetic experience: Freedom of the faculties
The starting point of Kant's inquiry is the way in which our mental faculties interact in aesthetic experience. Developing the division with which

he opens the *Critique of the Power of Judgment*, Kant offers us two models of how aesthetic judgments are made. In the case of ordinary cognitive judgments (e.g., "This is a rose"), our imagination (*Einbildungskraft*) provides a sense-impression which, although perceptually unified—or "synthesized" to use Kant's terminology—lacks a particular label, so to speak (e.g., "rose"). That is to say, the imagination offers us the perceptual impression of a rose even though we are not yet in a position to categorize or grasp it as such. In order for that to occur, we need the understanding to step in and apply the appropriate concept, rose, to the impression in question. The understanding thus "subsumes" the imagination's sense-impression under the suitable "determinate concept" (e.g., rose) thereby rendering the cognitive judgment fully intelligible.

With aesthetic experience, however, the psychology of judgment-making is different, for beauty cannot be, for Kant, a determinate concept in this sense. That is to say, when the focus of our experience is not something like "rosehood" but, rather, beauty itself (e.g., in "This [rose] is beautiful"), the understanding is unable to categorize our perceptual impression as beautiful, since there is no such concept for the understanding to apply to the sense-impression presented by the imagination. As a result, understanding and imagination enter into a harmonious state of "free play" in which neither of the faculties aim to subsume the material provided by the other. This state, Kant tells us, is pleasurable precisely in virtue of its freedom, and is what serves as ground for the aesthetic judgment.[4] To use Kant's words,

> [i]n order to understand whether or not something is beautiful, we do not relate the representation by means of understanding to the object for cognition, but rather relate it by means of the imagination . . . to the subject and its feeling of pleasure or displeasure. The judgment of taste is therefore not a cognitive judgment, hence not a logical one, but is rather aesthetic by which is understood one whose determining ground cannot be other than subjective. (2001, 1, 5:203)

Now, Kant's commitment to the idea that there can be no determinate concept for beauty does not mean that there is no such notion in the first place, or that it is nonsensical. Rather, what Kant is eager to highlight is that there can be no rules by which the concept of beauty can be applied. In other words, there are no fundamental principles that serve as reliable guides to whether or why beauty can rightly be ascribed (or not) to our sense-impressions. Importantly, there can be no rule in accordance with which someone could be compelled to acknowledge something as beautiful. Whether a garment, a house, a flower is beautiful: no one allows himself to be talked into his judgment about that by means of any grounds or fundamental principles. One wants to submit the object to one's own eyes. (2001, 8, 5:215–216)[5]

Aesthetic judgments must thus always be based on first-hand perceptual experience (rather than, say, testimony) and cannot be reduced to any kind of regulated or inferential process.

2.2. The validity of aesthetic judgments: Universality and necessity

So far, we have established that Kant conceives of aesthetic judgment as crucially different from cognitive judgment in two respects: first, the mental operations underpinning the judgment-making process (i.e., the "free play" of the faculties); second, the evidential ground upon which the judgment is based (i.e., the sensation of pleasure). However, we also know that it would be wrong to assume that Kant takes these divergences to imply that the two kinds of judgment have nothing in common. Perhaps most importantly, inherent to aesthetic judgment (despite being a judgment of taste) is "a claim to the assent of everyone" (Kant 2001, 32, 5:281), since the beautiful is "the object of a necessary satisfaction" (2001, 22, 5:240). On Kant's account, aesthetic judgments call for universal validity and are hence characterized by a powerful normativity.

To say that "Everyone has his special taste" would be to dismiss the very possibility of aesthetic taste, and to deny that there could be aesthetic judgments "that could make a rightful claim to the assent of everyone." (2001, 7, 5:213)

While we may agree with this, a question arises as to how the claim to universality and necessity can possibly be squared with the idea that pleasure is the evidential ground of aesthetic judgments. Kant's response to this problem lies in his conception of a *sensus communis* (communal sense) or the idea that all, or nearly all, human beings are endowed with sufficiently similar mental abilities to ensure that we undergo suitably similar experiences—if I experience something as beautiful then you will, too. As far as justifying our aesthetic judgments is concerned, we can thus appeal to this commonality: if my imagination and understanding engage in "free play" in a certain context, then—all other things being equal—so will yours.

Interestingly, this communal sense acquires a particularly significant dimension in light of the claim that there can be no rules for beauty (in contradistinction to ordinary cognitive judgments), no governing principles to support our aesthetic judgments. Kant himself points to the difficulty of his position in the "Antinomy of Taste," where he calls attention to the fact that although we frequently do argue about taste and its "claim to the necessary assent of others," we cannot establish a judgment's appropriateness "by means of proofs" since "[t]he judgment of taste is not based on concepts" (2001, 56, 5:338–339), that is, on rules for beauty. As a result, the necessity in question here is "exemplary." That is to say, rather than depending on principles or law-like regulations, aesthetic normativity is rooted in examples of beautiful things and our common experience of them. The absence of foundational principles in which to ground our aesthetic judgments is thus superseded by the shared psychological abilities that allow us, as human beings, to perceive, contemplate, and assess the external world with the same "aesthetic eyes," so to speak.

The explanatory power Kant places on this communal sense is thus of the kind we may expect from a universal predisposition to undergo similar experiences. But the experience in question here is still the sensation of pleasure that results from the harmony of the faculties—the only "evidence" we can have of being in the presence of something beautiful is still the feeling of pleasure. The challenge for Kant is, then, to secure the possibility of combining two seemingly incompatible ideas, namely, the objective ambitions of aesthetic judgments with their thoroughly subjective ground.

2.3. The ground of aesthetic judgments: Pleasure and disinterestedness

Kant's answer to that challenge is to qualify the kind of pleasure at work in aesthetic experience very early on in his account. Aesthetic pleasure, he tells us, is not just any kind of sensory enjoyment or gratification. In fact, it is fundamentally dissimilar to the enjoyment we may experience when we gratify our senses (such as when we scratch an itch) or when we do the morally right thing (such as help an elderly person cross the road). Kant distinguishes between the satisfaction of the good, sensory gratification, and aesthetic pleasure and adds that the pleasure occasioned by the harmony of the faculties is unique in being "disinterested." By this Kant means that the pleasure is not focused on any function the object may fulfill. Instead, disinterested pleasure is pleasure in something merely for its own sake, or for the sake of its form alone. In consequence, aesthetic judgment is "indifferent with regard to the existence of an object" (2001, 5, 5:209) in the sense that it is not aimed at nor is about the purpose the object in question may serve. For Kant,

> if the question is whether something is beautiful, one does not want to know whether there is anything that is or that could be at stake, for us or for someone else, in the existence of the thing, but rather how we judge it in mere contemplation . . . Everyone must admit that a judgment about beauty in which there is mixed the least interest is very partial and not a pure judgment of taste. (2001, 2, 5:204–205)

Disinterestedness thus differentiates aesthetic pleasure from other kinds of pleasure too idiosyncratic to ground universally valid judgments by detaching aesthetic contemplation from functional considerations, so to speak. In other words, any purpose that the object of aesthetic appreciation may serve does not enter into the reflective act of judging it beautiful.

2.4. What aesthetic judgments capture: Purposiveness without purpose

We judge something to be beautiful when it feels "just right" or when it gives us the impression of having successfully met some end. However, as we now know, aesthetic judgments can neither be based on private sensations nor on the notion of perfection since such judgments not only lay claim to universal validity and enjoy a well-founded normativity, but also cannot be reduced to rules or any application thereof. In Kant's words, aesthetic judgments are not about "objective purposiveness" (or the purposiveness of objects) targeted at "the sort of thing [an object] is supposed to be" (2001, 15, 5:228).

Having said that, there is room in Kant's theory for another kind of purposiveness, one which, although it is felt (since it based in the "free play" of the faculties), is nonetheless capable of underpinning Kant's conception of aesthetic judgment: "subjective purposiveness" or

"purposiveness without a purpose." Crucially, that which sets our faculties into free play is not the "matter" of sensation (i.e., the actual sense-
impression) but, rather, its "form," so that in enjoying something's form
what we grasp is, precisely, that the thing in question is suitable for
inducing the imagination and understanding into harmonious free play.
And this, for Kant, means that the forms that support the universal
validity claim must be "final" or "ends" for perception and contemplation. Beautiful things can thus be said to have the "form of finality"
since their purposiveness is one we ascribe to their form, and their form
is such as to benefit from being "just right" for setting our faculties into
free play. In that sense at least, they can be said to have met their end.
Most importantly of all, this purposiveness constitutes "the principle of
taste," which in turn is "the subjective principle of the power of judgment in general" (2001, 35, 5:286), grounded in the feeling of pleasure
and applied to art.

2.5. Aesthetic judgments about art:
Aesthetic ideas and genius

It should be clear, then, that according to Kant's account, when we
discern and contemplate beautiful form we are, fundamentally, engaging with one of our main mental faculty's guiding principles. But what
about when we create such form? What about the artists who seek to
produce it?

In addition to being endowed with the faculty of taste and sharing
the common sense that grounds the universal and necessary character
of aesthetic judgment, artists seek to improve their taste by examining
and engaging with examples of beautiful form in both nature and art.
The artist's goal is, therefore, neither to reach generalizations about
what most people find aesthetically pleasing nor to formulate some
rule that could serve as some kind of a priori guideline. Rather, the artist
examines exemplars of universally and necessarily pleasing form in order
to be able to recreate it.

To be aesthetically valuable, artworks must not only have beautiful form but also be capable of "animat[ing] the soul" or of conveying
"spirit" (2001, 49, 5:313). That special something that certain artists
can transmit through the creation of an artwork is what Kant calls an
"aesthetic idea," or a "representation of the imagination that occasions
much thinking though without it being possible for . . . language [to]

fully attain or make it intelligible" (2001, 49, 5:314). Being expressive of aesthetic ideas shows a work of fine art to be a work of "genius," which, in turn, is "a talent for producing that for which no definite rule can be given . . . [and] consequently originality must be its primary property" (2001, 46, 5:307–308). The aim of genius is thus to produce something that can serve as a paradigmatic example of what a work of fine art is and which can be followed (although not copied). In other words,

> genius really consists in the happy relation, which no science can teach and no diligence learn, of finding ideas for a given concept . . . and . . . hitting upon the expression for these, through which the subjective disposition of the mind that is thereby produced . . . can be communicated to others. (2001, 49, 5:317)

Artists of genius are thus those who can adequately express ideas in such a way as to animate our imagination and understanding without thereby relying on rules or other restrictions. Beautiful form infused with "spirit" can, therefore, engage us in a pleasurable (and extended) aesthetic contemplation, and it is this feature that makes some artworks works of genius.

2.6. Kinds of aesthetic judgments:
Pure and impure—beautiful and sublime

Judgments of beauty characterized by the form of finality we have discussed so far are undoubtedly the main target of Kant's inquiry. Yet, even though Kant would not, unlike most contemporary philosophers, classify judgments of the dainty or the dumpy as aesthetic strictly speaking, there is room in his account for at least some diversity. First, Kant draws an important distinction between judgments of "free" and "dependent" beauty, or between "pure" and "impure" judgments of taste. Whereas the "first presupposes no concept of what the object ought to be, the second does presuppose such a concept and the perfection of the object in accordance with it." Dependent beauty (e.g., the beauty of horses or churches) is "ascribed to objects that stand under the concept of a particular end" (2001, 16, 5:229), and so there is a sense in which the object's end or purpose does enter into the judgment of its beauty.[6] Instances of free beauty (e.g., the beauty of flowers or birds), on the other hand, please merely "for themselves" and the corresponding judgments are not in any sense reliant on the object in question attaining some kind of perfection or on fulfilling its purpose.

No less crucial is the division Kant outlines between judgments of beauty and another kind of reflective judgment which lays claim to universal validity, namely, that of the sublime. The beautiful and the sublime differ mainly in two respects: first, the sublime involves "ideas of reason" (i.e., those of cognition and morality) rather than aesthetic ideas; second, the sublime is not concerned with the form of finality presented by objects so much as with the representation of phenomena that seem limitless, and to that extent even formless. Thus for Kant,

> it is noteworthy here that even if we have no interest at all in the object . . . still its mere magnitude, even if it is considered as formless, can bring with it a satisfaction that is universally communicable, hence it may contain a consciousness of a subjective purposiveness in the use of our cognitive faculties: but not a satisfaction in the object, as in the case of the beautiful (since it can be formless) . . . rather in the enlargement of the imagination in itself. (2001, 25, 5:249)

The sublime invokes an impression of awesome grandeur, even enormity, and captures "that which is absolutely great," such as the pyramids of Egypt (2001, 26, 5:252), "the dark and raging sea" (2001, 26, 5:256), and "the starry heavens" (2001, 29, 5:270). These are sublime in virtue of their size and force—they make us aware of our physical limitations in comparison to them.[7]

It is interesting to note that, of all the notions Kant introduces in his aesthetic theory, that of the sublime is one of the most difficult to grasp. At times, his conception of it seems almost to merge with the beautiful; at others, it seems to be of a different dimension altogether. Either way, Kant's account is substantially enriched by the fact that, although his focus is always on a specific kind of experience—a particular form of interaction between mind and world—he imposes only the widest limits on what kind of form the object of this experience can take, be it a horse or the starry heavens.

3. Kant's influence

In virtue of his developing an aesthetic theory so resolutely lodged within a broader philosophical project, Kant's long-lasting influence has operated in two distinct ways. On the one hand, Kant's theory has most probably contributed more than any other to positioning aesthetics as a philosophical discipline in its own right, albeit one that remains closely connected not only to the philosophy of mind, epistemology, and metaphysics, but also the philosophy of religion and moral philosophy. For Kant's treatment of the sublime offers close connections with the sphere of religion, and, famously, beauty is said to be the symbol of morality (2001, 59). Aesthetics, conceived as an independent although not isolated area of inquiry, begins to form a significant part of the philosophical continuum largely due to Kant's third *Critique*.

On the other hand, Kant's aesthetic theory has had a profound effect on debates within aesthetics in both the continental and Anglo-American or analytic traditions. Certainly in the case of the latter, Kant's original treatment of the subject has shaped not only the questions we still ask today but also the manner in which they continue to be tackled—principally, the layered analysis of aesthetic experience, the concern for the epistemological reach of aesthetic judgments, and the ontology of aesthetic properties.

Perhaps most importantly, Kant's theory highlights three central ideas. The first is the scrutiny paid to the notion of aesthetic pleasure itself, and to the carefully delineated role accorded to it in the distinction between aesthetic judgments and cognitive judgments. The second is the insistence on the normative force of aesthetic judgments and their aspirations to universality. The third is the notion of aesthetic perception. This he takes to be not only the sole means by which we can acquire the appropriate grounds for aesthetic judgments, but also the concept through which aesthetic discernment is first and foremost to be understood. For the disinterestedness that qualifies aesthetic pleasure is more than a mere criterion for the kind of pleasure in question, it is a pointer to Kant's conception of aesthetic experience as a particular way of engaging with the world and of grasping its full character.[8] None of this is to say that these notions did not play key roles in earlier accounts of aesthetic experience. Hume, for example, emphasizes precisely these aspects of the aesthetic in his essay "Of the Standard of Taste." What is remarkable in Kant, however, is the degree of systematic analysis of the concepts introduced in order to explain the phenomenon at hand, resulting in a considerably richer and more complex theory as a whole.

While it is beyond dispute that Kant poses some of the most interesting questions concerning the aesthetic, the matter of whether we take Kant to have provided satisfactory answers to these questions is not. Generally speaking, the third *Critique* has met with controversy ever since its first appearance in 1790, and many readers have found its numerous loose ends and ambiguous terminologies to make for more trouble than truth. To twenty-first-century philosophers, some recurring difficulties have to do with the seemingly outdated and idiosyncratic definitions of, among other things, the main mental faculties and their interactions. Other problems arise from the vague formulation of obscure notions such as "purposiveness without purpose" or "form of finality." Finally, internal inconsistencies appear to plague the very idea that, for example, dependent beauty might be a kind of beauty in its own right despite relying on the notion of perfection and function. Likewise, on these lines, Kant seems committed to the unlikely suggestion that judgments of ugliness or negative aesthetic judgment are simply impossible.

These factors notwithstanding, the philosophy outlined in the third *Critique* is possessed of a range and depth of thought about the aesthetic with which it is difficult to find comparison. It is also true that there are very few subsequent theories that have not made use of Kant's theory in some way. Above and beyond the explanatory power held by the key concepts outlined in the final *Critique*, perhaps this is also a reflection of the evidence of profound concern on Kant's part to link our aesthetic experience of art and nature to our lives as rational and moral agents. In other words, perhaps it is because Kant's account of beauty is so ambitious both in its internal analytic rigor and in its possible application to the entire scope of what is valued by human beings, that we just do not seem able to stray very far away from the milestones he has laid out for us.

Notes

1 For Kant, a reflective judgment is a judgment that seeks to find "the universal for the given particular" (2001, Introduction IV, 179), as opposed to determining judgments that aim to subsume particulars under given universals.

2   The *Critique of the Power of Judgment* contains two main parts: the "Critique of the Aesthetic Power of Judgment" and the "Critique of the Teleological Power of Judgment." The common aim of these two parts is to shed light on the faculty of judgment in general. Kant further divides the first part into two books: the "Analytic of the Beautiful" and the "Analytic of the Sublime." I concentrate on the first of those two books.

3   Although some of these qualities are mentioned in the *Critique of the Power of Judgment*, they don't fall within the category of the aesthetic for Kant. For more on this question, see the sections on to the agreeable and the charming (2001, §§3, 5, 7, 13, 29, 42, and 51).

4   For a particularly clear exposition of this twofold structure, see Janaway (1997).

5   For Kant, only first-hand perceptual experience can serve as starting point for aesthetic judgment. This idea, nowadays better known as the 'principle of acquaintance' has been widely adhered to in the twentieth century. Lately, however, there has been some discussion about its applicability. For more on this question, see Budd (2003) and Sibley (1965).

6   We will briefly return to the notion of dependent beauty in the next section.

7   As McCloskey explains, there are two phases to Kant's judgments of the sublime: (1) negative phase (unpleasant and "contrapurposive"); (2) positive phase (pleasant and "purposive"). Also, for Kant, there are two different kinds of sublime: the mathematical and the dynamical (cf. McCloskey 1987, 94–104).

8   Kant's notion of disinterestedness, generally interpreted as a special kind of attitude adopted in aesthetic contemplation—aesthetic attitude—is characterized as a unique way of perceiving or grasping the aesthetic quality of a certain situation. For more on this notion, see Dickie (1964) and Stolnitz (1978).

Primary sources

Kant:

2001. *Critique of the Power of Judgment.* Paul Guyer and Eric Matthews (trans.). Cambridge: Cambridge University Press. Originally published 1790.

References and further reading

Budd, Malcolm. 2003. "The Acquaintance Principle." *British Journal of Aesthetics*, 43, 386–392.

Dickie, George. 1964. "The Myth of the Aesthetic Attitude." *American Philosophical Quarterly*, 1, 56–65.

Guyer, Paul. 1987. *Kant and the Claims of Knowledge.* New York: Cambridge University Press.

Hughes, Fiona. 2007. *Kant's Aesthetic Epistemology: Form and World.* Edinburgh: Edinburgh University Press.

Janaway, Christopher. 1997. "Kant's Aesthetics and the 'Empty Cognitive Stock'." *Philosophical Quarterly*, 47, 459–476.

Kukla, Rebecca. 2006. *Aesthetics and Cognition in Kant's Critical Project.* Cambridge: Cambridge University Press.

McCloskey, Mary A. 1987. *Kant's Aesthetic.* London: Palgrave Macmillan.

Savile, Anthony. 1993. *Kantian Aesthetics Pursued.* Edinburgh: Edinburgh University Press.

Sibley, Frank. 1965. "Aesthetic and Non-aesthetic." *Philosophical Review*, 74, 135–159.

Stolnitz, Jerome. 1978. "The 'Aesthetic Attitude' in the Rise of Modern Aesthetics." *Journal of Aesthetics and Art Criticism*, 36, 409–422.

Wenzel, Christian H. 2005. *An Introduction to Kant's Aesthetics: Core Concepts and Problems.* Oxford: Blackwell.

CHAPTER 6

G. W. F. HEGEL
(1770–1831)

Richard Eldridge

Georg Wilhelm Friedrich Hegel lectured on aesthetics in Heidelberg in 1818 and then in Berlin in 1820–1821, 1823, 1826, and 1828–1829. The text that we know as Hegel's *Aesthetics* was in fact compiled, edited, and published posthumously, in 1835, by the art historian H. G. Hotho, primarily from the last set of Hegel's lecture notes, supplemented by notes taken by students and by Hotho's own emendations. The earlier lecture notes were subsequently found and have now been published in German, though the Hotho edition remains the standard text in Hegel's official *Werke*. This edition is the one translated into English as Hegel's *Aesthetics* by T. M. Knox in 1975. It has been argued convincingly by Annemarie Gethmann-Siefert, the most important German scholar of Hegel's philosophy of art, that Hotho in preparing his text distorted Hegel's views, primarily by suppressing qualifications and revisions and by overemphasizing Hegel's concern with artistic beauty at the expense of his actual engagement with the meaningfulness of art (beauty to one side), especially in modernity. While Gethmann-Siefert has done important work in pointing to the significance of the earlier lectures, it is also possible to read the standard text with her warnings in mind and to focus on Hegel's account of the meaningfulness of modern works of art as it appears in the text prepared by Hotho.

1. Hegel as a theorist of modern art

Hegel approaches the philosophy of art as a distinctly modern theorist of the arts. First, he discusses the major modern, so-called fine

arts—architecture, sculpture, painting, music, and literature (epic, dramatic, and lyric poetry, with brief references to prose fiction)—and not,
for example, gardening, weaving, book illumination, or vase painting.
(Hegel of course did not know film, television, video art, conceptual art,
or performance art.) Second, the major problems about art that Hegel
treats are the familiar problems of the significance of art within modern culture. In contrast with the successes of modern natural science in
offering a person-independent representation of the physical world as
a system of material substances undergoing changes according to laws,
art traffics in imitations or imaginatively constructed, often fictive representations that aim at involving an audience imaginatively and emotionally. In the modern world, art is also no longer firmly embedded in cult,
ritual, or religion. Modern artists working in any medium are largely free
to choose their subject matters and methods of artistic rendering, without subservience to the needs of religious representation. Hegel distinguishes between free art (*freie Kunst*) and subservient art (*dienende
Kunst*) that serves aims extrinsic to art, as in industrial, technological, or
practical arts such as the design of tools or useful machines. Only the
former is the proper subject matter of the philosophy of art.

Once the making and the reception of works of art are significantly
free from either religious or practical purposes, and once it is clear that
artworks represent subject matters for the sake of imaginative and
emotional involvement, it is then all but inevitable to ask what the point
of the practices of making and responding to art is. Is art a serious business or not, in comparison with, say, either science or religion? Or is it a
matter primarily of entertainment or idle pleasure, so that no failure to
know anything or to be committed to anything attaches to anyone who
simply does not care about art? It may be thought that one likes or does
not like certain works as one pleases, and the place of works of architecture, sculpture, painting, music, and literature in a serious educational
curriculum may come to seem questionable. And if works of art have no
serious, extrinsic importance, practical or cognitive, then how can we
tell which things are works of art at all? The piano works of Mozart, the
paintings of Leonardo, and the novels of Goethe are all very different
from one another, not to mention the millions of variations of medium,
subject matter, and treatment found in the productions of more minor
or amateur artists. If we cannot regard certain central works as addressing an important problem of human life in an especially successful way,

then how, if at all, can we speak of works of art as members of a clear and identifiable kind? Perhaps the word "art" is nothing more than an honorific term that is empty of descriptive content.

Though he addresses these central questions about the nature and value of modern fine art, or free art, Hegel's approach to them is strikingly different from that of many modern philosophers of art. To begin with, unlike Hutcheson, Hume, and Kant, or in the twentieth-century Monroe Beardsley, the problems of evaluation and of the justification of judgments of taste play no role in Hegel's theory of art. Hegel takes it more or less for granted that there is a broad consensus, albeit with very rough edges, about what the most central media of art at various historical times have been and about what the most important achievements within those media are. It is simply out of the question, for Hegel, that anyone could deny the distinctive significance for their cultures of Homer's epics, the Greek sculptures of Phidias and Praxiteles, the religious paintings of Giotto, Bellini, or Raphael, the music of Bach and Mozart, or the poetry of Goethe. Undertaking to settle borderline cases exactly by reference to some postulated procedure for decision is a fool's errand. What is important for the philosophy of art is that certain works in certain media at certain historical moments have been important within their cultures, and the central task of the philosophy of art is to give an account of this importance.

Second, Hegel locates the significance of art in its role in cultural life in general, not in relation to the psychological needs of individuals. Unlike Hutcheson, Hume, and Kant, Hegel treats art as an essentially historical and cultural phenomenon. Rather than talking of the needs of human individuals, without reference to any historical epoch or culture, for images of freedom, for "deep" pleasure, or for metaphysical reassurance, Hegel instead undertakes to characterize how different forms of art under changing historical and cultural conditions have satisfied collectively experienced needs in strikingly different ways. While Hegel offers a general characterization of the task of art as such for all human beings at all times—art is the sensuous appearance of *Absolute Spirit*—it is also integral to his view that Spirit develops itself historically in relation to human life. We may take Absolute Spirit to be, very roughly, the union of collective, human rational activity at a historical moment with its proper object, that is, with the forms of social and individual life at a given moment that that rational activity is essentially devoted to understanding, justifying, and sustaining. Because what human beings collectively find most worth doing changes historically—both as their technological situation changes and as their understanding of their own needs and interests develops (thus affecting their technologies)—what art is concerned to express changes. What is, for human beings, highest—the forms of life and activity that predominantly solicit and demand their allegiance—changes, as both social life and the understanding of values develop from the world of the early Mesopotamian civilizations to the worlds of the Egyptians, Greeks, Romans, and medieval and modern Europeans. As a result, both what is to be expressed by art and the material media that are appropriate to artistic expression change and develop as well. Spirit "generates out of itself works of fine art as the first reconciling middle term between pure [but undeveloped, abstract, and empty] thought and what is merely external, sensuous, and transient, between nature and finite reality [on the one hand] and the infinite freedom of conceptual thinking [on the other]" (Hegel 1975, 8), as human beings seek to determine the appropriate uses of their rational powers to construct a way of life and to express their determinations in sensuous, material, artistic forms.

2. Art's function and the history of art

Given his social, collective, and function-oriented understanding of the nature and task of art as a historical phenomenon, Hegel proceeds, at once both normatively and descriptively, to characterize in more detail how specific media of art and how certain central works within those media have been historically salient in fulfilling art's function. His treatment is neither "neutral" and purely descriptive—all philosophical thinking is bound up in the discernment of functions and values—nor purely prescriptive—it is not the task of philosophy to lay down rules for art a priori, without regard for how artists have historically discovered what will work at specific moments to fulfill art's function. Instead he proceeds, as he puts it, lemmatically (Hegel 1975, 24), taking for granted art's function in response to the development of Spirit, and then picking out various important works and describing in more detail exactly how they fulfill art's function in their specific combinations of materials, forms, and subject matters.

As a result, given both the selectivity of Hegel's choice of examples and his extraordinarily broad brush narrative of humanity's developments, it can seem as though Hegel's elucidations of art's powers are arbitrary and heavy-handed: the product of his own less than well-founded version of an only semisecularized Christian redemption story and of his own haphazard preferences and happenstance encounters with specific works.

Two thoughts, however, can help to moderate this appearance. First, Hegel's account of the functions that art serves historically is plausible enough in immediately anthropological terms, independently of his grand story about humanity's development. As Hegel poignantly observes,

> [Man] has the impulse, in whatever is directly given to him, in what is present to him externally, to produce himself and therein equally to recognize himself. This aim he achieves by altering external things whereon he impresses the seal of his inner being and in which he now finds again his own characteristics. Man does this in order, as a free subject, to strip the external world of its inflexible foreignness and to enjoy in the shape of things only an external realization of himself. Even a child's first impulse involves this practical alteration of external things; a boy throws stones into the river and now marvels at the circles drawn in the water as an effect in which he gains an intuition of something that is his own doing. This need runs through the most diversiform phenomena up to that mode of self-production in external things which is present in the work of art. (1975, 31)

The claims that the making of works of art originates in impulses of this kind, that these impulses then develop as we change in relation to our social forms of life, and that audiences look to works of art in order to participate in the satisfaction of such impulses afford a compelling starting point for rooting the production and reception of works of art—something present in all cultures—in deep, shared, but historically evolving human needs.

Second, by attending to central cases of historically important art, Hegel fills in the details of his account of the historical development of art in an illuminating way. Throughout his historical survey, Hegel emphasizes that an understanding of the work—perhaps less than fully articulated, but nonetheless present within practices of reception—is essential to the artwork itself. As the expression in sensuous form of what human beings hold to be highest as a way of life, the artwork is an essentially communicative phenomenon. It articulates—in sensuous materials—a historically salient sense of what it might be for shared rational activity to find satisfaction in a way of life. The artwork does this through inviting and sustaining a variety of responses, including awe, reverence, appropriation in cult, worship, and "freer" modern, individual audience identification with the artwork as a crystallization of attention and gesture. Although in modernity, where individuals are freer to choose more specific and differentiated courses of individual life than were available in more traditional cultures, there is considerable scope for an individual artist's choice of subject matter, materials, and manner of working, and also for variations in individual audience response, the artwork remains in its essence, or successfully in its central instances, a vehicle of the articulation, expression, and communication of shared impulses and possibilities of self-recognition. It is culturally situated and culturally communicative; even where it is distinctively original, it is not the product of any arbitrary, chthonic, self-standing individual psychology alone. Combining technical mastery, internalization of the history of achievements in a medium, and awareness of the shape of rational activity in social life, the artist must find, more than arbitrarily invent, a way to speak in artistic forms to a historical present.

Hegel divides the history of art into four distinct phases. Strikingly, these phases are distinguished from one another primarily by reference to which form of art, given its material possibilities of expression, is most appropriate to the stage of development and self-understanding that rational activity has reached. Though many forms of art exist simultaneously in many historical moments, only one is centrally suited in any epoch to the task of Spirit's sensuous expression.

Hegel finds the beginnings of art as the expression of Spirit within the cults and religious practices of ancient Persia. The Zoroastrians worshipped light as the absolute source of all growth and value, but were able to express this understanding only in the most abstract and indeterminate forms, for example, in towers oriented as sites of religious ritual. The towers of Babel and Bal in their undifferentiated verticality express unarticulated awe directed at the sun, while their labor-intensive physical construction for this end unites peoples in the activity of expression. The lingams and distorted figures of ancient India express a similar abstract and undeveloped understanding of a natural life force as what is to be revered. In giving vague, indeterminate expression in sensuous forms to an understanding of what is sacred, the works of the ancient

Persians and Indians stand as forms of pre-art, highlighting the origins of all art in collective religious impulses.

Art proper begins with the Egyptians, the first people to develop a conception of the immortality of the soul in relation to the body. In the Colossi of Memnon at Luxor, in the figures of the Sphinx, and finally in the pyramids as tombs in which the body is preserved for further life, one finds an essentially abstract understanding of continuing life and its value. In virtue of the abstract referentiality of these works to continuing life, Hegel dubs this phase of art *Symbolic*. Architecture, specifically the building of such abstractly referential works rather than, say, of dwellings or places of work, is the medium of art naturally suited in its heavy, space-occupying materiality to this abstract referentiality, and it is the dominant form of art in its symbolic phase. The transition to the subsequent phase begins when the artificers of such works become increasingly aware of the significance of their own labors in giving particularized shapes to the sculptural figures they created, initially as decorations and supplements to predominantly architectural works, but later as self-standing works on their own.

The second phase of art proper is the *Classical* phase of the ancient Greeks. Here the gods are presented as human figures fully realized in sculpture, the central form of art in its classical period. In the work of classical Greek sculpture, the god or, later, the hero or athlete or public figure, is fully sensuously present. Hegel compares the Greek sculpture in its living presence to a thousand-eyed Argus (1975, 154) that manifests its sensuous meaningfulness to its audiences in their physical space, as it serves as a focus of worship and of the self-celebration of the Greek way of life. The understanding of the sacred that is expressed is no longer abstractly referential. Instead the sensuous presence of the sculpture as a living, meaningful unity of form and material expresses reverence for Greek achieved humanity. During this phase, and only during this phase, art is the highest, most adequate form of expression of the human self-understanding of the sacred.

The third phase of art proper is modern or, in Hegel's terminology, *Romantic* art. Greek self-confidence in the achieved humanity of the male Greek aristocracy broke down under the pressures of trade and increasing ancient cosmopolitanism. In the Roman form of life, both citizens and aliens came to live under forms of imperial law governing commercial transactions. As trade increased, individuals living under Roman rule found themselves increasingly forced to draw back from automatic immersion in any givens of social life, in order to ask themselves: what is expected of me in this transaction and by the law? How might I as an individual (rather than naturally, as a Greek) regulate my conduct in these circumstances? Christianity, as a religion of initiation through baptism and conversion, gave similar prominent expression to a sense of the powers of individuals to shape their courses of life.

As a result of these developments in socially embodied self-understanding, modern or *Romantic* art takes inwardness as its proper subject matter. Inwardness—a sense within the person of revering or honoring something, which sense is to be expressed continuously in future action—and *its* proper objects are now what is highest for us. The artistic media properly suited to expressing this sense of the importance of inwardness in sensuous forms are, successively, painting, music, and poetry (lyrical and dramatic literature).

In contrast with sculpture, the flat surface of a painting can show not only a single object or a local group of objects, but an object, in particular a human figure, in relation to a larger environment and horizon that might contain anything. Hence a painting can show a human figure devoted to or thinking about something of importance, preeminently the devotion of the Madonna to the child and the devotion of Jesus in his suffering to his task. The human sensuous beauty of Greek sculpture is abandoned in favor of the depiction of inwardness in relation to its surroundings and objects of devotion. In addition, the painting is made for a beholder, who must be conscious of his or her position and so of himself or herself as an individual. Instead of existing as a self-standing object in a public space that it inhabits on its own, a painting is essentially *for* a viewer. In many of its central instances, modern painting determines just one point of view (opposite the vanishing point) as primary for seeing the significance of what is presented. In the initial phases of the depiction of religious themes in Renaissance Italy, Giotto and Bellini picked up Byzantine motifs of reverence, but developed techniques of perspective, coloring, and the rendering of landscapes and multiple figures. Religious painting reaches its heights of technical accomplishment with Raphael, but begins soon thereafter to decline into Baroque mannerism as a result of the pursuit of increasingly dramatic effects oriented toward the painterly surface. A late phase of successful painting appears in Dutch and Flemish painting of everyday life, as in the Van Eycks and

David Teniers, where the music of colors is used to celebrate and accept modern, domestic, independent life.

Music develops the expression of inwardness even further, as it abstracts from all depiction. Its material is vanishing sound, organized into overall plots of "cadenced interjection" (Hegel 1975, 903) that represent abstractly the plights and possibilities of subjectivity. By organizing their acoustic material, composers invite audiences to follow and dwell in patterns of development, involving thematic statement, complication and resistance, and resolution. In its abstraction from definite depiction, music resembles architecture, but, unlike architecture, it is a form of art that is generated by and addressed to modern inwardness.

Poetry combines the temporal development of music with the specific representationality of painting. It is the universal modern art, the art most adequate to rendering anything in its significance in relation to human life and feeling. Hegel discusses ancient epic, especially Homer, as a precursor to modern poetry, but differing from it in its orientation to collective, tribal values and to a cruder form of technological life, where inwardness was not of importance. Dramatic poetry reaches one pinnacle of development with Sophocles and his depictions of collisions of right with itself, as in the clash in *Antigone* between Creon's insistence on public order and Antigone's standing on the values of family and piety. Among modern dramatists, Shakespeare is preeminent in his ability to depict fully individualized, passionately ambitious, articulate characters whose ego-driven individuality sets them at odds with their social circumstances, leading often to their tragic downfall, as the rights of reasonable modern social life must be reasserted, but sometimes to their comic self-overcoming. Modern lyric poetry is able to take into view any subject matter whatsoever, from daffodils in a field to the French Revolution, with the aim of achieving through the presentation freedom "not *from* but *in* feeling" (Hegel 1975, 1112). Though his treatment of it is exceedingly brief, Hegel notes that modern fiction, as in Cervantes and Sterne, can develop the "prose of life" (1975, 1107), in such a way that an attitude of "objective humor" (1975, 609, 1235)—that is, bemused acceptance of the happenstances of life—can be expressed and cultivated for an audience.

In each of the modern arts of painting (after its initial religious phase), music, and literature, and preeminently in literature, the task and achievement of modern, Romantic art is to express imaginative and emotional attentiveness to the particularities of modern life rather than, as it was with the Greeks, to embody the most adequate understanding of what is highest. That latter task is now allotted first to religion and then to philosophy. Hence "art, considered in its highest vocation" as the most adequate form of human self-understanding, "is and remains for us a thing of the past" (Hegel 1975, 11). We no longer worship art or worship by means of art; our attitude toward art involves more enjoyment, distantiation, and critical reflection. But this is neither to say that art disappears nor that it is insignificant for us. It is instead freed from direct subservience to (often inchoate) religious impulses, so that it may now explore and reconcile us to quite particular circumstances of life and feeling.

As noted above, it is possible to find Hegel's metaphysics of Spirit or rational activity—as essentially aiming at the achievable end of reasonable, freedom-embodying, and satisfying social life—to be heavy-handed: a last gasp, implausible refiguring of a Christian theodicy. Hegel seems, moreover, insensitive to the interest of the forms of radical artistic experimentalism (already discernible in his lifetime in the writings of Jean Paul) that would lead to modernism and postmodernism. Hegel remains always concerned more with art as a social phenomenon involving communicativeness than as a form of iconoclasm that resists social life. But despite these difficulties, Hegel's ability to organize the histories of the arts into a single overarching narrative, his connection of that narrative with the development of social life more broadly, and his detailed insights into the historical saliencies and material possibilities of meaning of individual forms of art are unmatched by any other philosopher of art. The works of other, later, function-oriented philosophers of art, art historians, and theorists of art (such as Gyorgy Lukács, Walter Benjamin, Erwin Panofsky, R. G. Collingwood, John Dewey, Theodor Adorno, and Arthur Danto) would be inconceivable in the absence of Hegel's work, and his specific understanding of art in relation to modern life can stand comparison with the best of their insights.

Primary sources

Hegel:
1975. *Aesthetics: Lectures on Fine Art*, 2 vols. T. M. Knox (trans.). Oxford: Clarendon Press. Originally published 1835.

References and further reading

Gethmann-Siefert, Annemarie. 2005. *Einführung in Hegels Ästhetik*, München: Wilhelm Fink.
Houlgate, Stephen, ed. 2007. *Hegel and the Arts*. Evanston: Northwestern University Press.
Kaminsky, Jack. 1962. *Hegel on Art*. Albany, NY: State University of New York Press.
Pippin, Robert. 2008. "The Absence of Aesthetics in Hegel's Aesthetics." In F. C. Beiser (ed.), *The Cambridge Companion to Hegel*. Cambridge: Cambridge University Press, 394–418.
Rutter, Ben. 2010. *Hegel on the Modern Arts*. Cambridge: Cambridge University Press.
Szondi, Peter. 1974. *Poetik und Geschichtsphilosophie I*. Frankfurt a. M.: Suhrkamp.

CHAPTER 7

ARTHUR SCHOPENHAUER (1788–1860) AND FRIEDRICH NIETZSCHE (1844–1900)

Scott Jenkins

Few philosophers have granted greater importance to the arts than do Arthur Schopenhauer and Friedrich Nietzsche. Schopenhauer maintains that aesthetic experience both makes possible a fundamental sort of knowledge of the world and serves the practical function of enabling us to cope with painful but ineliminable features of our lives. Nietzsche similarly opposes the view that the arts are little more than unnecessary but pleasant diversions—"a readily dispensable jingling of fool's bells in the face of the 'gravity of existence'"—and maintains that "art is the highest task and the true metaphysical activity of this life" (1999, 14). This affinity between the two philosophers is no accident. Nietzsche turned from classics to philosophy after discovering Schopenhauer's *The World as Will and Representation* in a Leipzig bookstore in 1865, and Schopenhauer's considerable influence on Nietzsche is visible throughout his writings. Though they do disagree on many points concerning individual arts, artistic production, and aesthetic experience, Schopenhauer and Nietzsche both regard the arts as capable of playing a crucial role within human existence. In this chapter I examine the individual features of their aesthetic theories in light of this claim concerning the importance of the arts.

1. Schopenhauer on metaphysics and aesthetic experience

Schopenhauer was concerned with aesthetics throughout his writings, but the core of his aesthetic theory is located in his most famous work,

The World as Will and Representation (orig. publ. 1819). As the title of this work indicates, Schopenhauer regards the world as a combination of will and representation, and these notions are essential to understanding his aesthetic theory. He borrows the notion of representation from Kant, who maintains that the world around us is a collection of appearances constituted by our subjective forms of representation. For Kant these are the forms of space and time, which are associated with sensibility, and a set of twelve basic concepts (such as cause and negation) that give structure to the sensations we receive in sensibility. Schopenhauer agrees with Kant's theory of sensibility, but he maintains that Kant's list of twelve concepts should be reduced to one intellectual principle. This is the principle of sufficient reason, which we might regard as a causal principle employed in cognizing the world around us. In addition to this knowledge of appearance, we are also acquainted with willing as our own inner nature. By way of a rather obscure argument that I will not consider here, Schopenhauer identifies the world in itself, behind our representations, as a kind of basic, primal will (1969, 105). Thus, in knowing the world as representation we are aware of the ways in which that primal will is manifest to us.

Schopenhauer asserts that aesthetic experience is quite different from knowledge of representations. While our knowledge of the world around us is always knowledge of particular objects, related to other objects through causal relations of various sorts, in aesthetic experience the sole objects of awareness are what Schopenhauer, following Plato, terms "ideas" or "forms." When looking at a painting of a tree, for example, we do not experience a particular tree, but rather the idea or form of a tree—what is common to all trees that do exist or could exist. This knowledge is claimed to be completely free from the principle of sufficient reason. As Schopenhauer puts it, "we no longer consider the where, the when, the why, and the whither in things, but simply and solely the *what*" (1969, 178). Thus Schopenhauer regards aesthetic experience as a certain kind of knowledge, which is distinguished from our day-to-day knowledge by having ideas and only ideas as its objects.

This understanding of aesthetic experience has some obvious virtues. It sounds quite reasonable to say that when we have such an experience we are in touch with something universal. Aesthetic experience often *feels* like a cognitive state in which we gain knowledge of a very general sort. In addition, Schopenhauer's view provides a compelling account of why we value aesthetic experience as much as we do. Many people agree with the Platonic thought that knowledge of the basic aspects of reality is most valuable for human beings. Thus if we accept Schopenhauer's view that aesthetic experience provides us with such knowledge (a view that Plato himself certainly did not hold), we have an explanation of why it occupies a prominent place in human activity.

Schopenhauer adds one very intriguing, original element to this account. On his view, aesthetic experience is not valuable only for what it makes possible, namely, a certain kind of knowledge, but also because it eliminates from our awareness the painful aspects of life that derive from our willing natures. In order to understand this element of the theory we must return to Schopenhauer's account of willing. A central feature of Schopenhauer's view is that "all *willing* springs from a lack, from deficiency, and thus from suffering" (1969, 196). This means that all of our daily activities are rooted in the suffering we experience when we lack what we want. On this pessimistic view, all instances of getting what we want are actually cases of release from suffering. More accurately, they are partial releases, because "for one wish that is fulfilled there remain at least ten that are denied" (1969, 196). And even if a person's wishes were somehow to become completely satisfied, her state would not be a pleasant one since she would be left in what Schopenhauer terms the "fearful emptiness" of boredom (1969, 312). Thus within our willing lives there is no release from suffering. The nature of willing ensures that for any willing being, "its life swings like a pendulum to and fro between pain and boredom, and these two are in fact its ultimate constituents" (1969, 312). This theory of willing certainly yields a bleak picture of human existence, but I will set aside worries about the theory to examine Schopenhauer's account of the relation between aesthetic experience and the will. This account holds significant value even if it involves an overly pessimistic view of human life.

Schopenhauer regards aesthetic experience as valuable in part because it temporarily frees us from the burden of having a will. When we engage with a painting or find ourselves in a setting of natural beauty, our apprehension of an idea takes place through our cognition of the object no longer being connected with our willing relation to it. As Schopenhauer puts it, "knowledge tears itself free from the service of the will" (1969, 178). We are no longer concerned with knowing how an object might satisfy a desire or potentially harm us (as we are when we see a tree as capable of sheltering us or falling on us), but instead merely contemplate the object itself and find ourselves in touch with the form of that object. In this way, aesthetic experience is freedom from the pains of willing. The entire locus of willing, suffering, and boredom is no longer present to us when we have an experience of this sort: "we forget our individuality, our will, and continue to exist only as pure subject, as clear mirror of the object" (Schopenhauer 1969, 178). This understanding of the state of the subject in aesthetic experience can be understood as a radicalization of a feature of Kant's judgment of taste, namely, its disinterestedness. For Kant a judgment in which a particular object is judged to be beautiful cannot be influenced by our interests or desires. To be sure, we do value beautiful objects and desire to engage with them. Kant's claim is that an interest in consuming or owning an object cannot be the reason why we judge it to be beautiful. Similarly, Schopenhauer holds that aesthetic experience offers a kind of freedom from will by ensuring that the causal relation of an object to the will is no longer manifest to us. However this experience comes to be, whether from "an external cause or inward disposition"—say, the sudden appearance of a sunset or the state of mind that enables a person to engage with a piece of art—the result is that "the peace, always sought but always escaping us on that first path of willing, comes to us of its own accord, and all is well with us" (Schopenhauer 1969, 196).

Schopenhauer's description of the process by which a willing subject becomes a "clear mirror" of the object plays a crucial role in his account of the production of art. The ability to create art, which Schopenhauer like many of his predecessors terms "genius," is the exceptional ability to enter a state that is objective in this sense. While all persons are able to apprehend ideas, the person of genius enters this state more easily and inhabits it for greater periods of time, thus becoming capable of reproducing an idea in art. The artworks that result from this process present ideas more clearly than natural objects do, and thereby facilitate our apprehension of ideas. Thus, Schopenhauer regards the aesthetic experience of art and of nature as different only in degree: "aesthetic pleasure is essentially one and the same, whether it be called forth by a work of art, or directly by the contemplation of nature and of life" (1969, 195). Artists facilitate the objectivity already possible within an experience of nature.

Schopenhauer's identification of aesthetic experience and objective experience creates a close connection between beauty and truth. It also suggests that any object could be, in principle, beautiful. After all, any object we might consider is associated with an idea that could become an object of experience. Schopenhauer freely embraces this conclusion. But he also stresses that one object can be more beautiful than another insofar as "it facilitates this purely objective contemplation, goes out to meet it, and, so to speak, even compels it" (1969, 210). This view underlies Schopenhauer's approach to the fine arts, which he sorts according to the kinds of ideas they present to us. This classification is not terribly compelling. It depends upon sorting ideas according to the ways in which they manifest the primal will underlying all things, and the order among ideas that Schopenhauer postulates is difficult to defend. In addition, by identifying the arts with particular kinds of ideas, Schopenhauer seems to eliminate what is most interesting about them. For example, his classification of the fine arts begins with architecture, which he sees as capable of presenting us with low-level ideas such as gravity, cohesion, rigidity, and hardness (Schopenhauer 1969, 214). Even if we admit that architecture presents us with such ideas, much of what is valuable in architecture goes missing if we seek its value in connection with these ideas alone. Similar points can be made about Schopenhauer's treatment of other fine arts.

Music is the one form of art that does not fit this scheme, and Schopenhauer's account of music as fundamentally different from other arts is a defining feature of his aesthetics. On the one hand, he maintains that music does not present us with an idea, as the other arts do. But Schopenhauer also insists that music is not without content because it is a "copy of the will itself" (1969, 257). That is, music is more closely related to the inner nature of the world than the other arts, which represent only the various forms in which the primal will is objectified. We can elucidate Schopenhauer's view by considering the relation he sees between music and individual states of the human will:

> [M]usic does not express this or that particular and definite pleasure, this or that affliction, pain, sorrow, horror, gaiety, merriment, peace of mind, but joy, pain, sorrow, horror, gaiety, merriment, peace of mind *themselves*, to a certain extent in the abstract, their essential nature, without any accessories, and so also without the motives for them. (1969, 261)

Here Schopenhauer distinguishes between a particular pleasure or gaiety, which always occurs in a particular context, and the universal pleasure or gaiety expressed in a lighthearted piece of music. The latter is universal insofar as it copies a subjective state of the will but leaves out all elements of the particular context. Thus, the gaiety of a piece of music applies equally well to all individual cases of human gaiety and expresses what is common in them. Schopenhauer's view gains intuitive support from the fact that the connection between hearing music and experiencing a particular emotional or motivational response is familiar to all of us. This connection, combined with Schopenhauer's assertion that the world in itself is in some sense will, leads him to claim that through music we experience the most basic level of reality.

2. Aesthetic justification in Nietzsche's *The Birth of Tragedy*

Nietzsche's first book, *The Birth of Tragedy* (orig. publ. 1872), is clearly influenced by Schopenhauer. Like *The World as Will and Representation*, it maintains that the arts are a fundamental source of knowledge, and it aims to make an argument for the importance of music within the arts generally. That argument can be difficult to identify in Nietzsche's wide-ranging account of ancient culture, Greek tragedy, the figure of Socrates, and the problems of nineteenth-century Germany (to name just some topics of the work). But all of these topics relate in some way to Nietzsche's view that the arts offer us a way to see our lives as worth living.

The central claim of *The Birth of Tragedy*, which appears twice within the work itself and also in a preface added to the second edition (1886), is that our lives can be "justified" (i.e., shown to be good, or choiceworthy) *only* in an aesthetic manner:

> [O]ur highest dignity lies in our significance as works of art—for only as an *aesthetic phenomenon* is existence and the world eternally *justified*—although, of course, our awareness of our significance in this respect hardly differs from the awareness which painted soldiers have of the battle depicted on the same canvas. (Nietzsche 1999, 33)

Nietzsche's use of the present tense is important. While *The Birth of Tragedy* draws on extensive knowledge of ancient Greece and presents a novel theory of Greek tragedy, Nietzsche's primary aim is to demonstrate that art forms like tragedy are of great value for his own time, and for human life generally. Nietzsche was particularly concerned with drawing attention to the operas of his friend and mentor Richard Wagner, which he saw as capable of playing the same role in nineteenth-century Germany that the works of Aeschylus played in ancient Greece.

Nietzsche presents tragedy as a response to a problem encountered by the ancient Greeks, that of going on living in the face of the "wisdom of Silenus." He recounts the story of King Midas learning from the forest daemon Silenus that "the very best thing is utterly beyond your reach not to have been born, not to 'be', to be 'nothing'. However, the second best thing for you is: to die soon" (Nietzsche 1999, 23). This pessimistic thought resonates with Schopenhauer's claim that willing beings cannot avoid suffering. It also appears in a number of different contexts in Greek culture, some of which Schopenhauer catalogs in his account of the "vanity and suffering of life" (1969, 586). By placing this thought at the beginning of Greek culture, Nietzsche is claiming that tragedy originated in the need to deal with this unsettling knowledge.

We can approach Nietzsche's theory of the birth of tragedy through considering his account of the one feature of tragedy that modern viewers are likely to regard as mysterious, the chorus. This group of people, who stand to the side of the action on stage and comment on it in song, can seem completely superfluous to someone accustomed to modern theater. But Nietzsche insists that Greek tragedy originally consisted of chorus alone, with no actors on stage, which requires that we accord to the chorus a central role within tragedy (1999, §7). Tragedy was born from the music of the chorus, Nietzsche claims, and an actor on stage is best understood as originally a vision of the singing chorus, one made possible by its song. In approaching tragedy this way Nietzsche is making use of Schopenhauer's metaphysics and aesthetics. First, he is taking the elements of tragedy to correspond to Schopenhauer's notions of will and representation. The chorus through its song makes possible the appearance of an actor on stage, just as Schopenhauer's primal will underlies and makes possible the world as representation. Second, Nietzsche distinguishes between music—the art form of the chorus—and the visual arts.

Nietzsche's description of this difference involves some terminology unique to his work. He uses the terms "Apolline" and "Dionysiac" (or "Apollinian" and "Dionysian" in some translations) to pick out two basic artistic powers present in nature and responsible for the arts (Nietzsche 1999, §2). The Apolline artistic power receives its name from the god Apollo, who is associated with the sun and light. Apolline arts are those that involve visual appearance, or images more generally. Examples include painting, sculpture, and epic poetry. The Dionysiac arts, such as lyric poetry and music, are associated with the god Dionysus due to their intoxicating effect on us. This division clearly derives from Schopenhauer's description of the difference between music and the other arts (though Nietzsche is critical of Schopenhauer's understanding of lyric poetry [Nietzsche 1999, §5]).

We are now in the position to understand the importance of Nietzsche's account of tragedy as "a Dionysian chorus which discharges itself over and over again in an Apolline world of images" (1999, 44). He understands tragedy as unique among the arts both in its mirroring of Schopenhauerian metaphysics and in its ability to combine both aesthetic drives. These two features of tragedy are essential to its ability to offer the spectator a response to the wisdom of Silenus. First, the spectator sees in tragedy the deep truth of Schopenhauer's metaphysics. The character on stage is only a product of the chorus, just as the world around us is only a product of the primal will, and there is nothing that character can do to avoid the calamities of the tragedy. Consider the case of Oedipus, who attempts to avoid his fate of killing his father and marrying his mother but ends up doing exactly that. Such a case is a dramatic presentation of what Schopenhauer and Nietzsche take to be a basic fact concerning our existence—that life is defined by unavoidable suffering.

This feature of tragedy would seem to make it unsuited to the task of providing a justification of existence. After all, the fact that our lives contain ineliminable suffering is the ground of the wisdom of Silenus. But tragedy does not simply state this fact, as a philosophical treatise would. Tragedy presents it aesthetically and transfigures this feature of our lives. Here Nietzsche's account of the two aesthetic drives present in tragedy becomes relevant. The intoxicating force of Dionysiac music produced by the chorus separates the spectator from his particular point of view, resulting in an ecstatic state in which the spectator associates himself with the mass of the chorus. And from that point of view, the spectator regards the events on stage as beautiful, Apolline appearance. What appears in this way is no longer a particular actor, or even a character such as Oedipus or Dionysus, but rather the *universal* predicament of any willing being. Thus, from the point of view of the chorus, a life of ineliminable suffering appears to be a good thing. Human life is justified aesthetically by appearing valuable from a point of view outside of it, one that Nietzsche somewhat fancifully envisions as that of a chorus of satyrs: "in this enchanted state the Dionysiac enthusiast sees himself as a satyr, and *as a satyr he in turn sees the god*, i.e. in his transformed state he sees a new vision outside himself which is the Apolline perfection of his state" (Nietzsche 1999, 44). This is why Nietzsche asserts that our awareness of our status as aesthetic objects is almost as rare as the awareness painted soldiers have of the battle depicted on the same canvas (1999, §5). The point of view from which our lives are justified shows up for us only when we engage with a tragedy, a Wagnerian opera, or some similar work of art.

One might wonder whether this aesthetic justification of life is ultimately satisfying. If it is only by occupying a point of view different from our own that we can find our lives to be choiceworthy, the wisdom of Silenus appears to be untouched. Nietzsche's claim that human lives are not worth living is directed at individuals who are the subjects of the suffering and frustration characteristic of human lives. Any such individual might ask, "Why should I care that my life is justified *from some other point of view*, one that I as a finite individual cannot actually occupy?" It may seem that tragedy merely covers up the fact that a human life is filled with suffering, and thus fails to redeem or justify the awful features of that life for the person who lives it. Nietzsche himself suggests this more pessimistic approach to his own position. In the final pages of *The Birth of Tragedy* he repeats his claim concerning aesthetic justification, but with the significant revision that it is only as an aesthetic phenomenon that existence and the world *appear* justified (Nietzsche 1999, §24). Could it be that for Nietzsche our lives are never actually justified? This possibility gains some support from his remark that both beauty and the "metaphysical solace" gained from watching tragedy are forms of "an illusion spread over things" that motivates us to keep on living (Nietzsche 1999, §18).

Even if Nietzsche did hold this pessimistic view, his admiration of tragedy—and of the arts generally—would still be understandable. His insistence that it is *only* as an aesthetic phenomenon that existence can appear justified grants to the arts a preeminent role in our lives. He argues in *The Birth of Tragedy* and later works that other ways in which we might regard our lives as justified (such as by appeal to their moral features, or their orientation toward the truth) are all internally unstable. It is largely for this reason that Nietzsche had such enthusiasm for the work of Richard Wagner. He hoped that through Wagner's operas a new tragic culture would emerge in Germany, and that the arts would be restored to their proper place within society. This did not occur. Nietzsche was disappointed to discover that most of the spectators at performances of Wagner's works in the Bayreuth opera house (which was constructed specifically for these performances and opened in 1876) were bourgeois citizens and not the Dionysian throngs he had anticipated. Around this time Nietzsche's friendship with Wagner came to an end, and he also gave up his allegiance to Schopenhauer's metaphysics. But his commitment to the importance of art and aesthetic experience did not wane.

3. Art, artists, and aestheticism in Nietzsche's later writings

The works that follow *The Birth of Tragedy* exhibit Nietzsche's turn away from the Schopenhauerian claim that the arts put us in touch with the most fundamental features of the world in itself. In *Human, All Too Human* (orig. publ. 1878) he denies both that these features are accessible to us and that knowledge of the world in itself is of value (Nietzsche 1996, §9). In later works Nietzsche goes so far as to deny that we can even make sense of there being features of the world radically independent of our knowledge (1976, 485–486). So why would we ever think that the arts disclose basic features of reality? Nietzsche accounts for this tendency by comparing aesthetic views like Schopenhauer's to beliefs in religion and astrology, claiming that because such beliefs make us feel happy and secure we are strongly inclined to hold that art, religion, and astrology put us "in touch with the world's heart" (Nietzsche 1996, 14). In reality, he asserts, they "belong only to the surface of things." In *The Gay Science* (orig. publ. 1882) Nietzsche expands upon this claim by asserting that objects in themselves are never beautiful or attractive (or, presumably, graceful, dumpy, ugly, etc.) (2001, §299). By this he could mean that nothing is *really* beautiful (though some things appear to be), or that while some objects *are* beautiful, beauty is a subject-dependent property of the object. Either way, Nietzsche is asserting that aesthetic experience does not put us in touch with fundamental features of reality.

Related elements of Schopenhauer's aesthetic theory also receive penetrating criticism. For example, Nietzsche denies that there is such a thing as an inborn, aesthetic talent that deserves the name "genius" (2001, §163), and he aims to debunk the claim that exceptional artists have "a direct view of the nature of the world, as it were a hole in the cloak of appearance." Nietzsche now claims that such an understanding of artists derives from the vanity and desire for power present in individual artists (2001, §164). In this, artists have much in common with religious leaders (2001, §150). These types act as they do, and possess the self-understandings they do, for the same human, all too human reasons.

Perhaps surprisingly, these critical remarks aimed at Schopenhauer (and to some extent, at his own early views in aesthetics) do not mark a turn away from aesthetics for Nietzsche. In later writings he insists that the arts are of foremost importance in the context of a human life. He discusses art, artists, and aesthetic experience throughout his works—both in the abstract and in connection with the many artists he admires (e.g., Stendhal, Beethoven, George Eliot, Wagner, Goethe, and Aeschylus). And Nietzsche finds the aesthetic qualities of his own works to be essential to them. He experiments with numerous different literary forms, writing short aphorisms, rhymes, treatises, a philosophical novel, and an autobiography, in each case pushing the limits of the genre. This emphasis on the aesthetic suggests a number of questions—What is Nietzsche's new aesthetic theory? How does he understand the activity of an artist? What is it, on Nietzsche's view, for something to be a work of art?

There is no easy way to answer these questions. In his later writings Nietzsche moves away from the essentialism in aesthetics of *The Birth of Tragedy*. He no longer attempts to provide a general account of what an art object is, what an artist does, or how a person ought to engage with a piece of art, which suggests that he takes these questions to have little value. This shift explains why so many of his discussions concern *particular* artworks or artists. There is, however, one general point to be made concerning Nietzsche's later interest in aesthetics, one that connects his later works to *The Birth of Tragedy* and to Schopenhauer. Nietzsche takes some artworks, and some instances of artistic production, to be worthy of our attention because they can guide the way we live our lives. He maintains that following what he terms the "death of God," we can turn to art in order to find replacements for old, discredited moral criteria for the goodness of a life, action, or state of character.

These replacement criteria are unabashedly aesthetic in nature. Nietzsche speaks, for example, of a process of *giving style* to one's character through concealing what is ugly in it, reinterpreting some tendencies, and accentuating others (2001, §290). The result of this process is a coherent character shaped by a particular sort of taste—not merely an accidental collection of traits. This aestheticist criterion of style enables Nietzsche to regard particular characters as good independent of moral criteria. It is important to note that Nietzsche's aestheticism is not simply nonmoral, but also strongly opposed to the moral thought that there exists a *single* standard of value that applies to all lives, actions, or characters. Just as there are countless ways in which a piece of art can be a good piece of art, and a wide range of tastes that might shape an artwork, there are on this view countless ways in which a life, action, or character can be good. In a section of *Daybreak* titled "To deploy one's weaknesses like an artist" Nietzsche provides the example of how Beethoven, Mozart, and Wagner—three quite different composers— employ their own distinctive techniques for unifying the weaknesses and virtues of their works in such a way that the resulting whole accentuates the virtues unique to those works (Nietzsche 1997, §218). The process of giving style to one's character takes precisely this form, and would likewise vary from person to person.

Nietzsche gives this aestheticist standard of value a prominent position in his later work because he now holds that it offers the only stable approach to valuing ourselves and our lives. He states, for example, that "one thing is needful: that a human being should attain satisfaction with himself—be it through this or that poetry or art; only then is a human being at all tolerable to behold" (Nietzsche 2001, §290). Thus a project of self-fashioning modeled on the act of artistic production is a central element in Nietzsche's later project of understanding the significance of human existence independent of a moral or religious context. It is through becoming the "poets of our lives" that those lives can appear choiceworthy (Nietzsche 2001, §299). This means that a core element in Nietzsche's *Birth of Tragedy* does not disappear as he distances himself from Schopenhauer's metaphysics. Nietzsche reminds us of this common feature of his earlier and later views when he states: "as an aesthetic phenomenon existence is still *bearable* to us, and art furnishes with the eye and hand and above all the good conscience to be *able* to make such a phenomenon of ourselves" (2001, §107). Life is still justified through art, but in Nietzsche's later works that justification takes place *within* the point of view of the individual person who aims to construct himself in accordance with aesthetic values.

Primary sources

Schopenhauer:
1969. *The World as Will and Representation*, 2 vols. E. F. J. Payne (trans.). New York: Dover. Originally published 1819.

Nietzsche:
1976. *Twilight of the Idols*. W. Kaufmann (trans.). In *The Portable Nietzsche*. New York: Penguin, 463–564. Originally published 1889.
1996. *Human, All Too Human*. R. J. Hollingdale (trans.). Cambridge: Cambridge University Press. Originally published 1878.
1997. *Daybreak*. R. J. Hollingdale (trans.). Cambridge: Cambridge University Press. Originally published 1881.
1999. *The Birth of Tragedy*. R. Speirs (trans.). Cambridge: Cambridge University Press. Originally published 1872.
2001. *The Gay Science*. J. Nauckhoff (trans.). Cambridge: Cambridge University Press. Originally published 1882.

References and further reading

Jacquette, Dale, ed. 1992. *Schopenhauer, Philosophy and the Arts*. Cambridge: Cambridge University Press.

Nehamas, Alexander. 1985. *Nietzsche: Life as Literature*. Cambridge, MA: Harvard University Press.

Neill, Alex, and Christopher Janaway, eds. 2009. *Better Consciousness: Schopenhauer's Philosophy of Value*. Oxford: Wiley-Blackwell.

Young, Julian. 1992. *Nietzsche's Philosophy of Art*. Cambridge: Cambridge University Press.

CHAPTER 8

BENEDETTO CROCE (1866–1952) AND ROBIN G. COLLINGWOOD (1889–1943)

Gary Kemp

What are artists most fundamentally trying to achieve? The average person today is likely to reply by saying that artists try to express themselves. From an historical point of view that might seem anachronistic; although Michelangelo, for example, might have been willing to sign on to such a claim, his position can hardly be taken as representative of his time. Other artistic figures during the first half of the sixteenth century and earlier would have probably settled for a job description as a craftsman of beauty, blushing perhaps at the individualistic idea that one might "express oneself" by such means. But perhaps they were being too modest. The eighteenth century saw the rise of the idea of *genius*, and in particular artistic genius; by the time Kant wrote the *Critique of the Power of Judgment* in 1790, the idea that a central task for the aesthetician was to explain or at least adequately to describe the phenomenon of the *individual artistic genius* had definitely taken hold. The ground shifted for the next hundred years among the writers most influential upon philosophical aesthetics, away from the focus on the individual and toward the Hegelian idea that the individual is in some sense a product of his or her time. Nevertheless, at the beginning of the twentieth century came the most definitive formulations yet of the idea that artistic genius is to be explained in terms of expression. First was the Italian Benedetto Croce's *Estetica come scienza dell'espressione e linguistica generale* (orig. publ. 1902)—translated in 1909 as *Aesthetic: As Science of Expression and General Linguistic*—and then *The Principles of Art* (orig. publ. 1938), by the Englishman Robin Collingwood (Collingwood translated and to some extent followed Croce). Despite the historicist point of view these two thinkers more or less shared, it must have seemed plausible that they were making manifest something that was always at work in art, even if the artists—for example, Michelangelo's contemporaries—were not fully conscious of it.

Both Croce and Collingwood were general philosophers with formidable systems on which they thought of their aesthetics as drawing. Yet, at least among philosophers, their ideas in aesthetics have won a good deal more attention in the past 50 years than their general ideas, especially in Croce's case, whose overall system is nowadays seldom studied. This is partly because their central idea about art remains very much the thing, if not among professional aestheticians where the Institutional Theory (see Chapter 18, section 2) and its variants are at present dominant. But it is also because the viability or at least the interest of either Croce or Collingwood's ideas in aesthetics survive their being detached from the general theoretical context in which they were first articulated. In what follows, then, I shall attempt to discuss their aesthetic doctrines in their own right.

1. Intuition and expression

For both Croce and Collingwood, all reality outside the mind—ordinary things like tables and trees—is in some sense a construction of the mind. Reality, in a word, is *ideal*. But that is largely irrelevant to what they have to say about aesthetics. We can proceed as if they held commonsense views about the distinction between mind and matter. Indeed it will not ultimately matter if we think of them as dualists—so that mind and matter are categorically distinct—or as materialists—so that mind is in some sense made up of or realized by matter.

It's worth separating the proposition that art is expression into two:

(1) If something is a work of art, then it is expressive.
(2) If something is expressive, then it is a work of art.

That is, expression can be seen as necessary or sufficient for something's being a work of art. For Croce and Collingwood, it is both.

Expression is logically or linguistically a *relation*: if something is expressive, there must always be something that it expresses, even if what is expressed is obscure or ineffable. Thus we might think that the things expressed could in principle be expressed by different things, just as a person might have been called by a name other than their actual name. So the horror or terror of Edvard Munch's *The Scream* could in principle be expressed by different paintings, or even by works of music, or poetry, and so on. Or that particular expressive content might never have been expressed at all. Munch himself might never have become a painter, yet might still have undergone the experience, which indeed he describes in his diary:

> I was walking along a path with two friends—the sun was setting—suddenly the sky turned blood red—I paused, feeling exhausted, and leaned on the fence—there was blood and tongues of fire above the blue-black fjord and the city—my friends walked on, and I stood there trembling with anxiety—and I sensed an infinite scream passing through nature. (Quoted in Heller 1973, 106)

So that moment was in his mind; luckily for us, he *was* a painter, and thus, later, he managed to transcribe the experience onto the canvas.

This is perhaps the commonsense account of what expression is (and is found, for example, in Tolstoy 1996), but Croce and Collingwood both claim that it is deeply mistaken. The key error in this account is to undervalue the process of expression, making it into a mere practical or instrumental phenomenon. In particular, it misses the fact that the process of expression is one of *becoming conscious* of an emotion or of a feeling. One cannot really know, or be conscious of, what it is that one is going to express, and then set about expressing it; indeed if one is genuinely conscious of it then one has already expressed it. For in order to be conscious of something, one needn't be able to name it or apply a concept to it. That is a further act of the intellect. Thus Croce distinguishes between *intuitive* and *conceptual* knowledge, and declares that "to intuite"—to become conscious of something—"is to express"; "intuitive knowledge is expressive knowledge" (1922, 11).

Collingwood offers a more nuanced psychological account. He writes, of an artist, that he is

> conscious of . . . a perturbation or excitement which he feels going on within him, but of whose nature he is ignorant. While in this state, all he can say about

his emotion is: "I feel . . . I don't know what I feel." From this helpless and oppressed condition he extricates himself by doing something which we call expressing himself. This is an activity which has something to do with the thing we call language: he expresses himself by speaking. It also has something to do with consciousness: the emotion expressed is an emotion of whose nature the person who feels it is no longer unconscious. It also has something to do with the way in which he feels the emotion. As unexpressed, he feels it in what we called a helpless and oppressed way; as expressed, he feels it in a way from which this sense of oppression has vanished. His mind is somehow lightened and eased. (1938, 109–110)

So the apparent separability of the work of art from its expressive content must be diminished accordingly: indeed, if it is not possible to conceive of the latter except in terms of the former, then the two are really one. The creation of a work art—the expression—and the becoming conscious of what one is expressing, are all the same thing.

This is likely to cause puzzlement. For it now seems to follow that one cannot become conscious of an emotion unless one creates a work of art! To address this worry, we must look at the particulars of the Croce-Collingwood theory of the work of art.

2. Ideality

About the work of art—the thing doing the expressing—Croce and Collingwood give a surprising account. We say, of Munch's *The Scream*, that it hangs in the National Gallery of Norway, that it weighs, say, 10 kilos, *and* that it expresses something like horror or terror. But for Croce and Collingwood, this is not strictly speaking correct. The expressive thing is not a physical object at all, but rather what Collingwood calls the "total imaginative experience" that one has when perceiving the physical object. It is a mental thing, an *ideal object*, and *not* just in the sense in which all reality is ideal. That is, even if, as suggested, we think of our two theorists as having espoused a commonsense view of physical reality, they would still hold that *works of art* are not physical things, but things that exist only in the mind, that is, only when one perceives them.

For Croce, the painting of pictures, the scrape of the bow upon strings, the chanting or inscription of a poem, are only contingently related to the work of art, that is, to the expressed intuition. By this

Croce does not mean to say that, for example, the painter could get by without actually painting; nevertheless what he is doing is always driven by the intuition. First, the memory of the intuition often requires—though only contingently—the physical work to sustain or further develop the intuition. Second, the physical work does remain necessary for the practical business of the *communication* of the intuition, that is, of making it available to others. The process of painting is a closely interwoven operation of positive feedback between the intuitive faculty and the practical or technical capacity to manipulate the brush, mix the paints, and so on:

> [T]he painter, who paints upon canvas or upon wood, but could not paint at all, did not the intuited image, the line and color as they have taken shape in the fancy, *precede*, at every stage of the work, from the first stroke of the brush or sketch of the outline to the finishing touches, the manual actions. And when it happens that some stroke of the brush runs ahead of the image, the artist, in his final revision, erases and corrects it.
>
> It is, no doubt, very difficult to perceive the frontier between expression and communication in actual fact, for the two processes usually *alternate rapidly* and are *almost* intermingled. But the distinction is ideally clear and must be strongly maintained . . . The technical does not enter into art, but pertains to the concept of communication. (Croce 1966, 227–228, emphasis added; see also 1922, 50–51, 96–97, 103, 111–117; and 1921, 41–47)

So Croce insists that the ideality of the work of art is fully consistent with the practical necessity of the physical work of art. Collingwood agrees, and provides some simple examples of works of art that exist purely in one's head—a tune that is not played or sung, or a poem that is not written or said aloud; both things nonetheless do exist as works of art.

In addition, the experience of a painting typically involves a great deal that no one would say is "in the painting," which is, after all, a flat canvas with paint on it. Not only do we see things that are not really present, but we also have impressions of space and mass, perhaps by means of what the art historian Bernard Berenson called "ideated sensations"—those involving imaginary kinaesthetic sensations (1954, 73–78). These phenomena are not literally features of the canvas, but they are in some sense features of the work. So our theorists include within the work of art proper all that would normally be ascribed to the (correct) interpretation of the artwork. That is, if *aesthetic* properties are essential to the work of art, and exist only in the mind of the perceiver, then the work of art exists only in the mind of the perceiver. (One may be reminded here of Locke's distinction between primary and secondary qualities, and of Berkeley's criticism of that distinction.)

What, then, of our worry that, according to the Croce-Collingwood account, there are no conscious emotions independently of art-making (§1)? Part of the answer is provided succinctly by Croce. We have "the illusion or prejudice that we possess a more complete intuition of reality than we really do" (Croce 1922, 9). We have, most of the time, only fleeting, transitory intuitions amidst the bustle of our practical lives: "The world which as rule we intuite is a small thing," he writes; "It consists of small expressions . . . a medley of light and color" (Croce 1922, 9). So part of the answer to our worry is that we are *not* as conscious of things—internal or external—as we like to pretend.

On the other hand, we make more works of art than we realize; Croce writes:

> [A]mong the principal reasons which have prevented Aesthetic, the science of art, from revealing the true nature of art, its real roots in human nature, has been its separation from the general spiritual life, the having made of it a sort of special function or aristocratic club. . . . There is not . . . a special chemical theory of stones as distinct from mountains. In the same way, there is not a science of lesser intuition as distinct from a science of greater intuition, nor one of ordinary intuition as distinct from artistic intuition. (1922, 14)

For Collingwood, too, our conscious experiences are normally unsustained, fleeting, and lacking in depth (1938, 307). They take place in a mind that is busy with other things at the same time, and which is dominated by other overarching purposes. Nevertheless, things that normally we would not say are "works of art" are in point of fact so, as proven by our acknowledging their aesthetic dimension. The way we talk to our intimate friends, walk beside the sun-dappled river, or eat a peach may have some aesthetic qualities. Life, then, is full of "artworks," even if they are mostly shallow, unworthy of comment. And there are times when consciousness settles on something, such that the mental activity does approach the character of art, in the ordinary sense of the word. Sitting in a park, for example, we might dwell on the look of an oak tree, or suddenly think of an original stanza of poetry, or a snatch of melody. These are instances of what Collingwood calls *imaginative expression*, and are closer to what we should ordinarily call works of art. But they are likely to be lost, unless some record of the experience is made. The "artist," then, is one who has these experiences more deeply than the average person, and who has mastered the practice of dwelling on and preserving them.

3. The role of feeling

The doubts we have so far explored concerned (2) from §1, the proposition that all expression is the creation of works of art. But one may also doubt (1), the proposition that all works of art are expressive. Is that really plausible? It is easy to cite what seem to be counterexamples; unlike Munch's *The Scream*, Mondrian's famous *Compositions* of the 1920s are not things you would naturally say *express an emotion*, and they are not any the worse for that. However, that sort of thing—the stripped-bare, vulnerable exposition of intense emotion as in much of Tchaikovsky or Billie Holiday—is not what our figures mean by the thesis that art is expression. There are two elements to this.

First, expression should not be confused with the *venting* or *betrayal* of emotion. One's tears may be said to "express" one's sadness, or stamping one's feet one's anger, but these can occur without the making lucid and intelligible of the emotion that is requisite for expression in Croce's or Collingwood's sense. Generally, we think of expressive behavior or gestures as being caused, at least paradigmatically, by the underlying emotion or feelings. Betrayal can even occur that is wholly unconscious; one can blush without noticing it. But for both Croce and Collingwood there is a sharp distinction between this phenomenon and artistic expression. The relation between expressive object and emotion is that of embodiment or realization, not of causation or inference. Whereas the former is the subject of aesthetics as just explained, the latter is a topic for the natural sciences, as, for instance, "in Darwin's enquiries into the expression of feeling in man and in the animals" (Croce 1966, 265; cf. 1922, 21 and 94–97). In an article he wrote for the *Encyclopedia Britannica*, speaking of such "psychophysical phenomena," Croce writes:

[S]uch "expression," albeit conscious, can rank as expression only by metaphorical license, when compared with the spiritual or aesthetic expression which alone expresses, that is to say gives to the feeling a theoretical form and converts it into language, song, shape. (1966, 219)

So long as we allow that *pretending* to betray an emotion is from an aesthetic point of view equivalent to the actual betrayal of the emotion—so that the outer form and not the inner causation of the phenomenon is what counts—some phenomena commonly termed artistic are surely cases of emotional betrayal. Indeed Collingwood singles out no less a musician than Beethoven, complaining that some of his music amounts to ranting, a display or betrayal rather than expression (Collingwood 1938, 123).

Second—and here we touch on more general aspects of Croce and Collingwood's respective philosophies of mind—the role, not precisely of emotion, but of *feeling*, is for both figures much wider than one initially suspects. Croce, like Kant, holds that mental states are always *active*, not reactive or passive, and he holds that each mental state is an holistic or organic whole, such that it can be analyzed—sliced up according to concepts—only by falsifying it to some degree. The engine, or the source of energy for this activity, is feeling. Thus feeling is necessarily part of *any* (mental) activity, including bare perception—indeed, it is nothing but the *will* in mental activity, with all its varieties of thought, desire and action, its varieties of frustration and satisfaction (Croce 1922, 74–76). Art, since it is the expression of such mental states, cuts through the falsifying effects of analysis into concepts to deliver the mental life in its purity. The only criterion of "art" is coherence of expression, that is, of the movement of the will.

Collingwood espouses a more down-to-earth conception of mental states that sounds a lot like those of Locke, Hume, and his contemporary Bertrand Russell, in that the basic materials of consciousness are sense-data. But his distinctiveness is that he holds that each datum—like a red patch—comes with an "emotional charge" (Collingwood 1938, 228–234); feelings are not separate items on the mental screen, like dots in a pointillist picture that exist alongside others, but aspects of each sensory item. Much of the time we pass over such charges, but when we attend to them, we find them more pronounced; crimson is felt to be angry in comparison with green, and so on (Collingwood 1938, 161).

The upshot is that for either figure, there is no such thing as consciousness without feeling. Thus neither Croce's nor Collingwood's theory is directly refuted merely by the existence of works of art that we would not ordinarily characterize as expressive. Assuming for the sake of argument that they are of equal merit, the distinction between Munch's picture and, say, a *Madonna* by Raphael does not reside in the *amount* of feeling in the two pictures, but in the *kind* of feeling in them. Thus, it is not surprising that we speak of a feeling *running through* a work of art, and of a lack of feeling as a universal condemnation of a work. To say the latter is to say that the work lacks that heightening of mental activity, of conscious attention to every detail, that is distinctive of the best works. In addition, the expressive character of, say, a brushstroke, cannot be divorced from other aspects of it, such as its color or its size and shape. The attentive spectator, then, in attending to such aspects, necessarily becomes conscious of their expressive character.

4. Criticisms

Both Croce and Collingwood were men of letters. And the title of Croce's first book on the philosophy of art was *Aesthetic: As Science of Expression and General Linguistic*—that is, the book presents not only a theory of art but a theory of language. That is no accident: Croce believes that poetry is the foundation of all language, and that all language is expressive: "an emission of sounds which expresses nothing is not language" (1922, 143).[1] Furthermore, he claims that drawing, sculpting, writing of music, and so on are just as much "language" as poetry; therefore, "*Philosophy of language and philosophy of art are the same thing*" (Croce 1922, 142, author's emphasis).

Collingwood essentially agrees. "In its original or native state, language is imaginative or expressive," he writes. "It is imaginative activity whose function is to express emotion" (Collingwood 1938, 225). We can speak of the "totality of our motor activities" as a "parent organism," of which every type of "language (speech, gesture, and so forth)" is an "offshoot" (Collingwood 1938, 246–247). Indeed, Collingwood holds that the *proposition* or *cognitive meaning* of a sentence is "a fictitious entity" (1938, 266). Every actual episode of thought is performed with its own particular degree and character of emotion; there is no such thing as the thought shorn of its emotional husk.

Neither figure really provides an argument for this view; both are rather violently set against logic or the philosophy of language as we would recognize them today. And even if all language were to have something poetic about it, it would not follow that language is *only* poetry, or that the semantical dimension of language does not exist, or is a false abstraction. There must be something that distinguishes a scientific treatise from a tune—in fact it must be the same thing that serves to distinguish *poetry* from a tune (it has to have sound *and sense*, as we say). So to say that drawings and tunes are equally good examples of language seems, at best, strained.

But I bring the view of language into the discussion for another reason. One could argue that poetry is actually a rather special case: it is unlike other forms of art in being *language*, and just because of this, one can readily imagine being the poet as one reads or hears the poem. With painting things seem to be quite different, and thinking primarily about poetry may well have blinded our figures to the difference. For, as the philosopher C. J. Ducasse pointed out, when we look at a vase full of flowers, it does not matter how much of an *aesthetic experience* we have in attending to it; in no sense do we create a "work of art" unless we draw or paint it (1929, 52–54). In the case of a poem, there is nothing analogous to the vase of flowers—the only thing to look to is the complete poem itself—and that may cause one to overlook the gap between artist and audience. Both Croce and Collingwood have lost sight of the ordinary distinction between passively contemplating and *doing* something—between looking and drawing, listening and playing, watching and dancing, but also between reading and writing. Of course there are important connections between the first members and the corresponding seconds, but that is not to say that there are not philosophically crucial distinctions between them.

The thesis that the work of art is an ideal object has been subject to severe criticism (see, most notably, Wollheim 1980, §23; cf. Kemp 2003). The problem concerns the question of the correctness, or at least the justifiability, of interpretations or critical responses. To say that the work of art is ideal is to say that it is necessarily private; it is inaccessible to any person besides whoever is having the experience. Thus, since one person's experience of Munch's *The Scream* is necessarily a different thing from any one else's, there is no such thing as Munch's *The Scream*, understood not as a material painting but as a work of art; there is at most only Munch's *The Scream*-for-me, Munch's *The Scream*-for-you, and so on. These experiences cannot literally be compared or said to agree or disagree, since a point of view from which to adjudicate is impossible. But that would surely go too far in the relativist or indeed subjectivist direction; as Hume pointed out, it is unreasonable to deny that certain things are aesthetically better than others, even if the point is too often debatable. So, although an idealistic theory can seemingly be developed consistently, the view is nonetheless exceedingly unattractive; contrary to Croce's and Collingwood's intentions, it renders art a diversion *away* from reality. Although both figures disowned this consequence, it is hard not to conclude that, on this view, art becomes a domain of fancy, of daydreaming, without any check upon vanity.

This problem evaporates if we withdraw the claim that the work of art is an ideal object, replacing it, in the case of painting, with the claim that the material painted object is the work of art. More generally works of art should be identified in some sense with something public, even if, in some cases such as music, it is a relatively vague matter exactly what constitutes the work. We can still insist that art is essentially expression; it is just that the things doing the expressing are what we ordinarily take them to be, namely, physical or otherwise public objects, not nonphysical or ideal objects. And we can substitute for the ideal thesis something close to it, which we can call the *experiential thesis*. Croce and Collingwood speak as one in holding that the artistic enterprise is answerable only to the experience of the work of art. In particular, the aesthetic *value* of a work of art is precisely the aesthetic value of the experience of it. The experiential thesis, then, first, insists on the equation between the value of the work and the value of the experience, but does not make it into a tautology, as it would be according to the ideal thesis; second, it adds a constraint on what experiences determine the value of the work, requiring them to be "of those who understand the work," or "of those who experience the work rightly," or some such thing. Of course, it will have to be more flexible than that; we don't want to imply that there is exactly one exact way to interpret or understand a work.

If that is plausible, then much rests on what we said in §3, on the role of feeling. The problem being responded to there was that it is on the face of things implausible to say that art is expression—or, in keeping our substitution of the experiential thesis for the ideal thesis, that artistic value is expressive value—in the face of apparent examples of fine works of art that are inexpressive, or minimally so. Croce's and Collingwood's response was that this objection insists on too narrow a conception of feeling; if the matter is considered more carefully, we see that feeling actually comprehends a much wider domain. But that depends too heavily on their respective theories of mind, which, not to put too fine a point on it, are doubtful and have vanishingly few advocates. Is there some other way to maintain that all aesthetic value is explicable as the expression of feeling? To answer affirmatively, one would have to explain other apparent values (such as the value of formal arrangement in a painting), in terms of the expression of feeling, or argue that those apparent values are not really aesthetic. Both options appear on the face of it to beg the question: if one restricts the domain of aesthetic value to what is intuitively or naturally called expressive value—so that some of what we had thought were aesthetic values fail to be—then we are still owed an explanation of why we should accept that all aesthetic value is expressive value in the first place; if one widens the domain of expressive value to include all that is legitimately called aesthetic value, so that we lose our intuitive or natural sense of "expression," then it is not at all clear that the technical term "expressive value" does not count as a synonym of aesthetic value, and the theory no longer has anything distinctive to tell us. Both figures have a good deal to say aimed at both targets—as well as on many things I've not discussed—but all the same the list of potentially troublesome phenomena remains long.[2]

Notes

1 Croce was here taking his cue from his great precursor, Giambattista Vico (1668–1744); see Croce (1922, 220–234).
2 This essay adapts parts of my Kemp (2009).

Primary sources

Croce:
1921. *The Essence of Aesthetic.* D. Ainslie (trans.). London: Heinemann. Originally published 1912.
1922. *Aesthetic: As Science of Expression and General Linguistic.* Revised edition. D. Ainslie (trans.). New York: Noonday. Originally published 1902.
1966. *Philosophy, Poetry, History: An Anthology of Essays.* C. Sprigge (trans.). London: Oxford University Press.

Collingwood:
1938. *The Principles of Art.* London: Oxford University Press.

References and further reading

Berenson, Bernard. 1954. *Aesthetics and History.* New York: Doubleday.
Ducasse, Curt John. 1929. *The Philosophy of Art.* New York: Dial.
Goodman, Nelson. 1976. *Languages of Art: An Approach to a Theory of Symbols*, 2nd edition. Indianapolis, IN: Bobbs-Merrill.
Heller, Reinhold. 1973. *Edvard Munch: The Scream.* London: Penguin.
Kemp, Gary. 2003. "The Croce-Collingwood Theory as Theory." *Journal of Aesthetics and Art Criticism*, 61, 171–193.
—. 2009. "Croce's Aesthetics." *The Stanford Encyclopedia of Philosophy*, Fall 2009 edition. E. N. Zalta (ed.). URL = <http://plato.stanford.edu/archives/fall2009/entries/croce-aesthetics/>.
Langer, Suzanne. 1942. *Philosophy in New Key.* Cambridge, MA: Harvard University Press.
Neill, Alex. 1998. *R. G. Collingwood: A Philosophy of Art.* London: Orion Books.
Sircello, Guy. 1972. *Mind and Art: An Essay on the Varieties of Expression.* Princeton, NJ: Princeton University Press.
Tolstoy, Leo. 1996. *What is Art?* A. Maude (trans.). Indianapolis, IN: Hackett.
Wollheim, Richard. 1980. *Art and Its Objects*, 2nd edition. Cambridge: Cambridge University Press.

CHAPTER 9

ROGER FRY (1866–1934) AND CLIVE BELL (1881–1964)

Susan Feagin

Roger Eliot Fry and Arthur Clive Heward Bell were widely read critics, art theorists, and champions of postimpressionist art at a time when it was highly controversial. Bell has received greater attention philosophically due to his definition of art as significant form and his radical claim that representation is irrelevant to the appreciation and value of art. Fry is better known as an art historian, and it has been claimed that he, more than anyone else, helped to change the taste of his age. Literature, music, theater, and the visual arts were important to both theorists, professionally and personally. They were both part of the Bloomsbury Group, a loose affiliation of artistically minded intellectuals in London whose members included, among others, the writer Virginia Woolf and her husband Leonard, the painters Duncan Grant and Vanessa Bell (Virginia's sister and Bell's wife), the biographer Lytton Strachey, and the economist John Maynard Keynes.

Methodologically, they used their own experiences of individual artworks as the starting point for their theories, not because they took their experiences to be definitive, but because they believed that the value of art lies in the experiences it affords, in which case they need to be analyzed and explained. It is hard not to be struck by the passion with which they write about the arts.

1. Roger Fry and the imaginative life

After graduating from Cambridge University, Fry traveled to Paris and Italy to study painting. Ultimately, he turned to writing art history, mainly on the "Old Masters," which secured his professional reputation. He became familiar with the work of Paul Cézanne in 1906 while Curator of Painting at the Metropolitan Museum of Art in New York City. After returning to London, he curated the groundbreaking exhibition "Manet and the Post-Impressionists" (1910), coining the term that is now used to describe French painting from 1886 to 1914. He founded the Omega Workshops (1913), a short-lived gallery that showed both art and craft in an effort to remove the distinction between them; works were unsigned and sold anonymously in an effort to break down the "cult" of the artist.

"An Essay in Aesthetics," originally published in 1909 and later republished in *Vision and Design* (1920), is a compact, systematic exposition of Fry's ideas about the nature and value of painting and drawing, "the graphic arts." He argues that realistic representation—imitation or verisimilitude—is not the goal of the graphic arts, for if it were, they would be valued only as curiosities or ingenious toys, which manifestly is not the case. It would also be a mystery why music and architecture, where representation plays little if any role, would be categorized as art along with painting and drawing.

The true value of the graphic arts, Fry proposes, is to enhance our imaginative lives, where we can focus our attention on the perceptual and emotional aspects of the experience itself. Whereas our day-to-day lives are dominated by the need to take practical action and to assume moral responsibility for our actions, our imaginative lives are free from these demands. "It is only when an object exists in our lives for no other purpose than to be seen that we really look at it" (Fry 1920, 25). Mirrors provide a rudimentary path into the imaginative life because their frames serve to detach our attention from practical concerns, and hence they facilitate attending to the perceptual qualities of the images within them. Fry thus distances himself from Plato, who took the function of painting to be imitation, and hence of no more value than mirrors. In his later essay "Some Questions in Aesthetics" (chapter 1 of *Transformations* 1926), Fry advances a similar claim about documentary film footage: because we are sitting in a theater without any possibility of participating in the action, we are freer to attend perceptually and emotionally to what the film presents to us.

Fry cleverly inverts the traditional view that the purpose of art is to copy external appearance in another way: "ordinary people have almost no idea of what things really look like, so that oddly enough the one standard that popular criticism applies to painting, namely, whether it is like nature or not, is one which most people are . . . prevented from applying properly" (1920, 25). This does not, of course, prevent people from *thinking* that they know how things look, even if "the only things they have ever *really* looked at [are] other pictures" (Fry 1920, 25, emphasis added). People unwittingly end up judging the realism of pictures by comparing them with the way their subject matter is represented in other pictures with which they are familiar, an idea developed in detail some 60 years later by Nelson Goodman.

Fry's views have much in common with the "art for art's sake" movement, which originated in France with the poet and theorist Charles Baudelaire in the mid-nineteenth century, and the "aesthetic movement" in England, whose most famous advocate was Oscar Wilde. These two movements were criticized for being too sensual and insufficiently moral, a criticism that Fry dubs "Puritanical," even though he seems to agree that a life dominated by the idea of art for art's sake to the exclusion of other values would be fairly superficial. Since there is no evidence that appreciating art increases moral behavior or awareness, Fry remarks, defending it on moral grounds requires "some very hard special pleading, even . . . a self-deception which is in itself morally undesirable" (1920, 21). He similarly denies that religion should be praised for its effect on morality (Fry 1920, 21), asserting that both art and religion are more plausibly justified by the way they develop a *spiritual* capacity whose expression is good in itself. The distinction between the spiritual exercise of the imagination, with its clarity and fullness of perception and emotion, in contrast with the practical and the moral, is a central tenet of Fry's view.

Fry is specific about what qualities in a work provide the requisite clarity and fullness of experience. First and foremost, a work should exhibit order among variety. Some theorists have proposed order among variety as a formula for *beauty*, but Fry distinguishes two types of beauty. There is beauty that is merely "sensuous charm," the sort of beauty derided by the Puritans, and which Fry seems to agree cheapens the notion of art's value. In contrast with sensuous beauty is "super-sensual" beauty, which is "concerned with the appropriateness and intensity of the emotions aroused" (Fry 1920, 31). These emotions are elicited not merely by individually pleasing elements, including representational elements, but by complicated networks of relationships that display order amidst variety. Further, two types of unity can produce this order. The more familiar type ranges over elements of a painting or drawing that are seen simultaneously, as is typical when a work of graphic art is easel-sized or smaller. Less familiar but equally important is the unity possessed by music and literature that depends on temporal relationships between successively presented parts of a work. Fry points out that painting can have this type of unity as well, citing as examples Chinese landscape scroll paintings that are too long to be perceived all at once. The scroll is gradually unrolled, so that we visually trace, for example, the course of a river or a series of mountains, experiencing a pictorial unity through time.

In addition to the two types of unity, Fry describes five "emotional elements of design" (1920, 33): rhythm, mass, space, light (and shade), and color. These elements are not merely objects of *visual* attention, but "connected with essential conditions of our physical existence" (Fry 1920, 34). This aspect of Fry's view has been underappreciated, yet it provides a useful resource for those who wish to argue for the relevance of the body in perception and aesthetic experience. According to Fry, rhythms echo gestures; masses have momentum and resistance; space, such as represented by inclined planes, is experienced proportionally to ourselves; and light is so important that we are sensitive to the most minute changes in it. Fry writes that these four elements of design "play upon . . . the overtones of some of our primary physical needs" (1920, 35) and that they combine with representation to heighten and complicate our responses. Scientific research since Fry's time has borne out his last claim about light, for example, establishing that a single photon of light can make a difference in one's visual experience. However, Fry makes an unnecessary concession when he opines that the fifth element, color, is not very critical to our "physical existence," and hence that its emotional effects are not so deep or clear as with the other elements of design. Even though the emotional resonances of particular colors are more variable, color vision in general has enormous practical benefits, as revealed by the difficulties faced by those with the rare con-dition achromatopsia, the absence of color vision.

Fry breaks with much theorizing of the eighteenth and nineteenth centuries that takes nature to be the major locus of beauty and the aesthetic. Of course there is beauty in nature, but according to Fry it is not distributed so as to provide sufficient enrichment to imagination, and nature contains a great deal of ugliness as well. Thus, so he argues, nature does not fulfill the perceptual and emotional needs of our imagi-native lives. Further, our consciousness that an artwork is made with the intention that it is "to be regarded and enjoyed" (Fry 1920, 37) allows us to put aside our practical concerns and to experience it for its intended purpose: the enrichment of imaginative life.

2. Fry and the relevance of representation

In "Some Questions in Aesthetics," Fry expands upon many of the ideas first articulated in "An Essay in Aesthetics." He reaffirms his method, examining his own experiences in response to art and inviting readers to examine theirs to see if they coincide. He distinguishes between appro-priate attitudes to art and to ordinary life, and emphasizes that the aes-thetic depends on responses to relationships within a work, rather than to individual elements within it. The case is the same for literature and tragic drama as for the graphic arts: it is "not the emotional intensity of the events portrayed," but "the inevitability of their unfolding, the significance of the curve of crescendo and diminuendo" (Fry 1926, 10), in brief, a work's overall structure or organic unity.

Though Fry is sometimes grouped with Bell as a formalist, he in fact abhorred the distinction between form and content. Content may be "envisaged," to use his well-chosen term, spatially or plastically so that there is a fusion between the two. That is, the expressive character of the plastic forms may not be identifiable independently of what they represent, and vice versa. However, Fry does distinguish between *repre-sentational content* and the way a painting or drawing may encourage a viewer to think about the *psychological life* of the persons depicted and the accompanying narrative, taking the latter to be a *literary* concern. An important question for him is whether the depiction of psychology or narrative is properly a function of the visual arts. Caricature, he proposes, as in the work of Honoré Daumier, provides a compelling case that it is. Nevertheless, Fry still questions whether psychological and plastic values can fuse as form and content can. He explores the possibilities by describing his own responses to an etching by Daumier and paintings by Breughel the Elder and Nicholas Poussin. These descriptions are rich and detailed, and worth emulating in any effort to develop a better eye for looking at art, independently of their role in the debate over psychology and representation.

Fry finds that, in his experience, the plastic and the psychological do not fuse as form and content sometimes do, and that he is always shifting back and forth between the two. Realizing that no enumeration of cases will prove that the psychological and the plastic *cannot* fruitfully cooperate, he suggests a reason why such a conflict would be inevitable: since one aspect involves "the spaceless world of psychological entities and relations" and the other involves "the apprehension of spacial relations," we are, therefore, "compelled to focus on the two elements separately" (Fry 1926, 23). Further, the discomfort induced by shifting our attention back and forth compromises the work's organic unity. He concludes that paintings and drawings may serve psychological ends that are proper to literature and drama, but that the result will be a mixture of two distinct arts, "the art of illustration and the art of plastic volumes" (Fry 1926, 27).

If we assume, for the sake of argument, that the psychological and the plastic *do* require a shifting of attention, does it follow that the psychological and the spatial cannot be aesthetically cooperative or mutually supportive? In "An Essay in Aesthetics," Fry mentions one possibility that he here ignores, that is, that the relationship between the psychological and the plastic may be experienced *through time*, as with Chinese landscape scroll paintings. That is, even if it is not possible to experience the work's unity at a single point in time, the overall unity of a work may be experienced in shifting one's attention between and among various aspects of it.

Fry might rejoin that the experience of scroll paintings, like theatrical presentations and reading literature, is guided *systematically* by the changing visual array, but the experience of a Rembrandt painting through time is not controlled in the same way. Therefore, the unity one attributes to the work may well not be present in one's experience of it. Debates continue among philosophers of art over the extent to which a shifting of focus of attention should be seen as a precursor to a unified aesthetic experience, or whether the shifting of attention is a temporally extended way of experiencing the unity that inheres in the work. A recent example of such a debate is the exchange between Ernst Gombrich and Richard Wollheim over the shifting of attention between pictorial depth and surface composition.

3. Clive Bell and significant form

Bell and Fry agree that any theory of art must be grounded in one's personal experience while recognizing that no individual person's experience is definitive. And both aspire to develop a theory of visual art that, with suitable modifications, has general application to other art forms such as music and poetry. Fry is less interested in defining art than in explicating its value and showing how favorable judgments of individual works may be defended. Bell, in contrast, takes a definition of art to be *essential* to a theory of art and argues that art includes all and only those objects that have significant form.

In "The Aesthetic Hypothesis," the first chapter of *Art* (1914), Bell claims both that theories of art must begin with the personal experience of a particular type of valuable emotion, the "aesthetic emotion," and that the objects that produce this emotion are what we call "art." The "central problem" of aesthetics is then to discover what property of artworks is responsible for producing this type of emotion. Bell opines that "only one answer seems possible": significant form (1914, 17). By *form* he means the relations of lines, colors, and shapes. Forms are *significant* when the relationships of lines, and so on, move us aesthetically. If something is art it must have, to at least a minimum extent, significant form. We can agree on this much, yet disagree about how good any individual work of art is, since we may disagree about the extent to which any individual work has significant form. It is the job of critics to help us see the significant form of individual artworks so that we have aesthetic emotions when viewing them. Enabling viewers to have such emotions is the way critics "prove" their evaluative judgments.

Bell's fundamental assumption that it is necessary to define art— that is, that "either all works of visual art have some common quality, or when we speak of 'works of art' we gibber" (1914, 17)—has been repeatedly attacked by philosophers. Most obviously, works of art may share a particular *set* of qualities, not just one. In addition, different artworks may possess overlapping sets of features without there being any single feature common to them all, a possibility inspired by Ludwig Wittgenstein's idea that objects designated by the same term might display patterns of family resemblances rather than one or more essential features. Contrary to Bell's claim, "art" used to describe a category of objects identified in one of these two ways would not be gibberish. Thus, we cannot conclude, simply because we use the term "art" meaningfully, that there must be a single quality that all works of art share.

In defining art as significant form, Bell advances a "normative definition" of art, which entails that, to the extent that anything is art, it is *good art*. Thus, paintings that fail to have any degree of significant form are not *bad* works of art: they are not works of art at all. A painting that we ordinarily might take to be a work of art, such as William Frith's *Paddington Station*, an example that Bell discusses, turns out not to be one. Some see this as a defect in his theory, since it is not how we would ordinarily use the word "art," but Bell himself is not shy about advocating a revision of what we normally think of as art. It is also sometimes objected that, on Bell's view, there cannot be any bad art. Indeed, he does require that all artworks are good to some extent—to the extent that they have significant form—but it is possible for a work to have so little significant form that it should be judged as a bad work of art overall.

More pressing is what makes a form "significant" and hence capable of eliciting an aesthetic emotion. If we had an account of what makes a form significant, we could, at least in principle, identify whether it is present in individual works without having to rely on having an aesthetic emotion or on the promptings of critics. Bell, as one might expect, does not think such an account is possible. Innumerable combinations and relationships of line, color, and shape will be significant, and there is no way to provide a definitive description in advance of what enables them to produce an aesthetic emotion. This is something of a letdown, but it is not clear Bell is worse off in this regard than any other theorist who attempts to identify what properties make an artwork aesthetically valuable. The history of aesthetics is littered with attempts to explain how a work can be good in virtue of its intrinsic properties when there is no independently verifiable description of what these properties are.

Nevertheless, Bell ventures a hypothesis about why certain combinations of line, color, and shape move us emotionally while others do not: artists feel aesthetic emotions in response to such forms in the world, or, in other words, "ultimate reality" (1914, 46), and they communicate those emotions to perceivers via such forms in their work. Bell denies emphatically that this speculation is part of aesthetics proper, which is probably just as well, though it is a little odd that he would see such important claims about the nature of human value as not part of aesthetics. Fry, in contrast, identifies many qualities as responsible for enriching our perceptual and emotional imaginative life, and he is less concerned about the boundaries of aesthetics per se, even referring to empirical psychological studies designed to identify factors that make unity in variety appealing (1920, 31–32).

Bell resists using the word "beauty" to refer to significant form since aesthetic beauty is too easily confused with both natural beauty and the nonaesthetic beauty of something that serves its practical function well (1914, 20–21). Like Fry, he breaks rank with a whole host of theorists from the eighteenth century onward who take the beauties of nature to be paradigm cases of the aesthetic. Bell also claims that the nonaesthetic beauty of things that serve our personal, practical interests, including sexual appeal, is not the beauty of significant form. Fry, of course, allows that "supersensual" beauty of unity in variety can enhance our imaginative life and hence be a locus of value in art, a beauty that he thinks can be, but only rarely is, present in nature.

Bell's definition of art as significant form has also been attacked as circular or vacuous, as if he simply defines art, significant form, and aesthetic emotion in terms of one another. However, the lack of an independent description of what makes forms *significant* does not make Bell's claims vacuous. Indeed, he makes a number of substantive claims that can be and have been critiqued: that particular aesthetic emotions vary but are all of the same recognizable type; that they are produced in the visual arts by a combination of lines, colors, and forms alone; that the *one* defining feature of art is significant form; and that the significance or valuable quality of form may be present to a greater or lesser degree. One may agree or disagree with Bell on any of these points, and some standard objections have emerged to the first three. One may deny that all aesthetic emotions are of a recognizable type, and hence that there is a particular type of emotion, an aesthetic emotion, at all.

One may deny that lines, colors, and forms *alone*, independently of representation, are responsible for an artwork's value as art. One may deny that the presence of significant form, independently of the intentions of the person who made it, is sufficient to make something art; and one may deny that an object that is intended to be a work of art fails to be one because the artist fails to endow it with significant form. The fourth claim, that the quality of formal relationships comes in degrees, as does the value of different artworks, has not received as much attention.

4. Bell and the irrelevance of representation

Next to his definition of art, the most controversial component of Bell's theory is his view that representation is *completely irrelevant* to art. He is more extreme on this issue than Fry, who saw representation as enhancing the possibilities for variety and modes of unification, though he was at pains to draw the line at psychological values and narrative storytelling. Since Bell sought a defining property that all artworks share, regardless of medium, it had to be a property that would be present also in music and architecture, which typically lack representational elements. He claims that forms are to be apprehended stripped of any representational significance, with the exception that, "if the representation of three-dimensional space is to be called 'representation,' then I agree that there is one kind of representation which is not irrelevant" (Bell 1914, 28).

Bell's claim regarding the irrelevance of representation has been challenged on both psychological and philosophical grounds. As a matter of psychological fact, the human perceptual system cannot perceive anything without categorizing it in some way. However, it is possible to distinguish representational content of a thinner variety, involving two-dimensional forms and three-dimensional space, from representation of a thicker variety, where what is represented is identified using utilitarian or artifactual categories (such as tables and chairs), or roughly "scientific" or commonsense categories (such as trees and fruit), or social or historical categories (such as battles and baptisms). If categorization of the thinner variety alone is psychologically possible, it is not clear that the psychological objection poses a real problem for Bell.

The philosophical objection is more difficult to combat. The objection states that even though it may be *possible* psychologically to separate form from content or representation of a thicker variety, it is not *desirable* to do so if one is interested in appreciating an artwork. Ignoring the thicker representational elements impoverishes art because it eliminates so much of what we appreciate about it. Cézanne, for example, did not merely paint shapes and masses, but weighty, shaped pears; in his works, representation and form, as Fry puts it, "fuse" and are mutually transformed. Though Bell's theoretical writing does not allow that representation and form can be conjoined, his art criticism, to his credit, often involves significant reference to representation.

Bell is aware that his rejection of representation is a radical move. He acknowledges that virtually all works of visual art contain a "descriptive element" and he attempts to explain why representation is virtually ubiquitous if it is irrelevant to the value of a work of art. Once again, however, he takes the proffered explanations not as part of his aesthetic theory proper. He observes that, in the history of art, two sorts of single-minded projects have generally led to aesthetic failure: the pursuit of pure form, and the pursuit of verisimilitude or "naturalistic" representation. With regard to the former, he hypothesizes that if an artist concentrates on form alone, to the exclusion of some particular artistic problem related to subject matter, the project is likely to be "too vague" to be carried out (Bell 1914, 53). For example, suppose one is interested in the depiction of volumes floating weightlessly in space. Such a project is not doomed to failure, as demonstrated by Mark Rothko's paintings, but Bell's point is that a project has more specificity and is hence more manageable when it is carried out by painting, say, apples and pears, rather than by attempting to paint floating volumes per se.

It is sobering that the champion of pure form was not convinced that totally nonrepresentational art had much of a future. It could be that Bell's overemphasis of two-dimensional form and undervaluation of plastic or three-dimensional form led him to underestimate the potential of nonrepresentational art, for example, in the rendering of plastic form in counterpoint to total flatness, or in relation to representing spatial anomalies. Fry, in contrast, declines to attribute much aesthetic importance to two-dimensional design alone, where there are no plastic values. In any case, Bell at least acknowledges and addresses the bigger question as to why representation is virtually ubiquitous in the history of art, when on his view it is aesthetically irrelevant.

Bell argues not only that the pursuit of pure form leaves the artistic problem too vague, but also that the pursuit of verisimilitude makes things "too simple" (1914, 53). Excessive concern with "naturalistic" representation was an important target for both Bell and Fry, for the post-impressionists, such as Cézanne and Matisse, were often criticized for their lack of verisimilitude. Bell notes that advances in photography (even in his day) make the replication of visual appearances obsolete as a goal for painting. He might also have mentioned that the ability to draw or paint a scene in perspective, if not "simple," is still a skill that can be taught to virtually anyone. Finally, there is the point made by Fry that although people may *claim* to judge paintings by how closely they resemble what they depict, in reality most people spend little time looking carefully at the world and are hence not even good judges of painting as imitation. Viewers of paintings routinely fail to notice the specific ways they do or do not resemble the volumes, mass, and rhythms of objects in space.

Bell has an additional way of deflecting the criticism that painters such as Cézanne are insufficiently realistic. He argues that reliance on realism is often "a sign of weakness in an artist" (Bell 1914, 29) and that it appeals to a similar weakness in perceivers who are insensitive to form in art and instead tend to "read in" the emotions of everyday life. Admitting that he himself does not have much understanding of *musical* form, Bell confesses that when attending concerts he tends to think about everyday human emotions, associated stories, and other "ideas of life." He is thus more honest in admitting his inability to appreciate music than many who are no less deficient in their abilities to appreciate visual art. The purpose of art is not realistic representation, but to present us with significant form whose value is, as he puts it, "independent of time and place" (Bell 1914, 33–34) and hence at least in principle universally accessible.

Primary sources

Fry:
1920. *Vision and Design*. London: Chatto and Windus.
1926. *Transformations: Critical and Speculative Essays on Art*. New York: Brentano's.
1939. *Last Lectures*. London: Cambridge University Press.

Bell:
1914. *Art*. London: Chatto and Windus.
1922. *Since Cézanne*. London: Chatto and Windus.
1927. *Landmarks in Nineteenth-Century Painting*. New York: Harcourt, Brace.

References and further reading

Bell, Quentin. 1995. *Bloomsbury Recalled*. New York: Columbia University Press.
Blocker, H. Gene. 1979. "Formalism." In *Philosophy of Art*. New York: Charles Scribner's Sons, 143–202.
Carroll, Noël. 1989. "Clive Bell's Aesthetic Hypothesis." In G. Dickie, R. Sclafani, and R. Roblin (eds.), *Aesthetics: A Critical Anthology*, 2nd edition. New York: St. Martin's Press, 84–95.
Curtin, Deane W. 1982. "Varieties of Aesthetic Formalism." *Journal of Aesthetics and Art Criticism*, 40, 315–326.

CHAPTER 10

JOHN DEWEY
(1859–1952)

Thomas Leddy

John Dewey was arguably the major figure in American aesthetics and philosophy of art in the first half of the twentieth century. With Charles Sanders Peirce and William James, Dewey is widely considered one of the three great American pragmatists. His numerous publications cover almost every aspect of philosophy. He was also a public philosopher who had an influence that went far beyond the halls of academe. Although neglected from the 1950s through the 1980s, his philosophy underwent a significant revival in the 1990s, partly thanks to a renaissance of American Pragmatism.

In everything he did Dewey sought to overcome rigid dichotomies, for example, those between mind and body, subject and object, art-world and the world of everyday life, high and popular art, creative process and creative product, and artist and audience. Contemporary aestheticians sometimes oppose these dichotomies, but none are as thoroughgoing as Dewey. Although Dewey wrote on aesthetic matters from time to time over his long career, his views on these matters find their culmination in his masterpiece *Art as Experience* (orig. publ. 1934). Here I will draw entirely from that work.

1. Continuity with everyday life

Dewey believes that in order to understand fine art one has to appreciate that upon which it is based. He replaces the idea that the work of art is a product with the notion that it is what that product *does in experience*.

Unfortunately, contemporary culture routinely sees great works of art as isolated from both the conditions that brought them into existence and their consequences. For Dewey, this hinders us from understanding art's nature. Hence, he opposes the idea that art belongs to a separate realm—what he calls the "museum" conception of art. Instead, the natural continuity between art and everyday life needs to be restored. This means knowing the soil out of which art grows. Thus, to understand the aesthetics of art one must turn first to aesthetics "in the raw"—to the fascination, say, the spectator has in baseball or the mechanic in his work.

Theorists undermine the value of art when they separate it from ordinary experience. This separation is due to our culture's commitment to the spiritual over the material and the mental over the physical. By contrast, people from "savage" cultures, not influenced by this dualist impulse, admire everything that intensifies their sense of immediate living. They take great care in making practical things such as rugs and spears. Also their dance, music, and painting are not seen as separate from religious celebration. In the same way, our ancestors saw the various arts as organically related to each other and to other aspects of their lives. In ancient Greece, the arts reflected the emotions and ideas associated with social life. Art only became separated from temple and forum through the modern rise of imperialism and capitalism. Imperialism called for museums as places to store loot, while capitalism encouraged the newly rich to surround themselves with signs of taste. Art objects became disconnected from their places of creation, turning into items for sale in the world market. Art came to be seen as a matter of subjective self-expression, and theorists saw aesthetics as merely contemplative. In contrast, Dewey sees art not as existing in a separate niche but as a celebration of everyday life. It develops, accentuates, and idealizes what is valuable in life. In order to understand art, we need to understand the full meaning of ordinary experience. We need to learn how everyday making of things grows into making works of art, and how everyday enjoyment grows into aesthetic experience. This should not be seen as a rejection of museums and concert halls but of their isolation from life.

2. The nature of experience

To carry out this task we need to review the nature of experience itself. Like other animals, humans have certain needs and desires which are often frustrated. We respond to this frustration by means of defense and conquest, seeking to recover equilibrium. Such recovery is not just a return to a prior state, but is enriched by what it passes through. If life becomes fuller in significance, it does so by transforming the factors it has overcome into aspects of something higher, achieving a new harmony. At the nonliving level of existence, form comes when equilibrium is reached. When incorporated by nonhuman animals this state is met by harmonious feelings. In humans, the rhythm of losing and regaining integration with the environment becomes conscious. Disorder brings on emotion, which is then turned into an interest in objects that can bring new harmony. Following this, the artist focuses on moments of tension in life for their potential to be resolved in a unified experience.

Change is necessary for aesthetic experience: it could not happen in a world of total flux or in one that is finished and static. The rhythm of breaks and reunions in life makes aesthetic quality possible. The moment when we pass from disorder into harmony is the most intense: think of the hour when a paper you are working on suddenly takes on form and meaning. This moment of harmony is also a new beginning which has its own potential for new struggles and resolutions. Yet, such moments, in which past, present, and future are unified, are rare. When they fail to occur the past is a burden full of regret. Happiness, which Dewey defines as deep fulfillment, is the result of a harmony that has been preserved through various tensions. The past is absorbed into the present while the future has an aura of possibility. Art celebrates this.

Dewey believed that art is valuable both as a means and as an end. It is not a means in the sense of being merely useful but in that it gives us a refreshed attitude toward ordinary experience. Animals and more primitive men are particularly apt at achieving the kind of harmony described. The tribal man, for example, is most alive when his senses prepare him for thought and action, as in hunting. Today, for Dewey, people fail to connect art and everyday life because our societal structures of work and consumption encourage compartmentalization. We separate sense and thought, both in practice and in theory. Dewey sought to overcome these separations.

Some would argue that Dewey neglects the differences between humans and animals. But he held that humans are different in that they take the unity of sense and impulse in animal life and infuse it with conscious meaning. Human lives are more complex than animal lives because they offer more opportunities for resistance and tension, for invention, and for depth of insight and feeling. Human rhythms of struggle and consummation are more varied and long-lasting, and the fulfillments more intense. Art is proof that humans can consciously achieve the union of sensation, need, and action found in animal life, yet at a more complex level. This view leads Dewey to downplay the distinction between fine and applied art. What makes a work "fine" is only that the artist lived fully while producing it. Most utensils today are nonaesthetic only because of the "unhappy" (capitalist) conditions of their production and consumption.

3. *An* experience

Dewey's theory of perception leads to a radically novel theory of experience. Experience is seen not as a passive collection of sensations but as something dynamic. Although there are experiences that have no meaning because incomplete or undeveloped, the true nature of experience is to be found in what Dewey calls *"an* experience." He initially describes this as the kind of experience that has a beginning and an end, the end being a consummation or fulfillment of what was promised in the beginning. Later he suggests that it exemplifies the nature of the thing experienced, as, for example, a dinner that sums up all that food can be. *An* experience has a pervasive quality that gives it its character. Moreover, each of its parts is organically related to the whole, each flowing into the next without losing its identity. The unity of *an* experience is not simply intellectual, practical, or emotional: *an* experience, whether of art or of thinking, has all three features, although—*after* the experience—we might find that one of these modes is dominant. Another feature of *an* experience is that it contains no dead spots: even the pauses carry something from the past and project something into the future (this is most notable in music).

Works of art are examples of *an* experience. However, Dewey's theory of experience has a broader scope than art. It is a critique of earlier forms of empiricism. Contra John Locke and David Hume, Dewey holds that the ideas constituting "real thought" are not separate and independent entities linked by association, but are phases of a developing aesthetic quality. Thus scientific and philosophical thinking can also be *an* experience. Such thinking differs from art only in that its material consists of abstract symbols rather than qualities. As with art, the experience of this kind of thinking satisfies us emotionally when it is both internally integrated and aesthetic. Even practical action can have the quality of *an* experience, as when one engages in a courageous act that develops toward a consummation. By contrast, nonaesthetic experiences and nonaesthetic trains of thought involve loose or mechanical connection of parts.

Dewey stresses that experience is emotional and that emotions are aspects of events and objects. It is emotion that gives *an* experience its qualitative unity and its aesthetic character. Yet emotions are not to be thought of as static: they are aspects of complex wholes that have their own development. *An* experience, for example, studying for and successfully taking an exam, includes both a doing (taking the exam) and an undergoing aspect (studying), and requires a balance between the two. The undergoing aspect can be painful and yet can be incorporated into a larger pleasurable whole.

Once we see conscious experience as including both doing and undergoing, we can see that the making and the experiencing aspects of art form an integrated process. Something is artistic when the qualities of the result control the process of production. Thus, the artist designs her work with the viewer in mind. Similarly, aesthetic experience should be linked to the process of production by creating one's own experience in such a way as to include relations similar to those experienced by the artist. *Identical* experience is not required, however. The experiencer can only bring the work alive for herself through recreating it in her own terms. Dewey's emphasis on both making and experiencing art leads to his seeing art as expression.

4. Theory of expression and of the expressive object

For Dewey, every creative process begins with an "impulsion." Impulsion, which is a movement of the entire organism, is the beginning of a *complete* experience. The organism, in trying to satisfy its needs, typically runs into resistance. It converts obstacles into something useful. In this process it becomes aware of itself, and this involves reference to the past. Expression is an ordering of the impulsion by way of incorporating past experience. Unlike emotional discharge, such as instinctive crying, expression brings inspiration to completion. The future is involved as well as the past, for future consequences are incorporated into the expressive object as meaning.

Artistic expression involves interaction of the self and surrounding environment over time. For this to happen there has to be a medium. Musical tones, for example, express only within the context of other tones; hence they do not express unless they are in the medium of the other tones. Yet expression is not a matter of applying a preestablished idea to some material. The artist only understands what she was trying to do at the end of the process, when the meaning initially stirred up finally becomes conscious.

The expression as act and the expressiveness of the product are organically tied: a graceful painting derives from a graceful act of painting. This view is contrary to that of later philosophers such as Monroe Beardsley who sought to disconnect the creative process from the creative product. Dewey, however, believed we should not view the art object in isolation from the vision of the artist who produced it, or from the aspects of the world that inspired it.

5. Representation, form, and rhythm

Art is representational, not in the sense that it copies the world, but in that it tells people about the nature of their experience. Meaning is not something projected onto the world. The world has concentrated meaning that art brings out. Tintern Abbey, for example, expresses *itself* in Wordsworth's famous poem about it. Art, then, does not just express the inner emotions of the artist. The artist gains passion from her relation to her chosen subject matter. The expressive object only comes about through the development of this passion in a medium. The painter, for example, gives the viewer a new object in which the scene portrayed and the emotion felt are fused in paint. For an object to be expressive, sensuous matter and prior experience must be incorporated together.

Dewey's analysis of form is strikingly different from that of Roger Fry and Clive Bell, whose formalist theory of art dominated the early twentieth century. Form, for Dewey, is a dynamic and temporal thing. It is an operation of forces that bring *an* experience to fulfillment. It is a matter of anticipation, tension, rhythm, accumulation, and consummation. Nor is consummation a static endpoint: there can be many consummatory moments in the experience of a work of art.

Dewey divides aesthetic experience into three stages: *rapturous seizure*, in which an inclusive qualitative whole is first experienced; *discrimination*; and *criticism*. *Discrimination*, also called analysis, considers parts as parts of a whole, and cannot ultimately be separated from synthesis. *Criticism* attempts to achieve objectivity, which is based on two factors. First, works of art are parts of the objective world and they are conditioned by materials and energies of that world. Second, for an object to be the content of aesthetic experience it must satisfy objective conditions that belong to that world. This is why the artist shows interest in the world, and in her materials.

The first and most important of these objective conditions is rhythm, which Dewey sees as crucial not only for music but for aesthetic experience generally. Rhythm already exists in nature: for example, the rhythm of the heartbeat, or that of dawn and sunset. Early humans saw these as having mysterious meaning related to their survival. This led them to create rhythms of their own. They brought the essences of animals and other natural phenomena to life in the rhythms of dance, sculpture, and painting. Reproducing the rhythms of nature generated a sense of drama in life.

6. What is common to the arts?

Dewey rejects the possibility of defining art in terms of necessary and sufficient conditions, for he thinks that definitions do not reveal some inward reality that is eternally fixed. There *are* essences, but only in the sense that there is the "gist" of a thing. That Dewey understands art *as* experience has often led people to think that he identifies art *with* experience, or with aesthetic experience. This is wrong, as there can be aesthetic experiences in science, philosophy, and practical life as well as in art. Neither does he define art as expression, although he sees the two as closely tied. He does tell us *when* there is a work of art, however. A work of art exists when the force of the object interacts in a positive way with the energies of the experience to produce a distinct reality that develops cumulatively toward a fulfillment.

There are also things common between the various arts. Dewey mentions four. The first involves the creative process. Whatever the medium, the artist begins with a certain mood which is then gradually differentiated while a pervasive quality gives the work its unity. Dewey associates this with what he calls the "background" of a work of art. Experiences, unlike *objects* of experience, are not clearly bounded. The background of *an* experience, although unconscious, extends infinitely. If the sense of that background becomes intense, the experience is mystical. A painting or poem can heighten the sense that everything exists within a larger whole.

A second commonality is that each art form has its own medium and its own sense modality. That different arts are in different media may seem to separate them dramatically. However, Dewey held that the medium simply concentrates all of experience into one sense modality. A medium is a means, but not a mere means. It is a means that is taken up into the outcome and is contained within it.

A third commonality is that each great work of art has parts that are capable of being perceptually differentiated indefinitely. This is in contrast to trivial works, from which we only get a kick. Great works give us something to dwell on. Observing how this happens sharpens our aesthetic perception.

A fourth commonality is that space and time are found in the matter of each art. Yet the mathematical approach to space and time does not apply here. In the arts, space and time are not empty containers or sets of relations. They are experienced qualitatively as changes of feeling.

7. What is different between the arts?

Although rigid definitions may be useful in the sciences and in logic, they are not so when differentiating the various arts, since they neglect both transitional forms and historical development. In particular, Dewey objects to the traditional division between arts of vision and arts of sound. Although each art medium focuses on an organ of perception, it incorporates other aspects of perception in the final experience.

Most theories fail to recognize that the artwork is *an* experience that has a temporal and cumulative nature. This is why Dewey opposes the idea of separating art into temporal and spatial forms. The seemingly spatial form of architecture has a temporal dimension: to appreciate a great cathedral one must explore it over time. He also opposes the idea of dividing art into representational and nonrepresentational forms. A work of *seemingly* nonrepresentational architecture *is* representational both in the way it expresses such phenomena as gravity and stress and insofar as it represents the values of the culture that produced it.

8. Art interpretation and criticism

A work of art is only complete when it is actualized in the experience of someone other than the artist. Even the artist working in isolation is thinking about the impact on the audience. To perceive a work aesthetically is to create something new, and, therefore, no two persons experience the same work. Indeed a work of art is recreated every time it is experienced, and changes as the viewer brings something different to it. Dewey thinks it absurd to ask what an artist meant by a work. What the work means is whatever you can get from it that gives it life. What makes a work universal is that different persons in different contexts can experience it in their own ways.

The function of criticism is not to render a verdict or even to merely give an impression but to enhance perception. Good judgment requires background knowledge and discipline. The business of the critic is to analyze the impressions we receive from an artwork in terms both of what causes those impressions and of their consequences. Dewey believes that, although there are no standards for critical judgment in the sense that there are scientific methods of measurement, there are criteria. Also, unlike scientific matters, the subject matter in art is qualitative. The criteria of art judgment are not rules but rather means of discovering what the work of art is. They are found in the relation of form and matter, in the nature of the medium, and in the nature of the expressive object. For example, an artist is unsuccessful if she does not fill the work of art as experience with meanings from prior experience. The business of criticism is to deepen experience *for others* through reeducating perception. Criticism fails when irrelevant or arbitrary. It also fails when the whole is reduced to a single isolated element, or the work is reduced to a mere object of economic, political or psychoanalytic analysis.

9. Art and civilization

Throughout his philosophical writing Dewey sought to reform society. This was no less true in his aesthetic theory. He saw his own time (the 1930s) as one in which relations between members of society were mechanical and external, and in which communication was constrained. Art, because it is a universal language, provides a partial escape from these conditions. The isolation of art in our society is a manifestation of social incoherence. It is also the product of the rise of science. Although science gives us a new conception of the physical world, we also retain views inherited from older moral and religious traditions. Thus, the moral and physical worlds are separated, resulting in philosophical dualism. Yet, although science strips things of their value, the world in which art operates remains the same. Thus, the death of art is not imminent since art is essential to civilization. Dewey defines civilization as instruction in the arts of life and the civilized person as someone who participates in the values of life by means of imagination.

The main trouble art faces today is with the nondemocratic nature of our economic system. That system entails a radical separation of the labor and leisure aspects of our lives. Like Karl Marx before him, Dewey believed that only a radical social change, one that would allow for more worker participation in the production and distribution of products, would improve the quality of experience in the lives of workers, giving them more aesthetic satisfaction in their work.

10. Dewey's reception

Dewey's aesthetic writings found a very wide audience. He was read by artists and art administrators in the 1930s and 1940s as well as by philosophers. He had a direct impact on Roosevelt's WPA, New Deal project, which was, for a while, the dominant force in the arts in the

United States. Many of the visual arts movements of the 1950s and 1960s, including Abstract Expressionism and Pop Art, were consistent with Dewey's ideas and were both directly and indirectly influenced by them. Environmental Art, Happenings, and Installation Art all owe something to Dewey.

In philosophy, Dewey had two sorts of critics in his own lifetime. Followers of Hegel, such as Benedetto Croce, believed he over-emphasized the material side of art. By contrast, fellow naturalists and pragmatists, notably Stephen Pepper, often argued (with little real understanding) that he had reverted to Hegelianism in this late work, especially in his advocacy of organicism. An organicist opposes philosophical reductionism, holding that there are some wholes, for example, works of art, which are not fully understandable in terms of mechanical relations of parts. Dewey *was* an organicist, but he did not agree with Hegel's more speculative position that all of reality is an organic whole. Finally, many writers from various schools had trouble with the continuities Dewey found between the aesthetic experiences of art and those of everyday life.

In the 1950s aesthetics underwent an analytic revolution. A famous article by J. A. Passmore (1951) argued that traditional aesthetics was dreary because it was too vague and Hegelian. After this Dewey's philosophy began to be neglected, although it still had influence on such figures as Monroe Beardsley, who adapted Dewey's idea of experience, and Nelson Goodman, who shared with him the idea that art is a kind of language.

The major thinkers of the 1970s and 1980s seldom mentioned Dewey by name, although some philosophers, notably Arnold Berleant and Marx Wartofsky continued to be inspired by him. Joseph Margolis has Deweyan strands in his thought, in particular his pragmatism and his idea of works of art as physically embodied and culturally emergent entities. The most widely recognized figure of the time, Arthur Danto, could be said to be anti-Deweyan in his emphasis on the artworld as an entity isolated from the cultural world, the world of "mere things," and in his tendency to downplay the role of aesthetics in art.

Revival of interest in Dewey came with a renewed interest in pragmatism launched by the writings of Richard Rorty, who, unfortunately, had little to say about Dewey's aesthetics. Also there was an increasing interest in applying aesthetics beyond the realm of fine art. Although Dewey did not always speak positively of popular art, the general tendency of his thought was to incorporate it into aesthetics. Thus, he could be said to be an inspiration for all the efforts to talk about the aesthetics of such art forms as jazz and comics. The development of an aesthetics of nature, for example, in the work of Allen Carlson, found inspiration in Dewey, as did the newer "aesthetics of the environment," spearheaded by Carlson and Berleant. Dewey has been even more influential in the recent development of an "aesthetics of everyday life," as in the work of Yuriko Saito. A particularly strong advocate of Dewey's aesthetics has been Richard Shusterman who has also developed his own theory of body-related aesthetics called *somaesthetics*. Those who wish aesthetics to be more multicultural can find many points of convergence with Dewey, as can feminist aestheticians. Also, those who wish to understand aesthetics in terms of evolutionary theory and neuroscience can find inspiration in Dewey's naturalism. Finally, Dewey's fierce love of democracy and his incorporation of liberal ideals into his theory make him a natural ally for political progressives. That said, the rediscovery of Dewey's aesthetic thought is very much incomplete, as proven, for example, by the existence to date of only one major scholarly explication, that of Thomas Alexander (1987).

Three things are most remarkable about Dewey's aesthetics. First is his vision of aesthetics as a series of connections and continuities: between everyday life and art, human and animal existence, primitive and civilized, and the rhythms of man and the rhythms of nature, among others. Second is his image of fully actualized experience as something that carries the past into the present and projects it into the future through development of a pervasive quality. Third is his attempt to move aesthetics from the periphery of philosophy to its center through emphasizing the role it plays not only in art but also in science and philosophy. These have been the insights most neglected since the analytic revolution, and the things most in need of revival.[1]

Note

1 Some passages here are adapted from Leddy (2006).

Primary sources

Dewey:
1987. *Art as Experience.* In Jo Ann Boydston (ed.), *The Later Works, 1925–1953, Volume 10: 1934.* Carbondale: Southern Illinois University Press.

References and further reading

Alexander, Thomas M. 1987. *The Horizons of Feeling: John Dewey's Theory of Art, Experience, and Nature.* Albany, NY: State University of New York Press.
Jackson, Philip W. 1998. *John Dewey and the Lessons of Art.* New Haven, CT: Yale University Press.
Leddy, Thomas 2006. "Dewey's Aesthetics." In E. N. Zalta (ed.), *The Stanford Encyclopedia of Philosophy*, Winter 2006 edition. URL =<http://plato.stanford.edu/archives/win2006/entries/dewey-aesthetics/>.
Passmore, J. A. 1951. "The Dreariness of Aesthetics." *Mind*, 60, 318–335.
Shusterman, Richard. 1992. *Pragmatist Aesthetics: Living Beauty, Rethinking Art.* Oxford: Blackwell.

CHAPTER 11

MARTIN HEIDEGGER
(1889–1976)

Joseph Shieber

Heidegger's views on the nature and function of works of art are best addressed within the context of his general views on the meaning of being. Heidegger approaches the question of being phenomenologically, that is, from the perspective of the human subject. From this perspective, Heidegger argues that artworks achieve something that no other type of thing can: only works of art are capable of revealing the world as it is, while some artworks are capable of bringing a new world into existence. Finally, Heidegger also sketches a rough hierarchy of artworks, according to which world-constitutive works are more genuine exemplars of being an artwork than those works that lack a world-constitutive function.

1. The framework of *Being and Time*

Understanding Heidegger's views on the nature and role of works of art requires understanding some of the features of his magnum opus, *Being and Time* (orig. publ. 1927). There, Heidegger seeks to investigate the meaning of being, by which he means not only the question of how it is that all existing things are understood (what he calls the "ontic" question), but also how it is that beings *are*—that is, how it is that we understand the being of beings (the "ontological" question).

According to Heidegger, all previous discussions of the nature of being focused exclusively on the former question—which properties of beings are essential and which accidental—and ignored the more fundamental question concerning the various ways of being. To better answer the ontological question, Heidegger distinguishes three modes of being of things: *readiness-to-hand* (*Zuhandensein*), *presentness-at-hand* (*Vorhandensein*), and *Dasein*.

The first mode of being, readiness-to-hand, characterizes the way that pieces of equipment make themselves available to us when we are actively coping with them. Consider some activity with which we are very familiar—say, cooking. This activity involves the employment of equipment: a pan, bowl, a whisk, a spatula, and so on. It is worth noting how, at least for an expert chef, those kitchen utensils are not, in the first instance, objects with which she relates from the perspective of a detached observer. Rather, in the practical context of cooking, those utensils and their user form a unity. All seem to the chef an extension of herself.

For the expert, when everything is functioning smoothly, each ready-to-hand object makes itself available in the context of the activity with which she is engaged—she never has to stop to consider where the proper tool is or what comes next. Of course, activities do not always proceed so smoothly: equipment malfunctions or is misplaced, one has to stop and consider the next step, or one's project misfires. In some cases, one is only aware of the sudden unavailability of a piece of equipment, as when the handle of the pan comes loose or the spatula goes missing. When those events occur, one simply finds another tool for the activity and remains focused on the task.

On other occasions, however, the disruption is so significant that one is led to step back from one's activity and reflect on the tools with which one is interacting. One might take a more detached view of those tools, considering, say, whether the pan's handle is attached with a bolt or a screw, or whether a wooden or metal spatula would work better. When one's relation to an object becomes detached in this way, the object ceases to be ready-to-hand and becomes, instead, merely present-at-hand.

It is in dealing with objects that are merely present-at-hand that one adopts toward them the attitude that is necessary for theoretical deliberation. One becomes conscious of one's position as a detached observer and becomes capable, more or less, of examining the features of the objects in one's environment in a disinterested, theoretical way. Thus, to deal with objects as merely present-at-hand is to adopt the stance of, say, the engineer, the research scientist, or the efficiency consultant.

The third of the three modes of being, *Dasein* (literally, "being-there"), is the mode of existence characteristic of the human. Unlike other beings, which can be either ready-to-hand or present-at-hand, those beings whose being is *Dasein* are capable of posing the onto-logical question that is at the core of *Being and Time*: "*Dasein* is an entity for which, in its Being, that Being is an issue" (Heidegger 1962, §41). Furthermore, *Dasein* is unique because it is devoid of essential attributes: "those characteristics which can be exhibited in [*Dasein*] are not 'properties' present-at-hand of some entity which 'looks' so and so and is itself present-at-hand; they are in each case possible ways for it to be, and no more than that" (Heidegger 1962, §9).

One implication, particularly relevant here, of the analysis of these three modes of being is that readiness-to-hand is both temporally and logically prior to presentness-at-hand. It is temporally prior in that, only when our practical activities go awry, we gain sufficient remove from them and see the relevant objects as merely present-at-hand. The ready-to-hand is also logically prior to the present-at-hand since, Heidegger emphasizes, we are "always already" embedded in practical contexts, in a world of objects ready-to-hand, prior to our achieving the sort of detached perspective on objects that are merely present-at-hand: "when something within-the-world is encountered as such, the thing in question already has an involvement" in a practical context that is the hallmark of the ready-to-hand (1962, §32).

2. The status of the work of art

Artworks, however, are neither equipment ready-to-hand nor mere objects to which we relate detachedly, as with the present-at-hand. Thus, they pose a challenge to the analysis of being given in *Being and Time*. Heidegger turns to this challenge in his 1935 lectures on "The Origin of the Work of Art," first published in 1950. There, he grapples with how artworks constitute a genuinely new category of things, over and above the present-at-hand and the ready-to-hand.

Heidegger does not fail to recognize that artworks have some of the properties that we can attribute to the present-at-hand or, for those artworks that are functional objects, to the ready-to-hand. As he grants, "there is something stony in a work of architecture, wooden in a carving, colored in a painting, spoken in a linguistic work, sonorous in a musical composition" (Heidegger 1971, 19). However, Heidegger notes, what makes a work of art what it is *qua* artwork is not exhausted by its material qualities (nor, of course, its function).

In order to do justice to the particular mode of being that character-izes the work of art, one must go beyond the categories of the ready-to-hand and the present-at-hand. As we saw, both of those categories involve *Dasein* in its practical context—either one's active, interested, interaction with the ready-to-hand or one's detached, theoretical, per-spective on the present-at-hand. Only the work of art makes possible for *Dasein* a perspective on being that is not bound to some practical context. For Heidegger, the work of art—indeed, only the work of art—"lets the world be" in both senses of that phrase: leaving the world alone—that is, not treating the world as the raw material for some technological project—and allowing the world to be present—that is, revealing the world as it is.

To develop and motivate his discussion of the being of works of art, Heidegger considers three paradigmatic artworks or types of artworks as a way: van Gogh's painting, *Shoes*, of a pair of worn leather hobnail boots; the architecture of the temple in classical Greece; and poetry. The example of van Gogh's *Shoes* demonstrates how artworks might open up a world that would otherwise be closed to us. The present-at-hand/ready-to-hand dichotomy presents us with a sort of dilemma: those for whom a given object is ready-to-hand have no perspective on the object at all, as it disappears into the context of activity, whereas those for whom an object is present-at-hand have a perspective on the object, but one that is disinterested and alienated from the context of equipment in which it has meaning.

Thus, in the case of *Shoes*, the user of the boots—perhaps a peas-ant, who takes for granted their well-worn leather, made comfortable by repeated use—fails to have any perspective on the boots at all, other than as a taken-for-granted piece of the context of equipment that is subsumed in the user's daily routine. Furthermore, we who are not the user, hence are not involved in the daily grind of his life, which gouges grime into the cracks of the leather, would also fail to get at the boots as they really are. By simply depicting the cast-off boots, the artwork reveals how integral they are to their owner's world: how worn they are and scuffed from his hardscrabble existence. In the case of *Shoes*, "the equipmentality of [the boots] first genuinely arrives at its appearance through the work . . . The nature of art would then be this: the truth of beings setting itself to work" (Heidegger 1971, 36).

Not all types of artworks perform this revelatory function in the same way. In the case of *Shoes*, the being of the objects revealed is still a being defined in relation to the owner whose poverty-stricken existence forces him to use the boots until the leather cracks and the soles wear through. That is, van Gogh reveals to us what Heidegger terms the *world* of the *Dasein* that is the boots' owner. However, it is a preexisting world, ready-made by the context of work, and want, of the boots' wearer. With his next example, the Greek temple, Heidegger suggests that some artworks not only reveal a world already there, but *found* a world, create a world that did not exist before the artwork brought it into being.

For Heidegger, the most genuine artworks create a world by ripping it out of the earth from which it is formed. Here, both "world" and "earth" are technical terms. World is where *Dasein* lives, the human environment populated by objects ready-to-hand. Earth is the opposite of world, radically other and hidden. Whereas it is the nature of the world to be open and easy to understand, constructed as it is out of the ready-to-hand, it is the nature of earth to remain concealed. Certain works of art derive their power from the tension between earth—which is concealed—and world—which is unconcealed—shaping meaning out of what, prior to the artwork, had no meaning.

An example of this sort of artwork is the Greek temple. Unlike van Gogh's *Shoes*, the temple doesn't depict anything. Rather, the temple first provides the context in which the projects of *Dasein* have meaning. It "first fits together and at the same time gathers around itself the unity of those paths and relations in which birth and death, disaster and blessing, victory and disgrace, endurance and decline acquire the shape of destiny for human being" (Heidegger 1971, 42). That is, in creating the temple the Greeks let their world be—they created the world in which their life events first acquired significance.

The artwork confronts us with the earth, the radically other reality of the nonhuman, which we ignore when we are engaged in practical tasks and misdescribe when we attempt to grasp the earth in the disinterested manner of the present-at-hand. At the same time, art brings forth from earth the world in which the ready-to-hand acquires its meaning.

Thus, Heidegger sees the meaning-constitutive role that certain artworks play as a function of their position at the place where earth and world collide. He describes this dual function of the artwork as both "setting up a world and setting forth the earth" (Heidegger 1971, 55). It is important to note that, for the Heidegger of "The Origin of the Work of Art," the truth communicated through art is a form of revelation, a reformation of the world. This is evident in the way in which Heidegger compares the meaning-constitutive function of artworks to the introduction of new political paradigms through the "act that founds a political state," or even religious revelation, the "nearness of that which is not simply a being, but the being that is most of all [i.e., God]" (1971, 62).

Indeed, for Heidegger, just as with the establishment of new political orders or new religious traditions, artworks establish communities. Artworks unite their creators, the ones who "put truth into the work," with audiences, those willing to suspend their "usual doing and valuing, knowing and looking" (Heidegger 1971, 66) to enter the world of the work. Only if audiences are willing to open themselves to the revelation of the work, to suspend their "usual doing and valuing, knowing and looking" in favor of an ecstatic "knowing that remains a willing, and willing that remains a knowing" (Heidegger 1971, 66–67), can the audience "put [the artwork] to work" (1971, 71)—that is, allow the artwork to construct a world.

Certain artworks, then—those that are, for Heidegger, most genuinely artworks—call into being a world that did not exist before they were put to work. Furthermore, as we have seen, Heidegger thinks of the world as fundamentally tied to the practical interests of *Dasein*. The primary way in which *Dasein* structures its practical interests, however, is by means of language: when we plan, we do so by means of talking to others—or to ourselves, *in foro interno*—about our goals and how best to achieve them. This means, then, that the most fundamental mode through which the world is structured is by means of language— hence, the last one of the three exemplars of artworks that Heidegger considers: poetry.

If language is the fundamental medium through which world is ripped out of earth, and poetry the artistic medium through which language is enriched and renewed and paradigm shifts concerning the medium of language are introduced, then poetry is the fundamental art form, logically prior to all others. The poetry of Homer or Hesiod does not simply depict a world that was already there in the way that, say, Van Gogh's *Shoes* does. Rather, through his poetry, Homer creates a new world, revealing a world that did not exist until his poetry brought it into being.

This, however, would not distinguish the poetry of Homer from the Greek temple—since both are world-constitutive. Unlike the Greek temple, though, Homer's poetry not only creates a world but also creates the very language through which the Greeks represented the world—through which they celebrated birth and death, memorialized disaster and blessing, and theorized about endurance and decline.

Primary sources

Heidegger:
1962. *Being and Time*. J. Macquarrie and E. Robinson (trans.). New York: Harper & Row. Originally published 1927.
1971. "The Origin of the Work of Art." In *Poetry, Language, Thought*. A. Hofstadter (trans.). New York: Harper & Row, 15–86. Originally published 1950.

References and further reading

Kockelmans, Joseph J. 1985. *Heidegger on Art and Artworks*. Dordrecht: Martinus Nijhoff.
Pattison, George. 2000. *Routledge Philosophy Guidebook to the Later Heidegger*. London: Routledge.
Young, Julian. 2001. *Heidegger's Philosophy of Art*. Cambridge: Cambridge University Press.

CHAPTER 12

WALTER BENJAMIN (1892–1940) AND THEODOR W. ADORNO (1903–1969)

Gerhard Richter

The thought of Walter Benjamin and Theodor W. Adorno has had a profound impact on the history, politics, and practice of aesthetic theory in the twentieth and twenty-first centuries. While the friendship between these two German-Jewish thinkers was often characterized by tensions and philosophical disagreements—especially over such issues as the applicability of aesthetic theory to media like photography and film, and over the methods of dialectical thinking—they nevertheless shared a deep intellectual connection. This notion is borne out not only by their extensive correspondence, which continued until Benjamin's death, but also by such empirical data as the fact that Adorno taught the first university seminar on Benjamin as early as the 1930s and that he, in his 1933 book *Kierkegaard: Constructions of the Aesthetic*, relies heavily on Benjamin's complex and far-reaching notion of allegory as the latter had developed it in his 1928 *Origin of the German Mourning Play*. The political philosopher Hannah Arendt, who knew both thinkers personally, once even went so far as to call Adorno Benjamin's only student. And after Benjamin's suicide in 1940, committed while fleeing Nazi persecution, it was Adorno—while in exile in the United States and, after the war, again in Frankfurt—who, in cooperation with Benjamin's other lifelong friend, the Jewish Studies scholar Gershom Scholem, played a central role in making Benjamin's work known to what would become a dedicated worldwide readership.

1. Theoretical context

Context Benjamin and Adorno sometimes are referred to as members of the first generation of the so-called Frankfurt School, an influential transdisciplinary group of cultural theorists and philosophers working between the two World Wars on projects that would transform their own conceptual roots (provided by Kant, Hegel, Marx, Freud, and others) into the concepts and strategies that came to be known as "Critical Theory." In contrast to what they considered to be the traditional bourgeois paradigm of largely *affirmative* modern thought—supplied by the mathematical logic undergirding Cartesianism—this group set out to devise a *critical* theory of experience and of society that would take into account the political implications and transformative potential of a radically dialectical perspective on the world of phenomena as it presented itself to them in light of the two sibling political formations of fascism and capitalism.

For all their differences in style, emphasis, and subject matter, Benjamin and Adorno, like most prominent members of the Frankfurt School, share a self-understanding of their work as inscribed within the modern aesthetic tradition that developed out of German Idealism (especially Kant and Hegel), German Romanticism (especially Hölderlin, Novalis, and Friedrich Schlegel), and aspects of Nietzsche's thought. Like Nietzsche, Benjamin and Adorno view the artwork not simply as a pleasant diversion from more important matters but rather as a privileged embodiment of the highest form of reflection, that is, as the space in which the experience of thought can be exposed to its own potentialities, contradictions, and conditions of possibility. But unlike Kant, for Benjamin and Adorno the realm of the aesthetic no longer can be viewed as having a mediating function per se (as when Kant mobilizes it, in the third *Critique*, as the mediating force between the precepts of pure reason and the commitments of practical reason). Rather, the aesthetic becomes the very locus in which reason—and the thinking of different modes of reason that, following Kant's Copernican turn, is indissociable from modernity—provides an account of itself to itself in terms that are not strictly bound by reason. What is to be gained from such an experience of the aesthetic is not so much an "aesthetic education" leading, as in the playwright Schiller's early appropriation of Kant, to the aesthetically mediated form of a moral political state; rather, it is a rigorous interrogation of the very foundations of cognition and the knowledge claims that are based upon it.

Insofar as the ceaseless interrogation of cognition that Benjamin's and Adorno's artwork may sponsor is a gesture toward the experience of freedom—among other things, the freedom from social injustice and needless human suffering—this liberatory potential is related to, but conceptually distinct from, the classical Marxian paradigm. In *The German Ideology*, Marx and Engels write: "In direct contrast to German philosophy which descends from heaven to earth, here we ascend from earth to heaven. . . . Morality, religion, metaphysics, all the rest of ideology and their corresponding forms of consciousness, thus no longer retain the semblance of independence" (1985, 47).[1] From the Marxian perspective, therefore, "life is not determined by consciousness, but consciousness by life," and any analysis of both the life and the consciousness of aesthetic production would have to take this determination into account (Marx and Engels 1985, 47). For Marx the artwork is, both in its modes of production and in the logic of its representation, the expression of a social determination—that is, it is part of a superstructure that stands in a tension-filled relation to what is not its own, the base structure. For Benjamin and Adorno, by contrast, the artwork simultaneously possesses a singular cognitive value apart from its material embeddedness in social determination. Its singularity and idiomaticity—namely, the multiple ways in which it refuses to be merely reflective of a reality external to it—evoke the experience of a certain *autonomia* (that which gives itself its own laws) rather than that of a mere *heteronomia* (that which receives its laws from elsewhere and, therefore, is, from the outset, unfree even when it advocates freedom). For Benjamin and Adorno, the question of the special cognitive status of this aesthetic *autonomia* deserves our attention. "This is not the time," Adorno argues, "for political works of art; rather, politics has migrated into the autonomous work of art, and it has penetrated most deeply into works that present themselves as politically dead" (1992, 93–94). The genuine artwork can never be a mimesis of what already is the case, even as a negation of what is the case. As a form of nonsynchronicity, its promise always resides in an unnamable elsewhere, an opening that is yet to be created.

How, then, does the question of cognitive and conceptual specificity within the artwork pose itself to Benjamin's and Adorno's respective projects? In what ways do the two thinkers attempt to respond to Schlegel's famous dictum that, when it comes to the philosophy of art, there is usually one thing missing, the philosophy or the art? As we will see, for both Benjamin and Adorno, albeit from different vantage points, the aesthetic cannot be reduced *merely* to cognition (in which case no artwork would be needed, because that cognition could be obtained through other means); nor does the aesthetic refuse itself to cognition outright (in which case it would remain merely unintelligible and, therefore, not an appropriate matter of sustained conceptual inquiry). Rather, the aesthetic is to be thought as the perpetually transitory space where the content of the artwork has not yet fully become cognition or knowledge, but rather provides, in the seriously playful realm of semblance, an intimation of conceptual and experiential *possibility*. This experience of possibility enacts itself across Benjamin's and Adorno's variegated aesthetic writings in multiple and heterogeneous formulations.

2. Benjamin's potentiality

The multiple loci of Benjamin's sustained engagement with aesthetic questions encompass such diverse themes as the concept of art criticism in German Romanticism (the topic of his 1919 doctoral dissertation); the aesthetics of imagination and color; the German Baroque mourning play; his theories of translation and translatability; his work on literary authors such as Hölderlin, Goethe, Keller, Baudelaire, Kafka, Proust, and Brecht; his meditations on surrealism and on proletarian children's theater; and his attempts to intervene in the aesthetic and conceptual specificity of such emerging media as photography, film, and radio. Subsequent to the German National Socialists' ascent to power in 1933, his work also addresses questions of Hitler's so-called aestheticization of politics, through which the fascist regime—for Benjamin the most aesthetically self-conscious in modern history—fatefully attempted to mobilize the sphere of art and semblance for its own political aims.

Working to call into question the aestheticization of the political, Benjamin, in all his heterogeneous writings on aesthetic issues, wishes

to respect the singularity of the aesthetic as the instantiation of conceptual and experiential possibility. He feels compelled not simply to apply
a general aesthetic system or conceptual doctrine to this or that particular work of art—a process through which the individual work of art
would be reduced to the status of mere example and, by extension, to
something indifferent and ultimately replaceable. Rather, he attempts to
reinvent his conceptual comportment toward the aesthetic experience
each time anew. Self-consciously eschewing the predictable gestures of
communicative transparency, his writing, therefore, requires its readers
to embark upon the laborious task of learning how to follow the text's
"own," at times strangely idiomatic, logic, and to compare this writing,
not with some external standard by which it could easily be judged,
but first and foremost *with itself*. In a 1926 letter to Scholem, Benjamin
refers to his own self-consciously elusive and figurative mode of argumentation as an unyielding desire to think and write in a style that is
"always radical, never consistent with regard to the most important
things" (Benjamin 1994, 300). Only this radicality, Benjamin suggests,
can ever hope to do justice to the singularity of the artwork *as* artwork
(rather than as pleasurable diversion or as mere illustration of a preexisting extraaesthetic "meaning") and to the very notion of a conceptually
significant aesthetic experience in relation to the specific artwork.

To approach an artwork in this way also means to engage the very
language in which the encounter takes place, that is, the language of
criticism, critique, and commentary. Here, the language of criticism not
only functions as an instrument for the transmission of certain ideas
about an artwork but also is called upon to provide an account of itself.
Incapable of remaining unaffected by the logic and experience of a particular encounter with a singular work of art, the language of criticism
is irrevocably altered by the experience for which no previous encounter could have prepared it. Benjamin's own rigorous engagement with
the language of criticism is encrypted in the first line of the epistemo-
critical prologue to his study on the Baroque German mourning play,
the so-called *Trauerspiel* book, as follows: "It is the property of philosophical writing to stand, with each turn [*Wendung*], once again before
the question of presentation" (1998, 27). This relentless and aporetic
insistence on the demands of a language that resists its author and its
subject matter each time it performs another *Wendung*, turn or trope,
a language that stubbornly refuses to become deceptively transparent,

decisively inflects the entire trajectory of Benjamin's engagements with the aesthetic. As if the discourse of aesthetic criticism were called upon to assume some of the artwork's own characteristics—without, however, thereby becoming an aesthetic object itself—in the massive collection of notes and fragments that were to be his material for a general theory of modernity, *The Arcades Project*, Benjamin confesses: "I have nothing to say. Only to show" (1999a, 460). Aesthetic critique proceeds by "showing"—as opposed to merely saying, a saying that would ignore the logic and requirements of its own strategic operations. It is here, as Benjamin's work in the realm of a specifically aesthetic mode of cognition and experience suggests, that the formal and the historico-political dimension of analysis and argumentation are dialectically intertwined and, indeed, are mutually saturated with the open-ended interpretive possibilities and unfathomable demands of the other.

For the Benjamin of the 1930s, whose preoccupations focus ever more relentlessly on issues of aesthetics and mediality in the broadest sense, the radical and apodictic modes of thinking and writing that are his signature could be said to coalesce around a set of issues that concern the relationship between historical—that is, genealogical—models of analysis and more strictly formal and structural ones. In fact, we could say that Benjamin's ways of thinking the aesthetic realm and medium-specific problems unfold according to a strategically unorthodox historicization. His groundbreaking approach to questions of media theory and mediality (although at the time there was no such thing as "media studies" in any formalized or institutional context) rely heavily on the genealogical mode of argumentation that is perhaps best condensed in the programmatic conviction, expressed in the "The Work of Art in the Age of Its Technological Reproducibility," that during *"vast historical spans of time the manner of human collectives' perception changes along with the collectives' entire mode of being-in-the-world.* The manner in which human perception organizes itself—the medium in which it takes place—is conditioned not only naturally but also historically" (Benjamin 2002, 104). For the mature Benjamin, the question of how to postulate the changing relationship of consciousness and perception to a work of art or a medium must not be limited to the phenomenological study of its appearance in the object world; it also must take into account the ways in which any approach to that phenomenal appearance is inflected by the historical transformations of the prevailing manner in which acts of seeing, listening, reading, thinking, and even feeling are performed. The determination of these large-scale temporal and epistemological transformations, however, always also concerns the history and logic of their medial and aesthetic specificity.

In keeping with this view, many of Benjamin's writings on art and mediality in the 1930s fasten upon a specific aspect of their historical unfolding, propelling him to compose, among many other works, "A Small History of Photography," "The Rigorous Study of Art," his texts on the production and dissemination of painting and the graphic arts, as well as his meditations on such topics as film, Chaplin, Mickey Mouse, the radio, the telephone, theater, children's books, journalism, newspapers, and the publishing industry (now conveniently collected in Benjamin 2008). According to the logic of this stance toward aesthetic phenomena, the critic's task is to construct the relays between an artwork's singularity and its universal conceptual demands by "erecting the great constructions from the smallest, sharply and cuttingly fitted building blocks," and to "recognize in the analysis of the small singular moment the crystal of the total event" (Benjamin 1999a, 461). This act of aesthetic recognition must be mindful of its own mediatedness, that is, of Benjamin's fundamental conviction—as he expresses in "Translation—For and Against"—that "there is no world of thought that is not a world of language, and one sees in the world only what is pre-conditioned by language" (2002, 249).

3. Adorno's resistance

While questions of aesthetic theory traverse the orbit of Adorno's entire oeuvre, they are most forcefully articulated in his unfinished opus magnum, *Aesthetic Theory*, posthumously published in 1970 (1997). Although for Adorno—the talented musician and erstwhile piano pupil of Alban Berg and Eduard Steuermann—music emerges as the most salient of the aesthetic realms in which philosophical questions may be posed, other arts such as literature and painting also lie within his work's purview. And yet, when *Aesthetic Theory* speaks of "art" (*die Kunst*), it typically does not simply mean the totality of the individual arts considered together; "art" rather becomes, as a cognitive category in its own right, the discursive placeholder within a larger philosophical project.

From Adorno's perspective, there can be no immanent medita-
tion on the realm of the aesthetic that is not also an enactment or
a determined negation of the social and political structures in which
the particular manifestation of the aesthetic—that is, the rigors of its
form—are embedded. Departing, however, from a more conventional
Hegelian-Marxian framework, what determines the political content
of an encounter with the aesthetic is neither its transmission of this or
that content, nor its revelation of a communicable message. Rather,
the aesthetic remains to be understood in terms of the specific and
formal ways in which it *resists* appropriation and instrumentalization.
We thus encounter the aesthetic, particularly in the domain of writing,
in a series of hieroglyphs that demand to be read but that also refuse
to yield their full meaning. Pointing to the ways in which "the concept
of *écriture* has become relevant," Adorno argues that "all artworks are
writing, not just those that are obviously such; they are hieroglyphs
for which the code has been lost, a loss that plays into their content.
Artworks are language only as writing" (1997, 124). While these hieroglyphs cannot be reduced to a singular truth statement or stable meaning without being canceled, they also cannot *not* be read. Rather, what
is at stake in interpreting the hieroglyphs of the aesthetic is the determination of the specific ways in which they resist determination. As
Adorno tells us, the "aim of the artwork is the determination of the
indeterminate" (1997, 124). Because the hieroglyphs of the aesthetic
reveal themselves in the form of enigmas, that is, as "script" in which,
"as in linguistic signs, its processual element is enciphered in its objec-
tivation" (Adorno 1997, 177), the artwork can only be understood as a
system whose internal laws are out of joint: "Each artwork is a system
of irreconcilability" (1997, 184).

Once this system of irreconcilability becomes visible in an artwork,
what reveals itself is that in "artworks nothing is literal, least of all their
words" (Adorno 1997, 87). This means that to read artworks and the
realm of the aesthetic to which they belong entails a decisive turn away
from the realist or mimetic effect that they may simulate on the surface.
In an act of dissimulation, they become thinkable and experienceable
only in and as something irreducibly figurative. One might call this their
material moment of inscription. Artworks become material and read-
able in what Adorno calls "their own figuration," that is, the allegori-
cal enactment of "the solution" to problems "which they are unable

to provide on their own without intervention." The specific intervention that the artwork can perform thus unfolds not in the sphere of
immediacy but precisely in the aesthetic and incommensurate event
marked—but not containable—by its inscription. This suggests, according to Adorno, that "every important work of art leaves traces behind
in its material and technique, and following them defines the modern
as what needs to be done, which is contrary to having a nose for what
is in the air. Critique makes this definition concrete." For Adorno, the
material inscription of the aesthetic event as a political act presents itself
in the figure of the scar: "The traces to be found in the material and the
technical procedures, from which every qualitatively new work of art
takes its lead, are scars: They are the loci at which the preceding works
misfired." A scar, as a trace of corporeal writing, marks the place of a
previous incision or injury. A sign of what no longer is, it also is a deeply
historical marker. The scar always occurs as a double gesture: it represents itself as the concrete and present image of a disfiguration, excessive in its reference to something that no longer exists, a signifier with a
signified but without a referent. The scar bespeaks that utopian moment
of coming to terms with and recovering from a traumatic injury, even as
it continues to render the forgetting of that trauma impossible. After all,
a scar is a sign both of healing and of danger: it always threatens to be
reopened. Seen from this perspective, the scar occupies a ghostly locus
between the various axes of time and of cognition. We even could say
that the figure of the scar, like Adorno's sentences themselves, not only
signifies the historical and theoretical complexity of material inscription,
but also embodies it. Following Adorno's lead, the history of Western
art and aesthetics deserves to be rewritten not in terms of teleological
succession but as an archive or constellation of scars. The scar, and "not
the historical continuity of [the works'] dependencies, binds artworks to
one another" (1997, 35).

For Adorno, the political function of the aesthetic paradoxically
is located in the very space in which it is inaccessible to instrumen-
talist reasoning and unmediated political intervention. Here, "art
becomes social by its opposition to society." Adorno argues that "by
crystallizing in itself as something unique to itself, rather than com-
plying with existing social norms and qualifying as 'socially useful,' it
criticizes society by merely existing, for which puritans of all stripes
condemn it" (1997, 225–226). Because even art that is socially and

politically engaged can become affirmative of the status quo by fulfilling the function of critique that the status quo already has assigned
to it—that is, by offering a critique that is co-opted by the system
that spawned it—Adorno prefers to think of the aberrant event of
art in terms of a "determinate negation of a determinate society."
Therefore, art "keeps itself alive through its social force of resistance"
without which it becomes, even in its critical forms, "a commodity."
Because "nothing social in art is immediately social, not even when
this is its aim," what art can contribute to society "is not communication with it but rather something extremely mediated: It is resistance"
(Adorno 1997, 226). For Adorno, there can be no resistance lodged
in an artwork that is not perpetually retreating from what it signifies
and from the determinate nature of the relays between it and the
contexts that mediate it.

In the particular case of musical aesthetics, a topic to which Adorno
devotes thousands of pages, we might say that to the extent that there
are strong mediating relays between music and philosophical thought,
these must be measured against, and modulated by, the fundamental
tension that traverses the explication of all aesthetic forms and that sat-
urates music in medium-specific ways. In other words, while the pleasure one derives from an artwork, especially a musical one, is certainly
open to analysis, any attempt to understand that work by means of the
precepts of reason alone—whether merely with an eye to its *illustrative*
function vis-à-vis this or that philosophical or political agenda, or in an
instrumentalizing attempt to translate aesthetic form and its irrational
pleasures into a rational system of concepts—will, sooner or later, bring
the question of art's raison d'étre to the fore. Adorno illustrates this
conundrum as follows: "When one asks a musician if music is a pleasure, the reply is likely to be—as in the American joke of the grimacing
cellist under Toscanini—'*I just hate music.*'" This leads to the following dilemma: "Whoever enjoys artworks concretistically is a philistine;
expressions such as 'a feast for the ears' give him away. Yet if the last
traces of pleasure were extirpated, the question as to the purpose of
artworks would be an embarrassment" (Adorno 1997, 13). As such, any
philosophical explication of music first of all must acknowledge that "art
stands in need of philosophy that interprets it in order to say that which
it cannot say, whereas art is only able to say what it says by not saying
it" (Adorno 1997, 72). Remaining faithful to the difficulty of this task

of simultaneously saying and not-saying would, therefore, constitute a perpetual challenge to any speculative analysis of musical aesthetics.

The difficulty of speaking philosophically about music is augmented when one considers that the proximity of music to discursive language, its linguisticality, continually offers a conceptual content that it simultaneously withholds. Does music *have* a language? If so, *is* it a language of its own? What kind of language would it be? If it can be conceded that music is or has a form of language—and the jury among musicians and theorists of music alike remains very much out on this point—how would the language of music relate to the language of speculative thought, its grammatical categories and organizing principles, its logic and its vocabulary? In his "Music and Language: A Fragment," Adorno argues that "music resembles language . . . in that it is a temporal sequence of articulated sounds which are more than mere sounds. They say something, often something human. The more sophisticated the music, the more penetratingly they say it. The succession of sounds is related to logic: there is right and wrong." He continues: "But what has been said cannot detach itself from the music. Music forms no system of signs" (Adorno 2002, 1). Thus, while music and language share certain modes of signification that, broadly speaking, could be construed as belonging to the vast realm of textuality, the content of music cannot be considered as belonging to the temporal gesture of its performance and cannot be paraphrased without being erased. In its failure to supply such reliable hermeneutic access to its arrangements of acoustic signs, music singularly denies itself, if not to citation, then certainly to summary and paraphrase.

This refusal to be summarized or paraphrased should not, however, be regarded simply as a deficit, since it constitutes a triumph as well as a failure. The triumph resides in the musical artwork's insistence upon remaining faithful to the difficulties that lie at the heart both of musical composition and of philosophical thought. In following this logic, one may recall Adorno's comments in *Negative Dialectics* when, apropos of his musical mentor Arnold Schönberg and the Second Viennese School, he writes:

An experience that Schönberg noted with regard to traditional music theory is confirmed in the case of philosophy: one actually only learns from it how a movement begins and ends, nothing about the movement itself, its course. Analogously philosophy would need first, not to turn itself into a series of categories but rather, in a certain sense, to compose itself. (Adorno 2000, 33–34)

He adds: "It must, in the course of its progression, relentlessly renew itself, as much from its own strength as from the friction with that against which it measures itself." For Adorno, it "is what happens in philosophy that is decisive, not a thesis or a position; its fabric, not the deductive or inductive single-tracked train of thought. Therefore philosophy is in essence not summarizable. Otherwise it would be superfluous; that most of it allows itself to be summarized speaks against it" (Adorno 2000, 33–34). Far from merely equating musical aesthetics with philosophy, Adorno emphasizes the shared compositional form and meticulously constructed aesthetic elements that, in the most rigorous and liberating musical and philosophical works, mitigate against a freezing of their sounds and signs into an apparently fixed and scannable database of meaning capable of being expressed in any number of ways that are independent of the resistant singularities of their forms. From this perspective, what the music of such figures as Beethoven (who, for Adorno, is Hegel set to music), Mahler, and Schönberg shares, or ought to share, with the orbit of philosophy is a resistance to paraphrase and a refusal to play along with the commodity fetishism of regressive listening that characterizes technocapitalism and the ideology of lucidity that demands remainderless and submissive transparency.

As with Benjamin, for Adorno the aesthetic encounter is one of possibility and unregimented, non-predigested experience. In this encounter, what comes to pass is the intimation of reason with its conceptual basis as well as its perpetual withholding in the guise of a singularly resistant form. It is here, in art's irreducibly double movement of disclosure and retreat, that the aesthetic assumes its own dignity. After all, as *Aesthetic Theory* reminds us, "only what does not fit into the world is true" (Adorno 1997, 59). Benjamin and Adorno are precisely the *misfits* who would have us linger with the many forms of exhilaration and mourning borne of this insight *in* (i.e., both into and contained within) the work of art.[2]

Notes

1   Here and elsewhere, I have occasionally modified the published English translations in order to enhance their fidelity to the original German.

2 For this essay, I have borrowed some arguments, sentences, and paragraphs from
   work on Benjamin and Adorno that I have carried out over the past decade or so,
   revising them and fitting them into a new framework.

Primary sources

Benjamin and Adorno:
1999. *The Complete Correspondence 1928–1940*. H. Lonitz (ed.), N. Walker (trans.).
Cambridge, MA: Harvard University Press.

Benjamin:
1994. *The Correspondence of Walter Benjamin 1910–1940*. R. Manfred and M.
Evelyn Jacobson (trans.). Chicago: University of Chicago Press.
1996. *Selected Writings*. Vol. 1: 1913–1926. M. Jennings et al. (eds.). Cambridge,
MA: Harvard University Press.
1998. *The Origin of German Tragic Drama*. J. Osborne (trans.). London: Verso.
Originally published 1928.
1999a. *The Arcades Project*. H. Eiland and K. McLaughlin (trans.). Cambridge, MA:
Harvard University Press.
1999b. *Selected Writings*. Vol. 2: 1927–1934. M. Jennings et al. (eds.). Cambridge,
MA: Harvard University Press.
2002. *Selected Writings*. Vol. 3: 1935–1938. M. Jennings et al. (eds.). Cambridge,
MA: Harvard University Press.
2003. *Selected Writings*. Vol. 4: 1938–1940. M. Jennings et al. (eds.). Cambridge,
MA: Harvard University Press.
2008. *The Work of Art in the Age of Its Technological Reproducibility and Other
Writings on Media*. M. W. Jennings, B. Doherty, and T. Y. Levin (eds.). Cambridge,
MA: Harvard University Press. Originally published 1936.

Adorno:
1981. *Prisms: Cultural Criticism and Society*. Samuel and Shierry Weber (trans.).
Cambridge, MA: MIT Press. Originally published 1955.
1992. "Commitment." In *Notes to Literature*, Vol. 2. Shierry Weber Nicholsen (trans.).
New York: Columbia University Press, 76–94.
1997. *Aesthetic Theory*. R. Hullot-Kentor (trans.). Minneapolis: University of
Minnesota Press. Originally published 1970.
2000. *Negative Dialectics*. E. B. Ashton (trans). New York: Continuum. Originally
published 1966.
2002. "Music and Language: A Fragment." In *Quasi una fantasia: Essays on Modern
Music*. R. Livingston (trans.). London: Verso.

References and further reading

Bernstein, J. M. 1992. *The Fate of Art: Aesthetic Alienation from Kant to Derrida and Adorno*. University Park, PA: Pennsylvania State University Press.

Marx, Karl, and Friedrich Engels. 1985. *The German Ideology*. C. J. Arthur (ed.). New York: International Publishers.

Richter, Gerhard. 2007. *Thought-Images: Frankfurt School Writers' Reflections from Damaged Life*. Stanford: Stanford University Press.

—, ed. 2010. *Language without Soil: adorno and Late Philosophical Modernity*. New York: Fordham University Press.

Weber, Samuel. 2008. *Benjamin's-abilities*. Cambridge, MA: Harvard University Press.

CHAPTER 13

MONROE BEARDSLEY
(1915–1985)

Noël Carroll

Monroe Beardsley was an American philosopher specializing in aesthetics. He was born on December 10, 1915 in Bridgeport, Connecticut and he died on September 18, 1985 in Philadelphia, Pennsylvania. He was married to the ethicist Elizabeth Beardsley. He was awarded his BA in 1936 from Yale University and did graduate work at Yale, receiving his Ph.D. in philosophy in 1939. Beardsley taught at several colleges including Mount Holyoke and Yale before he settled at Swarthmore, where he taught for 22 years. From Swarthmore, he moved to Temple University where he taught for 16 years, until his death. Beardsley was a major figure—if not *the* major figure—in establishing the discipline of analytic aesthetics in America. He was affectionately called "The Dean of Aesthetics" because of the seminal role he played in the field.

Beardsley first attracted wide attention for his work with the literary scholar W. K. Wimsatt (1907–1975) on what they called "the intentional fallacy"—the putative error of basing either the interpretation or the evaluation of a work of art on the intention of the author. Their best-known statement of the alleged fallacy appeared in their article "The Intentional Fallacy" (orig. publ. 1946), which was an expansion of the 1943 entry on the topic of intention in *The Dictionary of World Literature*. In 1949, Wimsatt and Beardsley also coauthored another famous article, "The Affective Fallacy." There they argued that the affective response of the audience was also irrelevant to the interpretation and evaluation of the artwork.

Both fallacies stressed that the artwork itself was the proper object of critical focus—not that which brings it about (the author's intention) or that which it brings about (the audience's response). The critic should perform close readings of the work and not dwell on where the work came from or what consequences issued from it. These arguments served the interests of the school of thought called the New Criticism, which dominated American literary criticism in the 1940s and 1950s. They gave teeth to the New Critics' slogan that one's reading should not wander *outside* the text where things like intentions and affective consequences lurk. Beardsley and Wimsatt provided the New Criticism with philosophical armor, which, in turn, reinforced the legitimacy of literary studies by arguing that it had a unique object of study—the literary work itself—and a correspondingly appropriate methodology—close reading.

In 1958 with the publication of his groundbreaking treatise—*Aesthetics: Problems in the Philosophy of Criticism* (reissued with a postscript in 1981)—Beardsley applied the tenets of the New Criticism to the arts in general, thereby legitimatizing the field of analytic aesthetics. Blending the kind of analytic philosophy that was coming to dominate the American academy with a tendency toward empiricism, Beardsley gave the aesthetician a method—what can be called *metacriticism*—and an object of study—what he first called an "aesthetic object" but later defined as the artwork itself. Metacriticism, à la Beardsley, consists of the examination of the concepts and modes of argument of the art critic. Thus, topics like representation and expression come in for close examination in *Aesthetics* and his subsequent investigations. Moreover, criticism itself has a unique object—the artwork itself. So metacriticism involves the analysis of the concepts appropriately deployed in the criticism of art.

Although Beardsley's ideas changed over the course of his long and productive career, in retrospect one finds his position to be remarkably stable. That is, seen retrospectively, the structure of Beardsley's thinking remains basically consistent throughout, despite some tinkering here and there. For instance, he never gives up on the idea of the intentional fallacy, although over the years he constructs new arguments on its behalf.

One change in Beardsley's approach, as already mentioned, is from his initial designation of the focus of criticism as the aesthetic object to the more ordinary concept of the artwork. And although Beardsley's propounding of a definition of art comes somewhat late in his career, we can see that it was holding his system together all along.

Beardsley was an immensely systematic philosopher. The keystone of his system is the notion of aesthetic experience, which, under the influence of John Dewey, Beardsley identifies as an experience of singular clarity and coherence, so singular, in fact, that the aesthetic experience is autonomous in the sense that it stands out or detaches itself from ordinary experience. When in the throes of aesthetic experience, we are free, released from antecedent concerns, and emotionally detached from events, such as tragic calamities, that might ordinarily threaten or oppress us.

Beardsley then goes on to define the art object as an intentional arrangement of conditions for affording experiences of marked aesthetic character. Here, the value of the artwork is construed instrumentally—the artwork is valuable for abetting aesthetic experiences. Beardsley requires that the artistic arrangement be intentionally contrived in order to distinguish artworks from things in nature that may afford aesthetic experience. The artwork is an artifact that in virtue of its features—such as unity, complexity, and intensity—provides the occasion for having nonnegligible aesthetic experience (so long as we batten upon the artwork itself and not the factors that brought it about or the consequences it may have for practical affairs).

Because Beardsley's theory of art is, broadly speaking, functionalist, he has the wherewithal to evaluate artworks specifically in terms of what they are ideally designed to bring about, namely, the promotion of aesthetic experiences of a nonnegligible magnitude. And artworks can be chided when they are incapable of delivering the requisite quotient of aesthetic experience. Moreover, when critics commend artworks, they can do so in virtue of the features of the artworks that afford aesthetic experience—features such as unity, complexity, and intensity of "regional qualities" (roughly Beardsley's name for expressive and/or aesthetic properties). That is, a canon of critical standards flows directly from Beardsley's experience-centered, functionalist definition of art.

Furthermore, given the structure of Beardsley's theory, he is able to hypothesize the importance of art for human life. The purpose of art is to engender aesthetic experience. Thus, whatever the value that art *qua* art possesses will depend upon whatever values attach to having aesthetic experiences. According to Beardsley, having aesthetic experiences is instrumentally valuable for several reasons. First, aesthetic experience is said to relieve tensions and quiet destructive emotions. Aesthetic experience also aids us in sorting out the jumble in the flow of consciousness in our mind, by virtue of its tendencies toward heightened clarity and coherence.

In addition to these contributions to mental health, aesthetic experiences enhance our perceptual faculties, enabling us to discriminate the elements of perceptual stimuli more and more subtly. Aesthetic experience also enlarges the imagination, notably expanding our ability to see affairs from the perspective of others. Moreover, aesthetic experience brings people together, fostering sympathy and social cohesion. And finally, aesthetic experience presents us with an ideal of human life; that is, human life may be modeled on artworks with their surpassing degree of unity, complexity, and intensity.

By speculating on the importance of aesthetic experience, Beardsley is able to answer the demand that Leo Tolstoy formulated in his 1896 treatise, *What is Art?*: that in order to be adequate, a definition of art must indicate why art is a significant human practice, one whose benefits outweigh the sacrifices it exacts. Because of the central role that aesthetic experience plays in Beardsley's account of art, it is often called an *aesthetic* theory of art. Indeed, aesthetic experience is so important to Beardsley's system that he calls his entire field of inquiry "aesthetics" rather than "philosophy of art."

Beardsley's system is immensely elegant due to the way in which the notion of aesthetic experience is fundamental to the notions of art and artistic evaluation, and even to the value of the very practice of art. Few theories of art are as neatly interconnected as Beardsley's. But for all of its admirable economy, it is open to a number of challenging criticisms. One way to appreciate its limitations is to look closely at Beardsley's concept of art.

According to Beardsley, an artwork is an intentional arrangement of conditions for the purpose of affording experiences of a markedly aesthetic character. On the one hand, this seems far too narrow and exclusive. Art of the twentieth century provides us with many examples of antiaesthetic art—intentional arrangements of conditions created in order to discourage and even thwart experiences with any aesthetic character, marked or otherwise. Ready-mades are a pertinent example here. In 1926, Marcel Duchamp, for example, exhibited an ordinary metal, canine grooming comb that was as dull looking as dull can be, and he did so intending to frustrate any attempt to use it to support an aesthetic experience.

Furthermore, Duchamp's ready-mades have been embraced by art historians, curators, collectors, art lovers, and artists alike as major contributions to the world of art. Yet Beardsley's theory of art cannot assimilate them. Beardsley, of course, was aware of this; his response was to deny that such ready-mades were art. Instead, he reclassified them as *comments* on art. However, this maneuver seems very ad hoc and stipulative. At this late date, given the history of modern art, the attempt to legislate that ready-mades are not art appears highly dubious.

Moreover, Beardsley's theory of art is not only too narrow, but also too broad. To see this, visit your local grocery store. There, you will see aisle upon aisle of products handsomely packaged to attract buyers. These have been designed at great expense. The commercial artists who created these colorful boxes surely intended these arrangements to afford appreciable aesthetic experiences. They wanted to make things that were pleasing to look at. Thus, they would appear to count as art on Beardsley's definition. But it is doubtful that most cereal boxes are art in terms of our ordinary understanding of that concept. Nor is this problem a marginal one, when one recalls the indefinitely large number of manufactured products—including automobiles and refrigerators—that are designed, very often successfully, to sustain experiences of a marked aesthetic character. In short, Beardsley's definition saddles us with too much art.

It might be thought that the way to prevent the preceding embarrassment might be to require that the arrangements in question be created with the *primary* intention that they promote aesthetic experience of a certain nonnegligible magnitude. However, that will result in rendering the theory too narrow again. The stain-glass windows in medieval European churches were not designed with the *primary* intention of affording aesthetic experience. They were intended to serve as pedagogical props that priests could use to educate their parishioners regarding the founding narratives of Christianity. Likewise, the Stations of the Cross in those churches were made with the primary intention of assisting the faithful in prayer and ritual. The artists and artisans who produced these works would be appalled at the suggestion that they made these things with the primary intention to abet aesthetic experience. Such a view they might regard as tantamount to blasphemy. They did not undertake the creation of these items in order to celebrate the autonomy of art from everyday life, but as instruments to assist the very purpose of life, which for them was salvation.

Thus, although one must admire the breathtaking, architectonic beauty of Beardsley's system, at the same time, one must approach it critically, as Beardsley himself did with respect to every leading theory in the philosophy of art of his time.

Primary sources

Beardsley:
1970. *The Possibility of Criticism*. Detroit, MI: Wayne State University Press.
1971. (With William K. Wimsatt.) "The Affective Fallacy." Reprinted in Hazard Adams (ed.), *Critical Theory since Plato*. New York: Harcourt, Brace, Janovich. Originally published 1949.
1981. *Aesthetics: Problems in the Philosophy of Criticism*, 2nd edition. Indianapolis, IN: Hackett. Originally published 1958.
1982. *The Aesthetic Point of View*. Ithaca, NY: Cornell University Press.
1987. (With William K. Wimsatt.) "The Intentional Fallacy." Reprinted in Joseph Margolis (ed.), *Philosophy Looks at the Arts*. Philadelphia, PA: Temple University Press. Originally published 1946.

References and further reading

Dickie, George. 2006. "Monroe Beardsley." In Donald Borchert (ed.), *Encyclopedia of Philosophy*, 2nd edition. New York: Thompson/Gale Publishers, Vol. 1, 508–510.
Kivy, Peter, ed. 2010. "Beardsley Symposium." *Journal of Aesthetic Education*, 44, 1–25.
Wreen, Michael. 1998. "Monroe Beardsley." In Michael Kelly (ed.), *Oxford Encyclopedia of Aesthetics*. Oxford: Oxford University Press, Vol. 1, 232–237.
Wreen, Michael, and Donald Callen, eds. 2005. "Symposium: Monroe Beardsley's Legacy in Aesthetics." *Journal of Aesthetics and Art Criticism*, 63, 175–195.

CHAPTER 14

NELSON GOODMAN
(1906–1998)

Alessandro Giovannelli

The American philosopher Henry Nelson Goodman produced ground-breaking work in different areas of philosophy, including metaphysics, epistemology, philosophy of language, and applied logic. He also helped revolutionize Anglo-American analytic aesthetics. His often unorthodox and radical views on a range of issues central to the philosophy of art energized the aesthetics debate of the second half of the twentieth century, opening up avenues of investigation that still continue today. His aesthetic views were given a systematic presentation in the seminal *Languages of Art* (1976), first published in 1968, but they were expanded and refined in later writings.

Goodman looked at issues in aesthetics, and especially in philosophy of art, out of a personal, deep love and respect for the arts (prior to his academic career, he directed an art gallery in Boston, and he remained an avid art collector all his life). Yet, a remarkable feature of his aesthetics is also its continuity with his proposals in other areas of philosophy. Indeed, Goodman provides a unifying theoretical key into the understanding of disparate parts of reality and human activity. His leading idea is that access to reality, whether through ordinary experience, science, or art, is made possible and modified by the use of symbols, and hence is ultimately a matter of interpretation. How we experience and understand any kind of reality—whether relevant to ordinary experience, the sciences, or the arts—ultimately depends on the classifications we cast upon the world—on the "predicates," linguistic and nonlinguistic, and combinations thereof that we "project" onto reality. We experience and understand the world in a certain manner partly because, for example, we project such predicates as "green" and "blue" onto those things that we call "emeralds" and "sapphires" (which, again, are what they are partly because of our projecting those predicates onto them; see Goodman 1983). Predicate projections do not reveal a pre-existing reality to us. Rather, reality is, quite literally, *made, constructed* by our categorizations. Hence, whether we are considering ordinary perception, scientific theories, or artistic projects, we should see these human, cognitive activities as contributing to "worldmaking," according to a constructivist metaphysical view Goodman first defended in *The Structure of Appearance* (1966), and then, in less formal terms, in *Ways of Worldmaking* (1978). Yet, Goodman is also a relativist: alternative and incompatible classifications may be acceptable. Emeralds and sapphires could be as adequately described as "grue" and "bleen," the two predicates Goodman famously devised in the context of his discussion of induction (1983). If "grue" is defined as "green when observed prior to a time *t* and blue otherwise," and "bleen" as "blue when observed prior to *t* and green otherwise," then nothing prevents describing emeralds and sapphires as we know them by these two predicates (an emerald, for example, is as green as it is grue). The reasons why we project "green" and "blue" instead, and project them in a certain way, are ultimately pragmatic: it is because of habit, of the "entrenchment" of those predicates rather than alternative ones (Goodman 1983).

Accordingly, there are as many worlds as the irreducible categorizations we can successfully devise. These are not just the worlds of the sciences—different worlds correspond to Newtonian and Einsteinian physics, for example—but also the worlds of the arts, artistic styles, and artistic works: we can think of Picasso's cubist paintings, for example, as bringing about a largely different world from that brought about by Masaccio's frescos. Which categorizations, hence symbols, are successfully projected over time—for example, which artistic styles are perceived as familiar and which ones as revolutionary, or which linguistic uses are considered literal and which ones metaphorical—largely depends on what is customary, entrenched within a given cultural, artistic, or linguistic community.

Fortunately, much of what Goodman has to offer regarding art does not depend on the rather controversial claim that talk of "worldmaking" ought to be taken literally.[1] Quite independently of his constructivism, Goodman still challenges us with a view of the arts as capable of bringing about new and important views on reality, and of doing so by means of works whose nature and meaning ultimately depend on conventions— old or new artistic conventions that operate in our cultures.

Goodman succeeds in proposing articulate theories on a range of aesthetic issues—pictorial representation and realism, artistic expression, metaphor, the ontology of art, meaning in different art forms (including the nonrepresentational arts), the notion of style, artistic merit, and even such specific issues as that of "variations upon a theme" in music and painting—starting from a remarkably simple basis: the primitive notion of "standing for," that is, symbolization. Works of art are concrete objects—a piece of canvas with paint on it, a carved chunk of marble, a series of uttered sounds, or ink marks on paper—that acquire artistic status, meaning, and value when they become symbols functioning within some system of rules. Hence, understanding what painting, or sculpture, or music, or literature is amounts to understanding how certain things acquire symbolic function, and symbolic function of a certain sort, within some systems of rules.

Two theses are fundamental to Goodman's theory of symbols: (1) symbolization, which is for him the same as reference, comes in different modes, and denotation or labeling (e.g., the relation between "dog" and dogs) is only one of them; (2) a symbol is a symbol of a certain kind only within a system of that kind (e.g., something is a picture only within a pictorial system). It is in this sense, then, that there are *languages* of art, although natural languages and other linguistic systems are by no means the only possible ones; there exist many other systems: pictorial, gestural, diagrammatic, and so on.

1. Modes of reference

One of Goodman's important contributions to philosophy is his investigation of kinds, or modes, of reference or symbolization (1976; see also Goodman 1984, chapter 3). *Denotation* is the relationship between a *label*, such as "Barack Obama," or "the 44th President of the United States," or the picture in an Obama campaign poster, and what it labels. As labels refer to things, so things possess the features attributed to them by whichever labels apply to them—that of being Barack Obama or the 44th US President (and also, of course, of being of such-and-such a height, a parent, and so forth, according to the respective labels). As said, labels are not limited to linguistic ones: pictures, sculptures, musical sonatas, and so on can also be labels that classify world items. Hence, the world or worlds we experience and try to understand are as much the result of linguistic categorizations as of categorizations brought about by paintings, sculptures, musical sonatas, and so on.

As mentioned, denotation is only one of the modes of reference. Think of the fabric swatches tailors use: they stand for a certain color and pattern, but they do so by (1) possessing those color and pattern features and (2) referring back to the labels that determine such feature possession (say, "red" and "tweed"), hence calling attention to those features. Thus, *exemplification* is that mode of reference that consists of "possession plus reference" (Goodman 1976, chapter 2). Of course, exemplification is selective: not all the labels that apply to a swatch are referred to by the swatch; typically, a swatch exemplifies color and pattern but not size or location, for example (Goodman 1978, 63–70). This mode of reference would be hardly relevant if it were limited to the world of tailoring and the like. Yet, Goodman claims exemplification to be as common as philosophically unrecognized a form of reference, with some central applications in aesthetics. Naturally, exemplification is key to the analysis of meaning—understood as symbolic function— in the nonrepresentational arts: paradigmatically, most music, dance, and architecture, as well as paintings with no representational content. Appealing to exemplification, Goodman can attribute to works that do not aim at representation a pervasive capacity of calling attention to some of their features, that is, of exemplifying them. Indeed, for Goodman exemplification pervades the arts even where representation *is* present. A poem's symbolic function, for instance, is not exhausted by what it says, hence denotes; that is why the task of the translator must be the "maximal preservation of what the original exemplifies as well as of what it says" (Goodman 1976, 60).

The analysis of artistic expression also appeals to exemplification, combined with a theory of metaphor. We have a metaphor, Goodman claims, when a symbol that normally refers to a certain (kind of) thing is made to refer to another (as when a man is called a "wolf"). Symbols, and labels in particular, do not work alone but rather as members of schemata, each ordinarily correlated to a certain realm of things. "Blue" and "green," for instance, belong to the same schema, usually correlated to colored things; likewise, "wild" and "carnivorous" are normally correlated to certain animals. A term is used metaphorically when it is successfully made to refer to the members of a realm different from that of its schema. When that happens, it is not just one label that is reassigned to a new referent, but rather a whole family of symbols to a new realm. Hence, if a metaphor like "Men are wolves" is successful, it typically bears other metaphorical attributions—say, that men are feral or that they have a pack mentality. Whether a use is metaphorical or not is relative to what are considered literal uses. Indeed, the difference between the literal and the metaphorical is, again, a matter of habit: literal uses of a term are often old metaphors that have just become literal applications (as when we refer to certain table parts as the "legs" of the table).

Artistic expression is, then, nothing but metaphorical exemplification. Specifically, an artwork expresses, say, sadness when it exemplifies a label, "sad," that metaphorically denotes it (metaphorically, since works of art literally do not have mental states). Indeed, for Goodman, expression is not limited to affective states such as emotions and feelings. *Any* feature (e.g., color, or shape, or movement features) can be expressed. Hence, we can say that a building expresses movement, dynamism, or being "jazzy" (Goodman and Elgin 1988, 40). Perhaps, Goodman's analysis of expression is most enlightening if considered as aimed at a general but not exhaustive account. For, if it is the case that a work of music expresses sadness insofar as it exemplifies a feature it only metaphorically possesses, then more could be said on what the metaphorical attribution of a mental state to a musical work amounts to, though that is not part of Goodman's project.[2]

The "routes" of reference are many. Other rhetorical figures can be explained, for Goodman, as requiring "transfers" of label schemata onto new realms, hence as "modes of metaphor": personification, synecdoche, antonomasia, hyperbole, litotes, irony, and so on (1976, 81–85; see also 1984, chapter 3). More generally, reference, whether by means of denoting or exemplifying, can also be *direct* or *indirect*. It is the latter when a symbol refers to its referent by means of referring to some other symbol or symbols. Indeed, symbols may combine in "chains of reference," where one symbol refers to another, such a symbol to yet another, and so on, giving rise to an instance of "complex" (vs. "simple") reference: an image of a bald eagle may represent the United States by denoting the member of a set, that of bald eagles, with those animals exemplifying a label as "bold and free," a label that in turn denotes the United States and is exemplified by it (Goodman 1984, 62).

Goodman appeals to the different modes of reference to account for a range of different notions. Addressing artistic style, for instance, he proposes that the stylistic features of a work make up a subset "of what is said, of what is exemplified, or of what is expressed" (Goodman 1978, 32). In particular, stylistic features are those symbolic properties of a work that allow us to position it in a certain place, time period, and artist's oeuvre. They help, in other words, in answering questions like "where?," "when?," "who?" with respect to a work—they function as a "signature" of sorts (Goodman 1978, 35). Even an issue like that of variation upon a theme, which Goodman extends from music to any art form, can be explained in terms of referential functions (Goodman and Elgin 1988). A musical passage, Goodman suggests, is a variation upon a theme when it both shares and differs, musically, from the theme *and*— via those same shared and differing features—it refers to the theme. Once again, the notion of exemplification, literal and metaphorical, is here explanatorily crucial, as the variation—Goodman submits—calls attention to the features it shares and it does not share with the theme. In painting, Picasso's forty variations upon Velázquez's *Las Meninas* dwell on selected aspects of the subject matter and other pictorial features of the original work.[3] The result is a series of what ultimately are to be considered *interpretations* of *Las Meninas*: we do not just see the Picasso's painting variations as derivative of *Las Meninas*, but also see the Velasquez's differently thanks to Picasso's insightful interpretations.

2. Types of symbol systems

Investigating the routes of reference is part and parcel of a more general project aimed at spelling out, as the subtitle of *Languages of Art* states, a general theory of symbols. For symbols refer the way they do—by denotation or exemplification, literal or metaphorical, direct or indirect—always within some *symbol system* or other. Further, whether a symbol is pictorial, or sculptural, or musical, and so on depends on the kind of system it belongs to: something is a picture because part of a pictorial system, a musical work because part of a musical system, and so on. Symbol systems differ from each other for their different syntactic and semantic rules, governing respectively how symbols can be formed and combined (e.g., how the letters of an alphabet can be combined into words and the words into well-formed sentences), and what and how they refer to what they refer to. In other words, a symbol system like the English language consists of a symbol *scheme*—that is, of a collection of symbols or "characters" (all the inscriptions of "a," "b," "c," etc.)—associated to a field of reference. The scheme is governed by syntactical rules, determining how to form and combine characters into new, compound ones; the system by semantic rules, determining how the symbols in the scheme refer to their field of reference.

The theory of symbol systems gives Goodman a way to address questions regarding ontology and the distinctions between the different art forms.[4] Questions like "What is a painting?" or "What is a work of music?" are answered in terms of the syntactic and semantic rules governing the different kinds of systems and how symbols are individuated within them. Of course, symbol systems may differ greatly for the realm that is associated to them—roughly speaking, for what their symbols are about. Yet, the different art forms cannot be differentiated by reference to content, distinguishing, say, painting from music for their referring, respectively, to a world of shapes and colors, and to one of sounds and aural structures. A painting may represent a sound (as perhaps Edvard Munch's *The Scream* does) or a musical piece represent colored, shaped objects (Mozart's *Requiem* may represent the flames of Hell). The notion central to Goodman's theory of symbol systems and hence to art ontology is that of a *notation*—in brief, a symbol system in which the marks that compose a character (say, all the inscriptions of the letter "a"—A, a, *a*, etc.) only compose that character, and in which to each symbol, that is, character, corresponds only one item in the realm, and to each item only one symbol (Goodman 1976, chapter 4). Musical scores get quite close to being symbols functioning in a notation in a Goodmanian sense. The English language has the syntactic but not the semantic characteristics of a notation: certain terms are ambiguous between two or more different possible meanings: "bank," for example, can refer to a financial institution or the land along a river.

The existence of a notation is what makes possible, in some art forms, a certain kind of multiple instantiation of artworks. You and I can both have our copies of Charles Dickens's *Hard Times*, and the same symphony can be performed on different occasions. Related, such art forms as music, dance, and theater allow for performances of the work thanks to the existence of a notation, within which the score or script specifies "the essential properties a performance must have to belong to the work" (Goodman 1976, 212). Notice that, in such art forms, the work is not the score or the script but rather the class of performances that are "compliant" with that score or script.[5] In contrast, paintings and sculptures do not work within a notation; hence, there is no copying of an original that would preserve its originality. A copy of a painting is *a copy*, not *an instance* of the original. This issue, then, has consequences on the question of forgery, and more generally on the relevance of a work's history of production to the identity, experience, and merit of the work (Goodman 1976, chapter 3). In certain arts—literature, music, and (if a notation is available) dance—copying the text or score preserves the identity of the work. In other arts—paradigmatically, painting and sculpture—if one were to pass a copy for an original, that would be a forgery, not an instance or performance of the original. The latter are the "autographic" arts, those for which it matters whether an item is the original or a copy; the former are "allographic." Notice how such a distinction is not the same as that between single and multiple art forms. In the art of etching, for instance, there are typically several instances of the same work—as many as the prints from the original plate. Yet, etching remains an autographic art: only prints from the original plate are instances of the work.

Goodman's proposals on what individuates artworks in those art forms that allow for some kind of notation seem to have odd results. Regarding music written in standard Western notation, Goodman claims that only those performances that fully comply with the score count as instances of the work (1976, 186). Hence, even one small mistake on the part of the performer, say, replacing one note with another when playing Beethoven's *Fifth Symphony*, disqualifies a performance from being an instance of the *Fifth*. On the other hand, since music is notational only with respect to the flags arranged on the staff, and not, say, indications of tempo, even radically differently sounding performances (in principle even one taking a whole year to be completed!) would count as instances of a work. It must be noticed, however, that Goodman sharply distinguishes the question of work identity from the question of the value of a performance, and that he is aware of the distance between ordinary usage and the requisites established by philosophical analysis. Thus, while "the most miserable performance without actual mistakes does count as . . . an instance [of a work], . . . the most brilliant perform-ance with a single wrong note does not" (Goodman 1976, 186). Yet, technical discourse is one thing, everyday speech another—Goodman cautions; he is "no more recommending that in ordinary discourse we refuse to say that a pianist who misses a note has performed a Chopin Polonaise than we refuse to call a whale a fish, the earth spherical, or a grayish-pink human white" (1976, 187).

Goodman's reference to actual artistic practice is particularly explicit with respect to architecture. Although this art form has developed something close to a notation, it is to be considered a "mixed and tran-sitional case" between an allographic and an autographic art (Goodman 1976, 221). In principle, two buildings built according to the same archi-tect's plates could be considered instances of the same work. Yet, in reality, the identity of architectural works is still fairly tightly bound to the history of production of each individual building.

In the case of literature, however, Goodman claims the identity of a work to be completely severed from the history of production. A novel or a poem as works of literature are the same as their texts. Of Jorge Luis Borges's famous Pierre Menard case—that of a fictional author try-ing to write a novel word-for-word identical to Cervantes's *Don Quixote* (Borges 1962)—Goodman and Elgin argue that the case fails to show that two works can have the same text (1988, chapter 3). All Menard might have been able to produce, they claim, is another inscription of the original text and work, and perhaps suggest a new interpretation of it. This syntactic approach to the identity of literary works, and the identification of works with their texts—a view Gregory Currie (1991) calls "textualism" and quite effectively criticizes—seem to conflict with powerful intuitions, and to have undesirable consequences. Two poems composed by two people independently of each other have a strong prima facie claim to be different works even if it were to happen that the two writers produce the same text; and there appear to be two authors at play. The Goodmanian proposal, instead, is that of attrib-uting the single poem thereby composed either to whoever happens to be the first writer or, if the texts are produced simultaneously, to both writers as authors of a *multi*authored work (Goodman and Elgin 1988, 63–64). In either case, it seems the proposal not only conflicts with our intuitions, but also implies a withered if not peculiar notion of authorship. Ultimately, Goodman's syntactic approach seems arbitrary in excluding the relevance to the identity of a work of the, broadly speaking, context of projection of a notational structure, whether linguistic, musical, or other.[6]

3. Pictorial representation

Goodman's analysis of pictorial representation, or depiction, has been heavily debated. Whatever its merits or flaws, it remains a clear, if radical, representative of a possible position on the issue: that for which the pictorial mode of signification is no less conventional, and no more "natural," than others, such as signification by means of language. For Goodman, at the core of depiction there is denotation: pictures (whether artistic or nonartistic) are labels for things, singular or multiple; respectively, a portrait of Napoleon represents Napoleon by denoting him and a picture of a beaver in a dictionary severally denotes all the beavers (Goodman 1976, chapter 1). Pictures acquire their meaning as symbols working within their systems, and such meaning (i.e., the picture depicting something) is ultimately a matter of convention, just like with any other sort of symbol. This may seem a strange thesis, since we would have thought that the relationship between a picture and, say, the dog it represents were more natural than the relationship between "dog," or "perro," or "hund," within the respective languages, and dogs. Yet, theories claiming that pictures relate to things by some natural relationship—the most traditional candidate being resemblance—are victims of the "myth of the innocent eye" (Goodman 1976, 7–10). Like perception, depiction is always relative to some conceptual framework, some system of classification, which allows us to see in the picture—as perception does in the world—certain things but not others, and see them in some ways but not others.

Whatever the case, that the relationship between a painting and its object is ultimately conventional need not be interpreted simplistically: the relevant conventions are not specific to the particular image (though, of course, there are distinctive conventions regarding, say, the iconography of Napoleon or the representation of religious figures in Western painting) but, rather, to all the pictures depicted within a certain tradition broadly conceived. They are general rules such as the use of outline, of the chiaroscuro, or of traditional perspective—and rules of which we are perhaps less aware, say, that a curved line in a certain context stand for a curved shape in the object represented. All of them are conventionally established rules of correlation between the members of certain pictorial systems and the realm of reference. And it is those correlations that are, for Goodman, ultimately conventional.

Realism in pictorial representation is also explained in terms of conventions, specifically of the acquaintance a viewer has with certain sets of rules of interpretation. Pictures that we consider to be more realistic are nothing but those depicted according to rules with which we are more acquainted. In sum, no picture or pictorial style bears a more natural relationship with what it represents than any other, hence requiring less or no interpretation. The interpretation is simply easier, more immediate, for pictures depicted according to familiar rules.

An apparent problem for a theory based on denotation is that of pictures that are of fictional or otherwise nonexistent things—say, pictures of Harry Potter or of unicorns—since they all, equally, denote nothing. Such pictures are nonetheless different from each other, Goodman glosses, in being denoted by different labels: "unicorn-picture" and "Harry-Potter-picture" respectively. Yet, a more fundamental concern might hide in the wings here, more general than that regarding pictures with null denotation. As Goodman himself emphasizes, consider that all pictures, whether they have a referent or not, singular or multiple, are denoted by predicates of the type "so-and-so-picture"; after all, a picture of Napoleon is in the first place a man-picture (indeed a man-in-uniform-riding-a-horse-etc.-picture). Independently of whether it denotes anything, a picture is the picture it is in the sense of its being denoted by a "so-and-so-picture" type of predicate. Hence, it is precisely to *this* question that a theory of depiction must offer an answer: what is it that makes a given picture a man-picture (we could say, a picture in which one can see a man) and not a dog- or a tree-picture? However, it must be emphasized that, for Goodman, philosophy cannot answer this question. Why pictures are classified in different ways (as unicorn-pictures, man-pictures, etc.), why certain shapes are correlated to certain kinds of objects, ultimately is a matter of habit within a cultural, artistic community, hence a question for anthropologists, not philosophers to answer. Philosophers only investigate the "routes" of reference—how the referential relationship applies between symbols and things, or between symbols—not the "roots" of reference—why certain symbols refer to certain things or symbols (see also Goodman 1984).

What Goodman does offer is an articulate and sophisticated answer to the more general question of what distinguishes pictorial symbols from symbols of other sorts (1976, chapter 6; see also Goodman and Elgin 1988, chapter 8). Pictures, as we have seen, are not symbols in notational systems. Specifically, pictorial systems are *syntactically* and *semantically dense*. In this, they are similar to certain diagrams and measurement tools: in brief, all those diagrams or instruments for which, in brief, any difference in the marks that compose them could in principle matter to meaning. When reading an analog watch, for instance, any difference in the position of the hands counts as a difference in the time indicated. Likewise, a change, no matter how small, in the marks composing a painting could affect its pictorial meaning. Indeed, with paintings it is not even the case that small differences in the marks make for small differences in meaning: just think of how even a minimal alteration to the lip area of Leonardo da Vinci's *Mona Lisa* could dramatically change the painting! Pictorial systems are also, in contrast to diagrammatic systems, *relatively replete*. That is, a larger number of features (color, shape, texture, hue, etc.) tend to be relevant while, with a diagram, generally fewer features (e.g., the relative position of the dots of a line) are. Hence, the difference between diagrams and pictures is only a matter of *degree*: typically, with a picture a smaller number of features can be dismissed as contingent or irrelevant.

4. Aesthetic status and artistic merit

For Goodman aesthetics really is, ultimately, a branch of epistemology and metaphysics, and this bears on his views regarding both aesthetic—or artistic—status and merit. For him, asking questions about the arts (Goodman did not really address questions regarding the aesthetics of nature) is continuous with asking more general questions regarding the

ways in which other forms of symbolization, hence of human knowledge, shape realities for us. Thus, artistic symbols are to be judged
for the classifications they bring about, for how novel and insightful
those classifications are, for how they change our world perception
and relations. The cognitive value of art—that is, art's contribution
to understanding—counts as artistic merit only because the symbols
involved and the experiences they bring about belong in some sense
to what Goodman calls "the aesthetic" (1976, chapter 6, and 1978,
chapter 4). Indicating the features that qualify certain symbolic activities and experiences as aesthetic or artistic is then important, though
more to see the commonalities between art and other human pursuits,
including science, than to isolate the realm of art from them.

Since to be a work of art is, for Goodman, to perform certain referential functions, the question "What is art?" should really be replaced
by the question "When is art?"—when does the performing of a symbolic activity qualify as artistic? No definition of art is possible; only
"symptoms" of the aesthetic can be indicated—features of a symbolic
activity that, when present, tend to qualify it as aesthetic, hence tend to
occur in art. There are five of such symptoms: syntactic density, semantic density, syntactic repleteness, exemplificationality (Goodman 1976,
252–255), and multiple and complex reference (1978, 67–68). These are
just clues that indicate but do not guarantee artistic status; and artistic
status is possible even without them.

Art has a general importance to the epistemic endeavor, which is
addressed with special clarity in *Ways of Worldmaking*. Works of art
can participate in worldmaking precisely because they have symbolic
functions (Goodman 1978, 102). As linguistic labels categorize the
world (and new, unusual labels as "grue" and "bleen" categorize it differently), so do pictorial labels, for instance, categorize it in a number
of ways (and some of them indeed in new ways). Literal denotation,
metaphorical denotation, as well as exemplification and expression, can
all contribute to the construction of a world. Cervantes's *Don Quixote*
literally denotes no one, yet it metaphorically denotes many of us
(Goodman 1984, 130). And artworks, by exemplifying shapes, colors,
emotional patterns, and so on, as well as by expressing what they literally do not possess, can bring about a reorganization of the world of
ordinary experience. Visiting a museum can change our perception of
the world, making us notice new aspects of reality and allowing us

to encounter a different reality (Goodman 1984, 178–180). Indeed, works of art may have effects that go beyond their medium; hence music may affect seeing, painting affect hearing, or both be affected by dance, and so on (Goodman 1978, 106). Especially in "these days of experimentation with the combination of media in the performing arts," Goodman glosses, music, pictures, and dance "all interpenetrate in making a world" (1978, 106).[7]

Notes

1 There is a sense, for Goodman, in which *we* make even physical objects, such as the stars (see his "On Starmaking" and, for discussion, the essays by Israel Scheffler and Hilary Putnam, among others, in McCormick, ed. 1996).
2 Contemporary theories of expression abound (see, for example, the works mentioned in Chapter 18, n. 10).
3 Nineteen of Picasso's variations are reproduced, and discussed, in Goodman and Elgin (1988).
4 On ontology, see also Chapter 18, section 3.
5 In *Languages of Art*, Goodman explicitly opts for a less formal exposition of his views, which defers from the nominalism he had defended since the time of his 1947 "Steps Toward a Constructive Nominalism," coauthored with W. V. Quine (reprinted in Goodman 1972, 173–198). The departure is only at the superficial level of exposition, however (Goodman 1976, xiii). Hence, for instance, his speaking of "classes" should not be taken as a commitment to their existence.
6 For an articulate critique of Goodman's construal of allographic arts, see Levinson 2011.
7 Rather unconventionally for a philosopher but consistently with his views, Goodman himself worked on three multimedia projects, using text, music, dance, and painting. One of such works, *Hockey Seen: A Nightmare in Three Periods and Sudden Death*, is briefly discussed in Goodman (1984, 69–71). Parts of this essay adapt Giovannelli (2010).

Primary sources

Goodman:
1966. *The Structure of Appearance*. Indianapolis, IN: Bobbs-Merrill.
1972. *Problems and Projects*. Indianapolis, IN: Bobbs-Merrill.
1976. *Languages of Art: An Approach to a Theory of Symbols*, 2nd edition. Indianapolis, IN: Bobbs-Merrill. Originally published 1968.

1978. *Ways of Worldmaking*. Indianapolis, IN: Hackett.
1983. *Fact, Fiction, and Forecast*, 4th edition. Cambridge, MA: Harvard University Press. Originally published 1954.
1984. *Of Mind and Other Matters*. Cambridge, MA: Harvard University Press.
1988. With Catherine Z. Elgin. *Reconceptions in Philosophy and Other Arts and Sciences*. London: Routledge.

References and further reading

Borges, Jorge Luis. 1962. "Pierre Menard, Author of the *Quixote*." In *Labyrinths*. New York: New Directions, 36–44.
Currie, Gregory. 1991. "Work and Text." *Mind*, 100, 325–340.
Elgin, Catherine Z., ed. 1997. *Nelson Goodman's Philosophy of Art*. New York: Garland.
Giovannelli, Alessandro. 2010. "Goodman's Aesthetics." *The Stanford Encyclopedia of Philosophy*. Summer 2010 edition. Edward N. Zalta (ed.). URL =<http://plato.stanford.edu/archives/sum2010/entries/Goodman-aesthetics/>.
Levinson, Jerrold. 2011. "Autographic and Allographic Art Revisited." In *Music, Art, and Metaphysics*. Oxford: Oxford University Press, 89–106.
McCormick, Peter. 1996. *Starmaking: Realism, Anti-Realism, and Irrealism*. Cambridge, MA: MIT Press.
Symposium: The Legacy of Nelson Goodman. 2000. *Journal of Aesthetics and Art Criticism*, 58, 213–253.

CHAPTER 15

RICHARD A. WOLLHEIM
(1923–2003)
Malcolm Budd

The British philosopher Richard Arthur Wollheim, whose interests, both inside and outside philosophy, were unusually wide, was, among other things, the finest aesthetician of his generation. He brought to the subject not only a powerful and creative mind but also exceptionally deep and extensive knowledge, a rich conception of the mind informed by his allegiance to and mastery of psychoanalytic theory, a passion for at least three of the arts (architecture, literature and, above all, painting), and a concern for the importance of art in human life. His profound interest in the human mind is reflected in the marked psychological orientation of his aesthetics.

Wollheim's first major statement on, and his principal contribution to, pure or analytic aesthetics is *Art and Its Objects* (1968). The distinctive conception of the philosophy of art it articulates was further elaborated in the second edition (1980), which contains six supplementary essays, and in other later writings, especially those collected in *On Art and the Mind* (1973) and *The Mind and Its Depths* (1993). A notable feature of his aesthetics is its assignment of conceptual priority to the philosophy of art over the aesthetics of nature. This is achieved through representing the aesthetic attitude to nature as the attitude of regarding nature as if it were art. This, I believe, is a definite mistake: if the aesthetic appreciation of nature (of the flight of a hen harrier, say) is understood as it should be, as the aesthetic appreciation of nature *as* nature, this precludes regarding it as something it is not—in particular as art. But I shall leave this aside and consider instead the topics he focused on in the philosophy of art, which was, after all, his prime concern. These were principally the nature of art, the ontological status of works of art, the meaning and understanding of a work of art, the nature of pictorial representation, and the nature of the expression by a work of art of psychological states or processes.

1. Art's nature, ontology, and meaning

About the ontology of works of art he argued in favor of three principal claims. The first is that for all works of art the identity of a work of art is determined by the history of its production: two objects that have a different history of production (produced, perhaps, by different people at different times) cannot be instances of the same work, no matter how alike they otherwise may be. (Of course, for this claim to have a fully definite sense, what constitutes one and the same history of production must be specified, as the existence of different impressions or editions of the same print or the restoration of paintings, for example, makes clear.) The second claim is that the fundamental distinction within works of art is between those that are *individuals* and those that are *types*, most being types, some individuals. And the third is that every work of the same art form belongs to the same category: if one poem is not an individual but a type, all poems are alike in being types, not individuals, and if one painting is an individual, all paintings are individuals, not types.

Although he acquiesced in the view that the central concern of the philosophy of art is to clarify the nature of art, his account of the nature of art is unusual. For he considered the concept of art to be of such complexity that the standard approach of attempting to provide an illuminating definition of the concept is inadequate. The right way of looking at the subject is, first, to eschew the normal spectator-oriented aesthetics in favor of one that does justice to both the point of view of the artist and that of the spectator. The aim of the artist is to give to the object he produces a meaning that is determined by the intentions that guide his activity—a meaning that can be grasped by the right spectators. (The notion of intention is here a very generous one, which includes more or less any psychological factor—desires, beliefs, emotions, commitments, and wishes, for example—that motivates the artist to work in the manner he has.) If the artist fulfills his intentions, the work is meaningful. The aim of the spectator is to understand the work, to grasp its meaning, which is a matter of retrieving the artist's intentions and perceiving the work in the light of those intentions. This requires the spectator to be adequately sensitive and informed, possessing knowledge of the work's "diachronic setting" or the aesthetic tradition to which it belongs, and usually much more knowledge than this, such as knowledge of artistic conventions and various truths about the world. But this understanding is not a cognitive achievement: it does not consist in recognizing that the artist intended the spectator to have a certain experience in perceiving the work. Instead, it is achieved by engaging with the work and undergoing the experience the artist intended it to provide: understanding a work is essentially experiential. Given that the subject must be looked at from both points of view, the philosophical focus must shift from works of art themselves to the so-called aesthetic attitude, understanding this as whatever is involved in regarding something as a work of art, which is intertwined with the complementary attitude of producing something as a work of art. Adopting this focus led Wollheim to the view that art should be thought of as a form of life (in Wittgenstein's sense), this form of life being such that for artistic activity and appreciation to be possible a complex, ramified structure of practices and institutions must exist, none of these elements being identifiable independently of the other elements in the structure. And having reached the conclusion that art is an essentially historical phenomenon, inevitably changing over time, with its changes affecting the conceptual structure that surrounds it, he suggested a recursive procedure that might be adopted for identifying which objects are works of art.

2. Pictorial representation and artistic expression

Two other important topics, to which Wollheim returned again and again, constantly reforming or refining his views, are pictorial representation and artistic expression, each of which, he held, depends on the exercise of both the artist's and the spectator's role. For both he advanced a psychological account, the nature of the phenomenon being definable in terms of a certain form of perception and the specific form of that perception the artist intended his or her work to receive. From his earliest writings he held that seeing an opaque marked surface as a representation essentially involves seeing it in such a way that one thing (a plane of color, perhaps) is seen as being behind or in front of another thing, so that, since most abstract paintings require this kind of seeing, pictorial representation is not restricted to figurative representation. Accordingly, since we see the surface of a painting, what is distinctive of pictorial perception is its particular twofold character. At first, Wollheim thought of this twofold character in terms of Wittgenstein's notion of seeing-as, but he soon changed this to seeing-in, thinking of seeing-in as a conjunction of experiences, one of seeing a surface and the other a form of seeing that involves the third dimension—seeing one thing in front of or behind another. But this conception of seeing-in was itself quickly replaced by his final view that seeing-in is a single experience with two aspects, the so-called "configurational" aspect is the visual awareness of the marked surface, the "recognitional" aspect is the visual awareness of, minimally, something being in front of or behind something else, more usually, many things being in front of or behind many other things—in other words, the representational content of the picture, which is usually a three-dimensional scene. Wollheim's final conception of seeing-in as the true account of pictorial perception has few adherents, not always because other accounts seem more plausible, and not necessarily in virtue of some feature inherent in my exposition of it, but because of a difficulty caused by Wollheim's refusal to countenance certain interpretations of seeing-in. The crucial issue concerns the recognitional aspect, the visual awareness of the depicted scene. What does this visual awareness of depth, of things three-dimensionally related, consist in? Three obvious candidates are these: a visual illusion as of seeing the scene, a perceived resemblance of the scene, an experience of imagining seeing the scene. But Wollheim firmly rejected all three. It is the apparent absence of any other plausible interpretation—and Wollheim not only did not offer one, but also considered that none was necessary—that primarily explains the lack of adherents.

Wollheim sought to elucidate artistic expression in terms of a form of perception that he called "expressive perception" and the artist's achievement in making a work that encourages a specific form of such perception. Now perception of this kind can be provoked by the landscape as well as by works of art, but I shall focus upon art only. Wollheim's conception of expressive perception directed upon a work of art always included the idea of the perception of a "correspondence" between the work and a psychological state: when we perceive a work as being expressive of a certain emotion, for example, the work seems to us to correspond to, to match or "be of a piece with," what we experience when in that emotional state. But this was only a partial characterization of this kind of perception and his full characterization underwent a number of changes. It finally crystallized into an analysis based on the psychoanalytic idea of the projection of emotion. But whereas standard psychoanalytic theory recognizes what Wollheim calls "simple" projection, Wollheim introduced another form of projection, not standardly recognized, so-called complex projection. Accordingly, Wollheim referred to a work's expressive properties as projective properties that are perceived by expressive perception. But he presented more than one characterization of the perception of projective properties. The two principal characterizations differ mainly in the presence or absence of emotion in the perceiver. One requires the observer to be experiencing the emotion that might be projected onto the work; the other drops this requirement. In both versions the emotion that might be projected "colors" the observer's perception of the work. However, only the second form is consistent with Wollheim's longstanding opposition to the idea that an artist, in creating a work as an expression of emotion, or an observer, in appreciating it as an expression of emotion, must feel the emotion that the work expresses. Despite this fact, his final formulation of the theory relies on the first version. Brought up against this and other difficulties in his position, Wollheim was prepared to concede that the crucial concepts involved in his theory, even in its final form, suffer from indefiniteness, so that the theory is merely programmatic (although he wondered, not altogether unreasonably in the case of painting, his prime concern, whether this might well be true of all philosophical theories of expression, the subject being still in its infancy).

3. Aesthetic value and applied aesthetics

Given Wollheim's passion for art it might appear strange that the topic of the evaluation of art figures so little in his work (although his own aesthetic judgments are manifest, even when not explicit). But as is explained in an essay in the second edition of *Art and Its Objects* that addresses the incidence and status of aesthetic value, the omission of the topic from the first edition was a deliberate distancing from certain tendencies of thought then prevailing in academic aesthetics. However, this essay itself is largely confined to enumerating and sketching the only views of the status of aesthetic value that he considers to have any plausibility. There are four of them: in Wollheim's idiosyncratic choice of terms, they are Realism, Objectivism, Relativism, and Subjectivism. I shall not attempt to summarize these views, but three of them liken the status of aesthetic value to the status of something else: for Realism aesthetic value has the status of a primary quality; for Objectivism it has the status of a secondary quality; and for Subjectivism it has "something of" the status of an expressive quality. The reason why Subjectivism holds that aesthetic value has something of the status of an expressive quality—an expressive quality being what Wollheim later called a "projective property"—is that Subjectivism, as Wollheim understands it, requires that at some point along the causal pathway between a work of art and an experience of it that grounds an aesthetic evaluation of the work, a projective mechanism intervenes essentially. Wollheim does not indicate the nature of this mechanism, but, as his thoughts about moral psychology make clear, he thinks of the projection as being some form of complex, not simple, projection. Although Wollheim does not commit himself to any of the four views he outlines, it seems probable that he favored Subjectivism. But given the variety of aesthetic value across the arts, for Subjectivism to be viable it would need a more nuanced account of projection than the one he proposed, in *The Thread of Life*, for moral value, where what is projected is "archaic bliss," "love satisfied."

Wollheim's work on aesthetics was not confined to general or analytic aesthetics but encompassed what he termed substantive aesthetics. His contribution to substantive or applied aesthetics is dominated by the massive work that is perhaps his masterpiece, devoted to what was his favorite art, *Painting as an Art* (1987). It contains a presentation of his theory of pictorial representation and the conception of the perception of pictorial expression that he held at the time. It also contains an application of his psychological theory of artistic meaning and understanding to the art of painting: a painting's meaning is revealed in the experience induced in an adequately sensitive and informed observer who looks at the surface of the painting as the fulfilled intentions of the artist led him to mark it. And it argues that a painting is a work of art in virtue of the manner in which the activity from which it issues is practiced. In addition, it advances a bold theory of the individual style of an artist. The notion of individual style must be distinguished from that of general style. General style is a merely taxonomic notion, consisting of a (fluctuating) set of features thought to be characteristic of paintings in that style. But individual pictorial style is not the set of characteristics associated with it. Rather, it is a generative affair, a matter of what in the artist's mind underlies and explains this set of characteristics. An individual style itself has psychological reality: it is a practical capacity that has been formed and lies deep in the artist's psychology, which causes the characteristics associated with it to be as they are and which enables the artist to fulfill his intentions. Wollheim recognizes that not all of a painter's works will derive from his individual style. He identifies three possibilities: prestylistic works, that is, works created before the style has formed; poststylistic works, works created after the painter's style had collapsed; and extrastylistic works, works in which an artist attempts something beyond the capacity of his style. Wollheim appears to rule out the possibility that an artist could possess more than one style at the same time, and although he allows that there can be changes in the enduring style of an artist, he maintains that an artist could acquire a different individual style only in a case of massive psychological disturbance. But perhaps the most interesting feature of Wollheim's book is his identifying, in addition to representational and expressive meaning, three other varieties of so-called primary pictorial meaning or content that a painting can achieve—textual, historical, and metaphorical meaning—and also what he calls "secondary" meaning, which is what the act of giving a picture its primary meaning meant to the artist; and his illustrating these kinds of meaning by a series of highly challenging interpretations of works by some of the painters he most admired.

Primary sources

Wollheim:
1968. *Art and Its Objects: An Introduction to Aesthetics.* New York: Harper & Row. Reprinted in 1970 (London: Pelican Books). Second edition with six supplementary essays published in 1980 (Cambridge: Cambridge University Press).

1973. *On Art and the Mind: Essays and Lectures.* London: Allen Lane.
1987. *Painting as an Art: The Andrew W. Mellon Lectures in the Fine Arts.* London: Thames and Hudson.
1993. *The Mind and Its Depths.* Cambridge: Harvard University Press.

References and further reading

Hopkins, Jim, and Savile, Anthony, eds. 1992. *Psychoanalysis, Mind and Art: Perspectives on Richard Wollheim.* Oxford: Blackwell.
van Gerwen, Rob, ed. 2001. *Richard Wollheim on the Art of Painting: Art as Representation and Expression.* Cambridge: Cambridge University Press.

CHAPTER 16

ARTHUR C. DANTO
(b. 1924)

Sondra Bacharach

Arthur Coleman Danto has published in a variety of fields in philosophy, but he is most famous for his systematic work in the philosophy of art, philosophy of art history, and art criticism. For nearly half a century, his writings in these areas have transformed the way aestheticians, art historians, and art critics engage with the disciplines. Throughout this time, Danto—himself a practicing artist and influential art critic—has maintained an intimate relationship with the artworld; indeed, his knowledge and expertise in the arts is by any standards extensive.

1. Danto's account of art

Danto's contributions to the philosophy of art are wide-ranging, covering the nature of beauty, issues in ontology and art interpretation—notably the role of intention in determining a work's identity, its meaning and artistically relevant qualities—as well as the philosophy of art criticism more broadly. However, by far, Danto's most significant contribution is his account of art, that is, his account of what makes an object a work of art. Indeed, a good portion of the contemporary discussions on the concept of art can be traced, directly or indirectly, to Danto's writings, especially to his seminal *The Transfiguration of the Commonplace* (1981).

Danto's account of art is first sketched in "The Artworld" (1964). Noticing the prevalence of artworks, by Pop artists, that appear indiscernible from ordinary objects, Danto realizes that the "method of indiscernibles" can be applied to art more generally: what makes the difference between ordinary comic strips, regular beds, real-world flags, and store-bought Brillo boxes, on the one hand, and the artworks by Roy Lichtenstein, Robert Rauschenberg, Jasper Johns, and Andy Warhol, on the other? The answer, he maintains, has to do with the nonmanifest or nonperceptual properties of the works. This is a novel way of thinking about art. Prior to Danto, definitions of art focused on the *manifest* properties of artworks—the way they looked, sounded, and so on. Any object that qualified as art did so in virtue of the object's manifest properties and, as a result, artworks were defined in terms of their visual, aural, and so on properties. Warhol's *Brillo Box* challenges this tradition: it was designed to look identical to its ordinary, store-bought counterpart. Indeed, *Brillo Box* is only identifiable as art, and distinguishable from nonart, by appeal to its nonvisual, conceptual, properties. Danto takes *Brillo Box* to raise the philosophical question regarding the nature of art, by presenting an artwork that cannot be differentiated from nonart in virtue of its manifest properties. Indeed, the moral of *Brillo Box* is a general one, regarding the relevance of conceptual properties as opposed not just to the manifest properties of an artwork, but to its physical, intrinsic properties more generally.

Of course, artworks that are indiscernible from ordinary objects predate both Danto and Warhol—just consider Marcel Duchamp's *Fountain* which is a signed ready-made urinal. According to Danto, however, *Fountain* makes a strikingly different comment on the nature of art than Warhol's *Brillo Box*. Duchamp originally submitted *Fountain* as a joke to the 1917 *Société des Artistes Indépendants* exhibition, under the fictitious name, Mr R. Mutt. The exhibition was supposed to accept any artwork submitted by any person who paid the six-dollar membership and entry fee. After a heated debate, however, *Fountain* was *not* accepted, on the grounds that the object was not a work of art. In response to this rejection, the *Blind Man*, a magazine published by Duchamp and two friends who knew the real identity of *Fountain*'s creator, carried an unsigned lead editorial, arguing that *Fountain* was in fact an artwork because the artist *chose* the work. According to the editorial, the meaning of *Fountain* was supposed to be that what makes an object an artwork is a *declaration* by the artist that it is such. *Fountain* shows that it may be sufficient for an artist to choose an object to transform it into an artwork.

Notice, then, that Pop art raises a fundamentally different philosophical challenge than Duchamp's art. While mere declarations by the artist might transform a urinal into *Fountain*, something other than artists' declarations distinguishes two perceptually indiscernible objects, like Warhol's *Brillo Box* and its ordinary counterpart from the hardware store. On Danto's view, the former, but not the latter, is an artwork because of the artistic theories surrounding the work. These artistic theories explain why an object is considered part of what Danto dubs "the artworld": "What in the end makes the difference between a Brillo box and a work of art consisting of a Brillo Box is a certain theory of art. It is the theory that takes it up into the world of art, and keeps it from collapsing into the real object which it is" (1964, 581).

We would not understand why Warhol made *Brillo Box* unless we also knew its relation to the theories of art that were endorsed by the so called New York School of the 1950s and 1960s. On Danto's view, the art theories of the artworld allow us to understand why an object is a work of art. As he famously proclaimed, "[t]o see something as art requires something the eye cannot decry—an atmosphere of artistic theory, a knowledge of the history of art: an artworld" (Danto 1964, 580). The artworld performs this central task, of individuating artworks from their indiscernible counterparts, by providing the art theories with which to interpret artworks. What makes an object art is that it can be interpreted, and what makes the artwork the *particular* artwork it is (and not some other, perceptually indiscernible artwork) is a function of the particular interpretations generated by the artworld of the time.

The notion of the artworld serves as the foundation for the formal definition of art that Danto advances in *The Transfiguration of the Commonplace* and that he refines in his later work (1997 and 1999). According to this definition, for something to be an artwork (1) the object must be about something and (2) the object must embody its meaning, where this *aboutness* and *embodiment* are determined by the interpretation for the artwork, an interpretation that, in turn, depends on the art-historical and art-theoretical context in which the artwork appears. Warhol's *Brillo Box*, but not an ordinary Brillo box, makes a statement about the kinds of objects that can qualify as art, and about the kinds of properties in virtue of which an object is art. *Brillo Box*, in other words, is importantly about the nature of art, and in virtue of this aboutness, it qualifies as a work of art. Of course, many works are about the nature of art (as, for example, Jackson Pollock's *Lavender Mist* is partly about the process of making a painting); but *Brillo Box* expresses what it's about in a particular way, namely, by looking identical to a Brillo box, rather than in some other way (as with the Pollock). The way that *Brillo Box* embodies its meaning, the way that it makes the statement that it does, individuates this work from other artworks.

For Danto, Warhol's work reveals an interesting insight into the viability of essentialism, the view according to which necessary and sufficient conditions govern the application of the concept of art. Classical attempts at defining art in essentialist terms have focused on identifying some standard feature of art as necessary and sufficient for an object to qualify as a work of art. Traditional definitions invoked a variety of different manifest properties of artworks, such as representational, expressive, or formal features. For Danto, what Warhol's work shows is not that we should reject essentialism, *tout court*. Rather, it shows that any plausible definition of art must be formulated with reference to an object's nonmanifest, as well as its manifest, properties. This is what distinguishes Danto's essentialism from the traditional essentialist accounts of art.

Danto's account of art has a significant advantage over earlier essentialist definitions: by appealing to nonmanifest properties, his definition is rendered immune to certain problems that have plagued these earlier definitions. The general problem for definitions that rely exclusively on manifest properties is that the development of art subsequent to any given definition may always produce some artwork that represents a counterexample to that definition, that is, is an artwork but lacks the very manifest property such a definition considers essential. Warhol teaches us that an artwork can have *any* manifest property and still be art, and hence that manifest properties are not essential to defining art. In this respect, Danto's essentialist definition of art, relying on nonmanifest properties, appears to be shielded from any possible counterexamples arising from future art.

2. Danto's historicism

One of the interesting consequences of the way that Danto's views are shaped by Warhol and the surrounding artistic theories of the artworld is that his definition of art is closely tied to art history: if what counts as art depends on the artworld, then what counts as art also depends on the particular moment in history at which an artwork appears in the artworld. Danto is sensitive to the fact that *Brillo Box* "could not have been art fifty years ago . . . It is the role of artistic theories, these days as always, to make the artworld, and art, possible" (1964, 581). As the artworld and related artistic theories evolve, so does the range of possible meanings that artworks may be about and embody. The evolution of art history determines the set of meanings that are possible at a given moment in the history of art. As a result, the development of an appropriate definition of art depends importantly on the development of art history and art theory: what is possible to discover philosophically depends ultimately on what is possible to discover art-historically.

An analogy may help explain how, on Danto's view, certain facts can only become epistemically accessible once the appropriate history of art has evolved. Consider the case of physics. In the eighteenth century, even the smartest physicist would have been unable to discover the central claims entailed by the theory of relativity. The physicist's knowledge is constrained by the current state of scientific theorizing. It would be impossible for *anyone* to uncover the truth of a physical claim entailed by the theory of relativity before the theory of relativity had been discovered; such claims could only be ascertained after the appropriate theories of physics had arisen. Similarly, even the smartest aesthetician would be unable to discover that, for example, aboutness is a necessary condition for an object to be an artwork, if the appropriate artistic theories were not already part of the artworld. We can only realize, for example, that aboutness is a necessary condition for an object to be a work of art once the relevant modernist theories of art that make artworks like Warhol's possible are in place in the artworld. Of course, it has always been, and always will be, a property that applies truly and correctly to artworks—even to artworks created before the existence of modernist art theories. If art history had not evolved as it did, then aboutness would still be a necessary feature of all artworks, but no definition could ever make reference to this fact. The definition of art is held hostage by what is possible in art history. As the relevant facts become historically available, so will the essence of art reveal itself through history.

3. Art history and "The End of Art"

While Danto is most highly regarded for his views about the philosophy of art, he is most criticized for his account of art history, and particularly the startling end-of-art thesis—presented in the 1984 essay "The End of Art" (reprinted in Danto 1986) but still maintained—that he takes to follow from this account of art history. Danto's account of art history is broadly Hegelian. First, he conceives of the history of art teleologically, such that it makes sense to say that art is striving for, or progressing toward, some goal, namely, formulating the question about the nature of art in its proper philosophical form. The history of art is construed as progressive and works of art are interpreted against the backdrop of art history. Further, since the history of art is constituted by different periods, each period contains its own internal development and the history of art during any given period is the history of works of art trying to achieve or realize a goal specific to that period. Second, the development of the history of art passes through distinct narrative phases at particular times: the representational period, ending with the invention of cinematography; the expressionist period, ending roughly with Fauvism; and the modernist period, ending with Warhol's *Brillo Box*. Each period is necessary to reach the next narrative, or level of art-historical development, and these narratives culminate in the realization of the final phase of art history: the modernist period, as it is expressed by the ultimate goal of the *master narrative*, in which art's goal is to formulate the philosophical nature of art. Finally, Danto emphasizes how contemporary art is striving to be reflexive, that is, to raise philosophical questions about the nature of its own existence and become conscious of its own self. Ultimately, art is about its own nature and that is why, in contemporary times, its reflexivity has become so overt.

Art becomes reflexive once Warhol arrives on the scene with *Brillo Box*. Danto argues that at this point artists have raised the central philosophical question about the nature of art. Moreover, since this question is essentially a philosophical one, Danto claims that it can only be answered by philosophers. Artists have been philosophically disenfranchised, and there is nothing more for them to do. As a result, Danto argues that art history ends in 1964 with Warhol's *Brillo Box*; after this point, we enter into the "post-historical" era—an era in which there is

no more art history in the sense of a progressive narrative of art's development, but there is still art-making. Because there are no more narratives governing art's development, anything goes in art today—the arts
have been freed from any constraints.

4. Critical assessment

There has been much critical debate over Danto's writings in all domains,
but the most recent criticisms continue to be preoccupied with two main
issues: the end-of-art thesis and the relation between Danto's essentialist definition of art and his historicist account of art history.

The end-of-art thesis is without a doubt his most controversial view.
Many of the criticisms of this thesis arise as a result of ambiguities over
what it means. Does it simply mean that painting in particular, rather
than art in general, has ended? Or does the thesis mean that art-making
has stopped but not ended? Does it mean that a *particular* narrative of
art history has been completed (say, the modernist narrative in which
art articulates its nature), or that the entire *master* narrative has come to
an end? Other criticisms center around the possibility of art coming to
an end with Warhol: why does art end with the raising, rather than the
answering, of a question? Why think that artists cannot answer a question about the nature of art, if they are capable of raising the question?
Further criticisms challenge the viability of his periodization of art history; for example, the expressionist period, in which art is purely expressive, fails to have an internal development: there is no clearly defined
goal for art whose aim is just to express, and hence no way to measure
the progress or development of the history of art during this period.

Still other criticisms challenge Danto's Hegelian conception of art history: the Hegelian model of art history diverges radically from Danto's
own characterizations of the art-historical narratives, if only because
Hegel could never have conceived of a period of art ending with Warhol.
All these challenges ultimately are designed to deny that art or art history has come to an end in any interesting or meaningful sense.

A second debate over Danto's views focuses on the relation between
his particular, essentialist account of art and his historicist account of art
history. Many commentators (e.g., Lee Brown, David Carrier, Michael

Kelly, and Noël Carroll) have argued these two accounts to be fundamentally at odds with one another. Brown was one of the earliest critics to challenge his account of art history and the related end-of-art thesis. More recently, Carroll has noted that the thesis conveniently indemnifies Danto's definition of art from the possibility of future counterexamples to his definition of art. After all, if there is no more art, there can be no more counterexamples to his definition, and Danto can rest assured that no future art could ever threaten his definition of art.

Primary sources

Danto:
1964. "The Artworld." *Journal of Philosophy*, 61, 571–584.
1981. *The Transfiguration of the Commonplace*. Cambridge, MA: Harvard University Press.
1984. *The Death of Art*. New York: Haven.
1986. *The Philosophical Disenfranchisement of Art*. New York: Columbia University Press.
1990. *Encounters and Reflections*. Berkeley, CA: University of California Press.
1992. *Beyond the Brillo Box*. Berkeley, CA: University of California Press.
1994. *Embodied Meanings*. New York: Farrar, Straus, Giroux.
1997. *After the End of Art*. Princeton, NJ: Princeton University Press.
1999. *Philosophizing Art*. Berkeley, CA: University of California Press.

References and further reading

Brown, Lee B. 1989. "Resurrecting Hegel to Bury Art." *British Journal of Aesthetics*, 29, 303–313.
Carrier, David, ed. 1998. *Danto and His Critics: Art History, Historiography and* After the End of Art. *History and Theory*, special issue, 37, 1–143. (Includes articles by Arthur Danto, David Carrier, Noël Carroll, and Michael Kelly, among others.)
Carroll, Noël. Forthcoming. *Arthur Danto's Philosophy of Art*. New York: Columbia University Press.
Rollins, Mark, ed. 1993. *Danto and His Critics*. Cambridge: Blackwell.

CHAPTER 17

KENDALL L. WALTON
(b. 1939)

David Davies

The contributions of Kendall Walton to philosophical reflection on the arts over the past forty odd years are striking both for their significance and influence and for their diversity. His work on the nature of visual representation in the arts, the nature of fiction and our emotional responses to it, puzzling aspects of our imaginative engagement with artworks, and the role of a work's provenance in its artistic appreciation has played a major part in structuring contemporary philosophical exploration of these issues. Walton has also enhanced the place of aesthetics in the broader philosophical culture, both by drawing on the latter in his work and by providing resources that have illuminated philosophical debates outside aesthetics.

1. Foundations of the representational arts: *Mimesis as Make-Believe*

To orient ourselves in Walton's corpus, we must begin with *Mimesis as Make-Believe* (1990), his magisterial work on the foundations of the representational arts. Representational artworks usually employ visual or verbal media, or, as in theater, some combination thereof. Paintings, for example, use a visual medium to *depict* their subjects, while novels use language to *describe* the things they represent. As a basis for clarifying the distinction between depiction and description, Walton offers a general theory of representation that applies both to artworks and more mundane things such as children's games. He describes a game where two children walking in a wood pretend that stumps are bears. In such a game, the stumps serve as "props" in the game of make-believe. A prop in a game of make-believe is a generator of truths in that game: facts about the props generate such truths. For example, that one stump is bigger than another makes it true in the game that one bear is bigger than another. Something acquires the status of prop in a game thanks to an understanding among its players, which Walton terms a "principle of generation." Given such a principle, whether something is true in the game is independent of whether anyone believes it to be true in the game. In the "stumps are bears" game, for example, a stump, even if unnoticed, makes it true in the game that a bear is lurking nearby. Props, then, *prescribe* what is to be imagined. This provides the basis for a general theory of *fictional truth*: a proposition is true in a fiction just in case there is a prescription that, in engaging with that fiction, we are to imagine that proposition.

Artistic representations, Walton argues, are also props in games of make-believe. A representation prescribes that we imagine certain things. The content of the prescribed imagining depends upon the relevant principles of generation, and the intended audience for an artistic representation understands what it prescribes because they understand these principles. Walton stresses the varied nature of the principles of generation operative in the arts. The occurrence of the name "Napoleon" in *War and Peace*, for example, prescribes that we imagine certain things narrated in the novel to be true of that historical figure. The title *Snowstorm at Sea* of one of Turner's more impressionistic paintings indicates the content of the prescribed imagining. Other principles of generation are more culturally specific. For example, the principles of generation operative in late fifteenth-century Italian Renaissance painting prescribe that, where a figure is depicted as extending her hand, palm forward, toward the viewer or another depicted figure, we are to imagine that she is issuing an invitation or welcome, rather than, say, a rebuff.

The difference between description and depiction is to be explained in terms of a more general difference in the kind of imagining prescribed. In the case of novels, readers are prescribed to imagine that certain events take place or that certain things obtain, and that they are learning this from a narrator. In the case of paintings, on the other hand, what is prescribed is that the viewer imagines that her seeing of the painted surface is a *seeing* of what the picture depicts. While what is true in the world of the work is determined by principles of generation, what is true in the world of the game *we* play with the work also includes facts about our relation to the world of the work as the confidants of narrators or as viewers of what is depicted.

Walton argues that his account of depiction in terms of imagined seeing captures what is left unelucidated in Richard Wollheim's talk of the "twofoldness" of our perceptual engagement with visual artworks, our seeing the subject of a painting *in* the array of pigment on canvas (Walton 1992). It also accounts, he argues (Walton 1990), for a crucial difference between our engagement with artistic representations and our engagement in ordinary games of make-believe. In the former, we are interested not only in the content that we are prescribed to make-believe but also in how the work's creator made these things fictional by manipulating the medium to produce a "prop" that articulates that content.

2. "Prop-oriented" make-believe, metaphor, and fictional characters

Walton draws an important distinction between "content-oriented" and "prop-oriented" make-believe (1993). While props usually serve our interest in participating in games of make-believe, sometimes regarding something as a prop in an actual or potential game may provide an illuminating way of thinking about that thing. This offers an insight into how many metaphors work. Consider Romeo's classic metaphor "Juliet is the sun." This invites us to consider a possible game of make-believe in which certain features of Juliet, as prop, make various things true of the sun (say, that it is a source of life). This leads us to focus on these features of Juliet, which are the ones that Romeo wishes to call to our attention by using the metaphor. Thinking of many metaphors in terms of prop-oriented make-believe helps us to understand the merits and demerits of alternative views of metaphor, such as the idea that metaphors provide "frames" for thinking about their subjects (Moran 1989), Walton argues.

Prop-oriented make-believe also helps explain our ability to talk about entities that don't exist, including fictional characters like Romeo (Walton 2000). When participating in prop-oriented make-believe, we usually pretend to say one thing but actually assert something else. In such a case, we often assert something about the real-world circumstance that generates a particular fictional truth. Walton claims that this applies to existential statements of the form "*X* exists" or "*X* does not exist." In uttering the sentence "Sherlock Holmes does not exist," we make believe that "Sherlock Holmes" refers to someone and that there is a property of "existing" that the referent of "Sherlock Holmes" doesn't possess. What we are really asserting, however, is that the attempt to refer using a particular linguistic expression fails. A similar analysis applies to uttering the sentence "Sherlock Holmes is a fictional character," though here we also identify the reason why we fail to refer. Walton offers, here, a *fictionalist* account of existential statements, which maintains that such statements are part of a "useful fiction" that doesn't commit us to the things we seem to be talking about. Walton's general account of fictions has inspired fictionalist accounts of other discourses, for example, talk of numbers in pure mathematics (see Kalderon 2005).

3. "Transparent pictures"

Both paintings and photographs can be means of depiction. But it is often said that photographs have a kind of "realism" that paintings lack. Such "realism" is neither a matter of photographs' relative fidelity to the look of things nor of their capacity to engender illusions. Rather, Walton argues, paintings and photographs differ in the kind of epistemic access they give to their subjects (1984). A photograph provides us with a *new way of seeing*. It is *transparent*, in that we literally *see* its subject *through* it, albeit indirectly by means of a picture. Cameras then are, like glasses, mirrors, and telescopes, "aids to vision." Paintings, on the other hand, are not transparent. What we see when looking at a painting is a *representation* of *X*, not *X* itself. Photographs, too, are representations, insofar as they prescribe certain imaginings. In looking at a photograph of *X*, while I *literally*, *indirectly* see *X*, it may be prescribed that I *imagine* that I am *directly* seeing *X*. Also, a photograph through which I indirectly *see* one thing can serve as a depiction of something else which I *imagine* seeing in the photograph. In looking at a still from *Casablanca*, for example, I indirectly see Humphrey Bogart and Ingrid Bergman while imagining that I see Rick and Ilsa.

Walton argues that we acquire information about the world from photographs and from paintings in different ways. In general, if we learn about *X* from an image *I*, then *I* must be *counterfactually dependent* on *X*: if *X* had been different, then *I* would have been different in certain systematic ways. When we learn something from a drawing or painting, this dependence is "intentional"—mediated by the *beliefs* of the artist *A*. If *X* had been different, then a painting of *X* would have been different only if *A* would have formed *different* beliefs about *X*. Only if we take *A* to be reliable in her belief-formation can we claim to learn, from her paintings, about the objects they depict. With a photograph, on the other hand, as with ordinary seeing, the dependence of *I* on *X* is *not* mediated in this way by the beliefs of the artist. A difference in *X* would result in a difference in *I*, whatever the photographer's beliefs about *X*. That is why, for instance, unwanted subjects such as an intruding passer-by may appear in photographs but not in paintings.

However, as Walton recognizes, this isn't sufficient to establish that we *see* through photographs. A mechanical device that produced *descriptions* might exhibit nonintentional counterfactual dependence, but we wouldn't thereby *see* what was described. A further necessary condition for seeing is that our susceptibility to *make mistakes* reflects similarities among things of the type seen. We may visually mistake a dog for a fox, or a sheep for a goat. But, in the case of the device that produces verbal descriptions, we might mistake a "dog" for a "hog" or a "Goat" for a "Coat." The claim is that looking at *photographs* of *X*s can lead to the same kinds of mistakes as looking at *X*s. Indeed, this is a characteristic that distinguishes depictions in general, and not just photographs, from descriptions. Critics, however, have questioned the sufficiency of Walton's proposed conditions for seeing, claiming that seeing *X* also requires "egocentric information" as to how *X* is related to us spatially and temporally (see Currie 1995, chapter 2). But Walton disputes the claim that this provides a reason for denying that we see things through photographs (2008b).

4. The "paradox of fiction"

A much-discussed "paradox" concerning our imaginative engagement with fictions is our ability to respond affectively to something we don't believe to be true. The paradox arises if, as many philosophers do, we subscribe to a *cognitivist* view of the emotions, which maintains that there is an essential cognitive component to an emotional state like fear. Famously Walton considers the case of Charles, who claims to be "terrified" by the green slime in a film that he is watching (Walton 1978). If the cognitivist theory of the emotions is correct for emotions like fear, then it seems that Charles's affective response to the green slime cannot be terror, or any similar emotional state, since he lacks the required beliefs. Only if one has certain kinds of beliefs, and perhaps also certain kinds of desires, can one be said to be genuinely afraid of something. Or, if Charles's affective state *is* terror, then he must be holding inconsistent beliefs—believing, for example, both that the slime doesn't exist (to explain why he remains in his seat) and that the slime does exist (to explain how he can satisfy the cognitive requirements for being genuinely terrified of the slime).

Walton's solution to the paradox draws on his more general account of our engagement with fictional representations. The receiver of a fiction comes to believe that certain things are true in the story and thus that, to properly engage with the fiction, one should make believe those things. But such a make-belief may produce physiological and affective responses in the receiver. It is Charles's belief that it is fictionally true that the slime is heading toward him, and his making believe that this is so, that causes him to experience the feelings he reports on this occasion. But, since this occurs in the context of Charles's imaginative engagement with the fiction, these feelings provide further input to the game of make-believe that Charles is playing, and make it true *in that game* that Charles is actually terrified. Thus, *in the game of make-believe* that Charles is playing as a result of viewing the film, it is indeed true that he is terrified of the slime. But he is not *really* terrified of the slime. Rather, as said, it is true that Charles is terrified of the slime only in the expanded game of make-believe generated by Charles's imaginative engagement with the film. In a later paper, Walton explores difficulties presented by our imaginative engagement with fictions that ask us to imagine things in conflict with our moral beliefs, such as that it is morally permissible to kill infants if they are female (1994). This paper has spawned a considerable literature on what has become known as the "puzzle of imaginative resistance" (e.g., Gendler 2000), although Walton himself rejects this way of labeling the issues (2008a, 47–59).

5. Artistic categories, artistic style, and aesthetic empiricism

In two important earlier papers (1970 and 1979), Walton argues for the bearing of facts about an artwork's history of making on its appreciation as a work of art. The target, here, is the "empiricist" view that only a work's "manifest" properties—those properties given to a receiver in a perceptual encounter with an instance of the work—can bear upon its proper appreciation. We can distinguish here between "narrowly" and "broadly" manifest properties of an instance of a work. The narrowly manifest properties comprise the nonaesthetic properties of the artistic vehicle—the distribution of pigment on canvas, for example. The broadly manifest properties are the aesthetic properties that a suitably sensitive viewer will see in its nonaesthetic properties—formal properties, expressive properties, and representational properties. The empiricist maintains that, given the sensitivity of the receiver, a work's narrowly manifest properties uniquely determine its broadly manifest properties, and thus its properly appreciable properties.

By contrast, Walton argues that the properly appreciable properties of a work are not uniquely determined in this way (1970). They also depend upon the *kind* of work it is, where this may *not* be narrowly or broadly manifest. Which appreciable properties we ascribe to a work, he maintains, depends upon the *category of art* under which it is apprehended. Artistic categories are defined in terms of three kinds of features: those that are *standard* or required, those that are *contra-standard* and are proscribed, and those that are *variable* and do not bear upon categorization. For example, being two-dimensional and having a picture-plane are standard, and having moving parts is contra-standard, for works belonging to the category "painting." The aesthetic properties we experience a work as having depend not merely upon our sensitive response to its narrowly manifest properties, but also upon whether these properties are standard or variable for the category under which we apprehend it. Two art objects with identical narrowly manifest properties might possess different aesthetic properties if apprehended under different artistic categories. Furthermore, Walton maintains, the aesthetic properties that are *correctly* ascribed to a work are those it possesses when apprehended under the category to which it actually belongs, where this is determined by facts about its provenance. Thus aesthetic empiricism is wrong to claim that such facts do not bear upon the proper appreciation of artworks.

To illustrate his argument, Walton invites us to imagine a culture with a category of artworks called *guernicas*. What is standard for a guernica is that a work, when viewed at right-angles to its frame, has the pictorial properties of Picasso's painting of that name. What is variable includes the topology of the work, guernicas being understood to be three-dimensional, bas-relief-like entities whose artistic value depends crucially upon their topological features. An object possessing the narrowly manifest properties of Picasso's work, while highly valued as a painting, would presumably be quite uninteresting as a guernica. Or, if it *were* an interesting work qua guernica, this would rest upon entirely different considerations from the ones that ground the interest and value of Picasso's work as a painting—its radical minimalism, for example.

In a second paper, Walton argues that the notion of artistic style is properly understood in terms of a style of *action* involved in the making of a work, rather than being a property of the product of that action taken independently of its history of making (1979). The style we ascribe to an artwork reflects the way it appears to have been made. This will apply, for example, to "aesthetic" aspects of style, such as being passionate, pretentious, exuberant, playful, sensitive, or sentimental. Although a work's stylistic properties are linked to how it *appears* to have been made rather than to how it was actually made, Walton stresses the importance of locating the work in the actual historical context of its making if we are to correctly identify how it appears to have been made, and thus the qualities that constitute its style. The idea that a work's expressive properties depend not merely upon its manifest qualities but also upon how we take those qualities to have been produced has been developed by Jerrold Levinson (1990). He defends the idea that the expressive properties of musical works are often grounded in the kinds of actions that are involved in producing the sounds that we hear. Levinson takes this to show that prescribed instrumentation is partly constitutive of a musical work.

These two papers stress ways in which determining the aesthetic and artistic properties of an artwork requires that we locate the artistic vehicle in the work's context of making. They have played an important part in arguments against the kind of empiricist view of artistic appreciation that held sway at the time they were written. Taken together with the very influential work on depiction, fiction, transparency, and imagination already surveyed, they firmly establish Walton's place as one of the key thinkers in contemporary aesthetics. The implications of his insights both within and beyond the philosophy of art are still being explored and will be for many years to come.

Primary sources

Walton:

1970. "Categories of Art." *Philosophical Review*, 79, 334–367. Reprinted in Walton 2008a.

1978. "Fearing Fictions." *Journal of Philosophy*, 75, 5–27. Reprinted, with a "Postscript," in Walton (Forthcoming).

1979. "Style and the Products and Processes of Art." In Beryl Lang (ed.), *The Concept of Style*. University Park, PA: University of Pennsylvania Press, 45–66. Reprinted in Walton 2008a.

1983. "Fiction, Fiction-Making and Styles of Fictionality." *Philosophy and Literature*, 7, 78–88.

1984. "Transparent Pictures: On the Nature of Photographic Realism." *Critical Inquiry*, 11, 246–277. Reprinted in Walton 2008a.

1990. *Mimesis as Make-Believe: On the Foundations of the Representational Arts*. Cambridge, MA: Harvard University Press.

1992. "Seeing-In and Seeing Fictionally." In James Hopkins and Anthony Savile (eds.), *Mind, Psychoanalysis, and Art*. Oxford: Blackwell, 281–291. Reprinted in Walton 2008a.

1993. "Metaphor and Prop-Oriented Make-Believe." *European Journal of Philosophy*, 1, 39–57. Reprinted in Walton (Forthcoming).

1994. "Morals in Fiction and Fictional Morality." *Proceedings of the Aristotelian Society*, Suppl. Vol. 68, 27–50. Reprinted in Walton 2008a.

2000. "Existence as Metaphor?". In Anthony Everett and Thomas Hofweber (eds.), *Empty Names, Fiction, and the Puzzles of Non-Existence*. Chicago: CSLI Publications. Reprinted in Walton (Forthcoming).

2008a. *Marvelous Images: On Values and the Arts*. Oxford: Oxford University Press.
2008b. "On Pictures and Photographs: Objections Answered." In Walton 2008a,
    117–132.
Forthcoming. *In Other Shoes and Other Essays*. Oxford: Oxford University Press.

References and further reading

Currie, Gregory. 1995. *Image and Mind: Film, Philosophy and Cognitive Science*.
    Cambridge: Cambridge University Press.
Gendler, Tamar. 2000. "The Puzzle of Imaginative Resistance." *Journal of Philosophy*,
    97, 55–81.
Kalderon, Mark Eli, ed. 2005. *Fictionalism in Metaphysics*. Oxford: Oxford University
    Press (especially Stephen Yablo, "The Myth of the Seven," 88–115).
Levinson, Jerrold. 1990. "Authentic Performance and Performance Means." In *Music,
    Art, and Metaphysics*. Ithaca, NY: Cornell University Press, 393–408.
Moran, Richard. 1989. "Seeing and Believing: Metaphor, Image, and Force." *Critical
    Inquiry*, 16, 87–112.

CHAPTER 18

SOME CONTEMPORARY DEVELOPMENTS

Alessandro Giovannelli

The last six chapters of this book already bring us into the aesthetic debates of our times. In many ways, Monroe Beardsley could be seen as continuing a somewhat traditional approach, one built around notions such as aesthetic experience, aesthetic object, and aesthetic attitude, and which is instantiated, albeit in very different ways, by Kant, Schopenhauer, Fry, Bell, and Dewey. Yet, already with Beardsley, we encounter a feature that became characteristic of contemporary Anglo-American aesthetics: attention to a plurality of questions regarding the arts: from representation to expression, from interpretation to evaluation, from artistic ontology to the nature of metaphor, and so on. The aesthetics of the last four decades has followed suit, covering a range of issues that go well beyond what can here only be touched on in passing and selectively. Indeed, philosophical aesthetics in the twentieth and twenty-first centuries seems to have undergone, progressively and increasingly, an evolution not unlike that which has occurred in other areas of philosophy, to wit, philosophy of science or, even better, the philosophy of the different sciences: a process of progressive specialization and, at the same time, a reduction of the distance between philosophical analysis and the practices it addresses. Indeed, various *philosophies* of the different arts—for example, of literature, film, music, but also poetry, horror film, jazz music—have emerged. Less and less can aesthetics in the Anglo-American tradition be accused of being "armchair" philosophy or analysis of some alleged, simplistically construed "language of art criticism." Rather, for philosophical investigations on art it is now almost an imperative that they be conducted with sufficient awareness of actual artistic and art-critical practices, and with close attention to actual artistic examples. Related to such an evolution are two other characteristics of at least some contemporary aesthetic investigations: their relationship with other art-related disciplines, on the one hand, and their relationship with wholly other disciplines and programs, especially scientific ones, on the other. Paradigmatic of the former is the work currently done in philosophy of film and philosophy of literature, which have arguably inherited some of the questions that traditionally were central to film theory and literary theory (say, on what distinguishes cinema from other art forms, or on the role of authors, narrators, and characters in the appreciation of narratives). Paradigmatic of the latter is the influence of cognitive science on aesthetics (and, to an extent, of aesthetics on cognitive science), for instance, in addressing issues regarding the imaginative engagement between readers or viewers and narratives' characters. Finally, it should be noted how philosophical attention has also opened up to art forms of a mass or popular sort: from rock music to cinema, from television to comics, from pulp literature to advertising.

Much of what goes on in aesthetics today will not find adequate, if any, coverage in what follows. Rather, I here selectively concentrate on some of the most lively areas of aesthetic debate today, hoping to exemplify, through them, the above-mentioned trends. The issues are arranged, for the most part, in a progression from the most general ones to some rather more specific ones.

1. The aesthetic: Attitude, properties, and pleasure

Philosophical discussion on the "aesthetic" comprises different questions, albeit related ones, depending on whether the focus of the investigation is the experiences that are deemed aesthetic or the properties that such experiences focus upon and by which they are perhaps brought about. The loosely Kantian idea, that adopting a distinctive kind of attitude—an aesthetic attitude—is essential to making an experience an aesthetic one, was given renewed emphasis, in the twentieth century, by Edward Bullough, who claimed that an aesthetic attitude is one that centrally involves distance from practical concerns (Bullough 1912, which is widely anthologized). To give a contemporary example in illustration, think of looking through a polluted landscape where, indeed thanks to the pollutants floating in the air, objects acquire a softer look, light is diffused in interesting ways, shapes and colors change unexpectedly: an aesthetic attitude requires taking distance from, bracketing, setting aside, the noxious nature of those fumes. Whether the aesthetic attitude is best described in this or some other way (another classic reading is Stolnitz 1960, for which an aesthetic attitude is one of "contemplation"), it has certainly been subjected to criticism. Famously, George Dickie (1964) called it a "myth": once analyzed, he claimed, the so-called aesthetic attitude is not special at all, but is rather just a matter of close attention and focus on an object.

Aesthetic experiences may be made possible, or at least be qualified as aesthetic, in virtue of targeting aesthetic properties. These need not be limited to beauty and ugliness, and are usually conceived as comprising a wide range of properties, from formal ones (e.g., being "balanced"), to content-related ones ("realistic"), to expressive ones ("somber"), and so on. The most influential paper on aesthetic properties is Frank Sibley's 1959 "Aesthetic Concepts" (2001), in which the author offers a list of aesthetic properties, and proposes that they be understood as based on and rooted in, but not inferrable from, an object's more basic, nonaesthetic perceptual properties.[1] (A more recent, and quite comprehensive, mapping of aesthetic properties is found in Goldman 1995.) Sibley's appeal to *taste* as the capacity required to discern such properties left it mysterious how, on the ground of nonaesthetic perceptual properties, one manages to perceive aesthetic ones. Kendall Walton's claim that the correct perception of an artwork depends on the application of the appropriate "categories of art," of course, goes precisely in the direction of specifying some of the factors that are at play in the experience of an artwork's aesthetic properties. The distinction between aesthetic and nonaesthetic properties has been questioned by Ted Cohen (1973) and Marcia Eaton (1994), who have differently argued that, for so-called aesthetic qualities, nonaesthetic applications can be easily found, and for so-called nonaesthetic qualities, aesthetic applications.

If aesthetic properties can indeed be individuated, they may be thought to help us in explaining the value of art as well as the aesthetic value of parts of nature; we attribute beauty, for instance, to paintings as well as to natural scenes. This has suggested—as in the tradition that emphasizes the role of aesthetic experience and aesthetic attitude—that aesthetic properties are independent of and conceptually prior to art; after all, beautiful landscapes existed long before paintings—and paintings of beautiful landscapes among them. Recently, however, Berys Gaut (2007) has articulated a view of aesthetic properties that in a sense makes them depend on art.[2] Aesthetic properties are evaluative properties, he claims; specifically, they are properties that make an object valuable as art. Natural objects, too, can have some of those properties; and certainly one need not be cognizant of this or any other view of aesthetic properties to appreciate them individually. However, what makes them unified under the concept of the aesthetic is, for Gaut, ultimately a relation to art.

One strand of the discussion regarding aesthetic properties is ontological: are they real properties? Do they actually exist independently of our conceiving of them? A *realist* position, affirming that aesthetic properties do exist, and exist in a mind-independent way, has been defended, for example, by Nick Zangwill (2001) and Jerrold Levinson (2006). By contrast, Goldman (1995) defends a sophisticated form of *antirealism*, one that emphasizes the irreducibility of certain aesthetic disagreements, specifically—and most damagingly for the realist stance, in Goldman's view—disagreements among "ideal critics."[3]

The issue of the aesthetic encompasses also the question of aesthetic pleasure: out of the many pleasures one can have in life, what is distinctive of those we deem aesthetic? Specifically, what distinguishes merely sensory pleasures—say, the pleasure derived from chewing on a candy or being massaged or having an orgasm—from aesthetic pleasures as had from looking at a painting or reading a novel or staring at an iceberg? Levinson (1996) has characterized aesthetic pleasure as deriving from an attention not just to an object's qualities—for example, the spatial balance manifested in a painting or, say, its insightful treatment of a subject—but also from the unique complex of lower-level properties that brings about such qualities. Though Levinson's focus is on works of art, an extension to nature seems warranted. Hence, similarly perhaps, an aesthetic pleasure prompted by a natural object, such as the iceberg, cannot be limited to enjoying the pleasing-to-the-eye shapes and colors, but must derive from reflecting upon what makes the iceberg be what it is and look what it looks like.[4]

Regarding art, there is in Levinson an emphasis on the unique *manner* in which an artwork brings about its content and character, an awareness of which must be integral to the aesthetic appreciation of a work. It is then not surprising that Levinson (2006) would also argue for the impossibility of pornographic (as opposed to erotic) art: when an item is projected—and hence, most likely used and enjoyed—pornographically, for the purpose of sexual arousal, an item is necessarily not projected as art. The pornographic use and enjoyment, we could say, is simply too oblivious to the formal features of a work that bring about the intended, nonaesthetic, pleasure. This thesis, in opposition to what was earlier argued by Matthew Kieran (e.g., 2005), has been at the center of a small but growing debate, once again proving the vitality of contemporary aesthetics and the richness of its interests (see Levinson and Maes, eds. Forthcoming).

Indeed, aesthetics owes part of its richness to its capacity for enlarging its scope to questions that are neither about art traditionally conceived nor about nature. Hence, nowadays we encounter aestheticians interested in the philosophy of food and drink (Korsmeyer 1999), the philosophy of humor and jokes (Morreall, ed. 1987; Cohen 1999), and the aesthetics of the everyday (Saito 2007).

2. Definitions of art

The question "What is art?" became all the more pressing in the twentieth century due to the development of various avant-garde artistic movements. Since the early 1900s, artists seemed to become less and less interested in producing items endowed with aesthetic qualities and conducive to aesthetic experiences as traditionally understood. (Artists interested in *ready-mades* or in the art of the *found object* in fact seem more interested in recontextualizing and reconceptualizing objects than in producing or creating them, in a strict sense.) Such developments naturally represent a challenge for aesthetic theories of Beardsley's sort, which link artistic status to the capacity for bringing about aesthetic experiences.[5] Indeed, under the influence of the philosophy of the later

Wittgenstein, and in response to the revolutionary spirit of much mid-twentieth-century art, skepticism regarding the possibility of offering a definition of art arose. In an influential and still widely anthologized essay, "The Role of Theory in Aesthetics" (1956), Morris Weitz (1916–1981) claimed that the creative character of art—in virtue of which new styles, artistic movements, art forms, and so on continuously emerge—makes the concept of art and its related subconcepts (e.g., "novel," "tragedy," "comedy," "painting," "portraiture") "open concepts," allowing for no explicit definition (much as with Wittgenstein's famous example of "game"). Of new objects it is decided whether or not they fall under such concepts only thanks to "strands of similarity" (or what Wittgenstein called "family resemblances") between them and other objects that have already been categorized that way. And sometimes a new concept, though related to already existing subconcepts of art, will have to be invented, as when some of Alexander Calder's work cannot quite be called a "sculpture," and is hence dubbed a "mobile." Any attempt at indicating a set of necessary conditions (unless aimed at some special purpose, as with concepts like "(extant) Greek tragedy," which allows for no new cases, and can thus be "closed") will always have to face possible counterexamples of works that, although undoubtedly works of art, or sculpture, or what have you, fail to satisfy such conditions. Further, we must recognize, for Weitz, that "art" and its subconcepts have both a descriptive and an evaluative use: by the former, we differentiate an item from items of a different kind (say, a novel from such other types of writing, such as medical handbooks or historical essays); by the latter, we praise the object. And we often do both things at once. Definitions of art, such as "art is expression" or "art is form" (see Chapters 8 and 9), which at the descriptive level are doomed to fail, ought rather to be recognized as evaluative, "honorific definitions," which ultimately recommend certain ways of making art, and are valuable in helping to focus debate over criteria of evaluation that would otherwise be overlooked.

A contemporary and somewhat different proposal that denies art the possibility of being defined is Gaut's "cluster" account of arthood (see Carroll, ed. 2000): an artifact or a performance—being the product of an action is the only necessary condition all artworks must fulfill, for Gaut—is a work of art when it possesses features comprised in one of several "clusters" of jointly sufficient features for arthood (say, possessing positive aesthetic properties, being expressive, being intellectually challenging, etc.). The list of possible clusters and of possible features, however, necessarily remains open, and new features and new clusters are always possible in the future.

The real turn in definitional attempts came with the *institutional* theory of art, found somewhat embryonically in Arthur Danto's 1964 landmark essay, "The Artworld," but which received its canonic formulation in Dickie (1974). In a nutshell, the theory claims that the status of art is *conferred* upon an item by members of that institution that can be called "the artworld." This allows for a ready-made like a snow shovel, which would otherwise belong to a hardware store, to be turned into a work of art—known as *In Advance of the Broken Arm* (1915)—when an artist like Marcel Duchamp presents it for exhibiting, or an art curator includes it in an exhibition, or an art critic writes an essay about it, for those acts implicitly or explicitly confer upon the item its artistic status. Dickie (1984) himself later reformulated his view in ways that in fact downplay the institutional character of the artworld—which indeed does not seem to have the characteristics of an institution—and foreground what he calls the "inflected" (or mutually involving) nature of art and associated concepts.

Whatever the specifics of the versions of the institutional theory, its break from the more traditional definition is that of not pointing to some quality or function—be it representation, expression, or the capacity of eliciting aesthetic experiences—but rather to a relation between artworks and some background situation. Once the relation between artworks and this background situation is construed not in terms of a quasi-institutional artworld but rather in terms of art's concrete past, the major alternative to the institutional theory, the *historical* definition, emerges. Originally proposed by Levinson in his 1979 "Defining Art Historically" (2011), the historical (or intentional-historical) approach is still at the center of contemporary debate. Roughly, in Levinson's proposal, which he has been refining in subsequent essays (1996, 2006), the artistic status of an item derives from the intention of the maker of the artwork, which—although not necessarily art-aware—successfully links the item to the preceding history of art. Specifically, something is an artwork if the work is intended for one or more of the "ways of regard" (ways of being treated, assessed, received) in which items previously recognized as works of art have been properly regarded: say, with a painting, being looked at for certain color features, appreciated for balance, engaged with for its expressivity, among many other things.

Stephen Davies has proposed an influential framing of definitional attempts (1991), centered on the distinction between "functional" and "procedural" definitions (paradigmatic of the former is Beardsley's aesthetic definition, and of the latter, Dickie's institutional definition), with historical definitions representing a third type of approach (one that, for Davies, suffers from leaving unspecified whether its central reference is to historically evolved functions or procedures). Davies himself shows a preference for an institutional, hence procedural, account, though one that he tentatively qualifies through reference to both the historical development of the institutions proper of the artworld and a limited appeal to aesthetic function. On the other hand, Robert Stecker much more explicitly combines the historical with the functional approach in his "historical functionalist" theory (1997).

3. Ontology of art

Perhaps the most basic fact about works of art is that they are *artifacts* in a broad sense (broad because the "making" of an artwork may just amount to the recontextualizing of a ready-made or found object *and* because conceptual art may have at its core the formulation of ideas, categories, thoughts, rather than the production of any artifact narrowly understood).[6] Beyond this basic fact, however, artworks exhibit the most remarkable ontological diversity. The ontological issue is largely coincident with that of distinguishing between different types or modes of art. Discussion has proceeded in terms of a number of fundamental distinctions, the first and most natural one being that between *singular* and *multiple* art forms. Paradigmatic of the former are painting and carved sculpture: the work has only one instance, say, the painted piece of canvas or the shaped block of marble that is in front of us. Paradigmatic of the latter are literature (including theater), music (including opera), cast sculpture, etching, engraving, photography, film, and dance. Of course, what counts as a multiple artwork may depend on the artistic conventions internal to a practice and sometimes to a specific artistic project. Architecture, for instance, though having all the potentials for being a multiple art form, most often is taken to produce site-specific works, or at least works that are bound to a construction process, and hence unique, singular works. (Saint Peter's in Rome seems bound to its specific site and, if an Egyptian pyramid preserves its identity in spite of relocation, it does so because of a link to the original construction process.) Further, what is true of the paradigm cases of an art form might fail to be true of some variations of the same art: Polaroid photos, for example, are singular, not multiple. The singular/multiple art distinction is normally accepted, with the notable exception of Gregory Currie's (1988) claim that, in principle, all art forms are multiple. Currie invites us to imagine a world where superxerox machines exist, capable of duplicating, molecule-by-molecule, say, a painting, hence showing, he argues, that art forms like painting are singular only contingently (for criticism, see Carroll 1998, Levinson 1996; for a more sympathetic critique, see D. Davies 2004).[7]

Among those arts that are normally considered multiple, the production of the instances of the work may happen in fairly different ways. Accordingly, the principles of individuation of proper instances of a work vary radically. Within some arts—paradigmatically literature and classical music—we find *notations*; in others—say, etching or cinema—we do not. The identity of a novel, for example, seems to be preserved by a word-for-word (including punctuation) correspondence with the original, and one that can be compatible with great differences in features that are irrelevant to both the work's identity and aesthetic value, say, the fonts used throughout different prints of the same novel. By contrast, a film screening or a cast statue is an instance of a work in virtue of having being produced from a template of sorts (Carroll 1998): the film stock (which, of course, might itself be one of the many prints of a film) or the statue's mold.

A distinction of crucial importance within the multiple arts is that between those for which the realization of a work requires a *performance* and those for which no performance is possible. The distinction is a general one: of etching, for example, we can say that, although a multiple art, it does not require and cannot receive a performance, but only an instancing. Yet the distinction becomes especially relevant when applied to those multiple arts for which some notation exists. A novel, so it seems, is accessed with no need of a performance; plays and symphonies (which have notations in scripts and scores) are instead accessed through performances, which in some sense realize the work.

What seems crucial of performances is that they require or amount to *interpretations* and that they can be judged artistically in their own right: there are good and bad performances of *Hamlet*, for example. The notion of performance has been widely investigated (D. Davies 2011 is the most recent work on the matter), especially with respect to music (see, for example, S. Davies 1994, Kivy 1998, and Levinson 2011). Interestingly, however, the role of performance in other arts, for example, the "performance" of reading a poem, even of reading it to oneself, has also been explored (Kivy 2006). David Davies (2004) has argued that *all* works of art, even those outside of the classical paradigm, are to be considered performances, specifically, performances by the artists who produced them. On the other hand, not all music qualifies as a performing art, or not in the same way. For example, of rock songs it has been argued that their identity is bound to the studio recording a band or singer produced as the master of a work (Gracyk 1996). If so, then rock songs would have an ontological status that is not so different, in this respect, from that of movies.

It is worth mentioning that the real-world identity of a work may not always be fully determinate and compliant to the paradigms of theory (not even of theory that in earnest tries to account for actual artistic practice): of Shakespeare's plays there exist significantly different texts, and a filmmaker may offer differently edited versions of the same film.

4. Art interpretation

Theories of interpretation—answers to the question of what, if anything, determines the correct interpretation of a work or the work's meaning broadly construed—have been developed primarily with respect to literature. Yet, the issue is clearly relevant to engagement with artworks produced in any art form or medium. When we appreciate an artwork, hence value it as a work of art, the appreciation or evaluation targets *the work* and *its* features only if such features, or at least their artistic relevance, are correctly attributed to it. Relatedly, interpretations of artworks may—indeed one would expect they would—open up opportunities for artistic appreciation, by calling attention to artistic features that would have otherwise passed unnoticed.

The primary division on the issue of interpretation, at least within Anglo-American aesthetics, is that between intentionalism (or more precisely, actual intentionalism) and anti-intentionalism, with the former being the view according to which the meaning of a work constitutively depends on the author's or artist's intention. A classic defense of intentionalism was offered by E. D. Hirsch (1967), while more recent defenses comprise those by Noël Carroll, Gary Iseminger, Steven Knapp, and Walter Benn Michaels (conveniently assembled in Iseminger, ed. 1992) and Paisley Livingston (2005). The debate over intentionalism revolves in part around how best to understand the notion of intention, and on the possibility for a work to fail to have the meaning the artist intended, without thereby being meaningless, and for works to have meanings their producers never intended them to have.

Anti-intentionalism may take what can be called a *formalist* direction, along the lines suggested by Wimsatt and Beardsley in their famous paper (see Chapter 13, on Beardsley) and the New Criticism school in general: the meaning is *in* the work itself and, quite independently of the author's intentions, it is to be discovered and extracted *from* the text alone. A contemporary defender of an approach of this sort, though one more nuanced than that associated with the New Critics, is Daniel Nathan (in Iseminger, ed. 1992). The debate on this type of view naturally concentrates on whether the very notion of meaning, as applied to literature and art in general, can be severed from at least some appeal to intentionality.

Anti-intentionalism can also take a *constructivist* direction, one that emphasizes the role of the reader or critic in projecting meanings on to a work.[8] A contemporary defender of the constructivist approach is Michael Krausz (in Iseminger, ed. 1992), who to some extent follows Joseph Margolis (see, for example, Margolis 1995). It can be here noted only in passing that, of course, not all constructivist views are alike; most notably, while Krausz, like Richard Rorty (1931–2007), for example, concentrates on the meaning-producing power of the reader who approaches a text, Stanley Fish sees instead the production of meaning as residing in entire interpretive communities. One concern with respect to constructivism has to do with its perhaps admitting too much in terms of what count as acceptable interpretations, including for instance, anachronistic interpretations (something that Wollheim 1980 notes as a fatal objection to this approach).[9]

In addition to contributing to a better understanding of the notion of intention, progress in this area has been facilitated by at least two other developments: attention to the existence of different *levels* of meaning and attention to the different *aims* that may be part of the interpretive critical enterprise. There is a basic, textual level of meaning, amounting to the meaning of a word sequence according to the conventions of language; such *word-sequence* or *textual* meaning need not be the same at the *utterer's* meaning, the meaning a speaker (writer, artist) intends to convey by the use of an utterance (which, of course, is here just short for, say, a whole novel or, more generally, work of art). Yet, the meaning of the utterance in its context of production—*utterance* meaning—need not coincide with the meaning *intended* by the utterer. Finally, what can be dubbed *ludic meaning* (from the Latin for "play") encompasses meanings an utterance may be seen as suggesting under possible, and often rather adventurous, construals. The above-summarized distinctions are suggested by Levinson (in Iseminger, ed. 1992), who defends a middle-ground position between those characterized above, one that regards *utterance meaning* as the notion central to the enterprise of interpreting a literary work and artworks in general. Levinson's *hypothetical intentionalism* identifies the meaning of a work with what is delivered by an optimal projection of meaning—that is, a hypothesis of intended meaning that is best attributed to the artist/author in question. Such projecting or hypothesizing must occur in light of all relevant, meaning-influencing considerations: the artist's actual intention, the artist's overall oeuvre, the historical context of the work's production, and so on, and in light of the type of work (say, a painting or, perhaps more specifically, a portrait) the artist actually intended to produce.

Which approach to art interpretation is preferable might partly depend on the different aims of an interpretive enterprise, as argued by Stecker (2003). And different criteria of correctness or acceptability perhaps apply to different aims. In any event, the question of what determines the meaning of artworks ought to be distinguished from the question of the possible truth of so-called *critical pluralism* (as opposed to *critical monism*): can some works allow for multiple and yet not reconcilable interpretations? (Krausz, ed. 2002). One way of defending an affirmative answer is by pointing to the interest of not limiting the interpretive investigation of works just to interpretations that are true, but rather expand it to interpretations that, though not true, are otherwise acceptable (Stecker 2003). Indeed, perhaps one of the central values of art is what can be called "interpretation-centered" value: a work's capacity, that is, to notably engage our interpretive abilities (Stecker 1997).

5. Affective engagement with fictions and narratives

Affective engagement is often central to our encounters with art. Some works are said to express emotions.[10] Often, perceiving (reading, viewing, listening to) an artwork provokes a variety of affective states in us, with emotions, moods, and desires being the most central ones. Indeed, responding in a variety of ways seems to be part and parcel of properly apprehending many artworks. And, of course, it is common experience to bond with fictional characters and come to care for them. Within the representational arts, most typically with narrative works, affective engagement prompts several philosophical issues, most prominently these: the so-called paradox of fiction, that is, the apparent paradox of our having emotional responses toward characters and events that we know to be fictional (see Chapter 17, on Walton); the paradox of negative emotions, that is, of how it can possibly be desirable to experience prima facie unpleasant or painful emotions, such as pity toward a fallen hero or fear for a monster (see, respectively, Budd 1995, and Carroll 1990); and the exploration of the types of imaginative, affective mechanisms of engagement that narratives and their characters invite.

At the origin of contemporary debate on the paradox of fiction is a famous paper by Colin Radford (1975, followed by a series of other papers by the same author), arguing that our responding to fictions ultimately commits us to irrationality. In rejecting Radford's type of conclusion, most contemporary debate has turned around two approaches, roughly: Walton's *make-believe theory*, for which at least some responses to fictions have a make-believe status and the *thought theory*, for which emotional responses to fictional characters and events target thoughts or unasserted propositional contents, say, the thought that Desdemona is being killed by Othello (Lamarque 1981; Carroll 1990; Dadlez 1997). Recent developments have also emphasized the importance of distinguishing between different kinds of emotional responses, say, between a viewer's self-oriented response of fear for oneself (for instance, as prompted by a fictional monster portrayed in a movie) and the viewer's other-oriented response of pity for a character (Neill 1993).

The paradox of negative emotions (addressed by Levinson with respect to music in a very influential 1982 paper [2011]), with respect to horror has been given a cognitivist solution by Carroll (1990). Audiences, he claims, are attracted to horror fictions, in spite of the unpleasantness of being scared of/disgusted by some monster (which for Carroll is essential to horror), out of curiosity toward the nature of the monster and, quite typically at least, by the "erotetic" (from the Greek for "questioning") nature of such narratives, which raise, and then often answer, a multitude of questions, including the overarching question of whether humankind will be able to prevail over the monstrous presence. The more classical version of the paradox of negative emotions, however, is the one targeting tragedy (see Chapter 4, on Hume). To the paradox of tragedy Susan Feagin (1983) has offered a "metaresponse" solution: we don't enjoy feeling fear and pity with respect to the tragic events and hero, but we do enjoy responses about those responses, since such metaresponses allow us to recognize ourselves as being capable of caring for others. An articulate and nuanced solution to the paradox is offered by Budd (1995), who emphasizes how the suffering the engagement with tragedies brings about is inextricably bound to what we value in the experience of a tragedy: a heightened understanding of the reality of human life, made of a first-person insight into ways of suffering and of an increased comprehension of reality offered by the play as a whole, together with an admiration for the hero's character traits and quality of consciousness and for the writer's capacity of looking at the most tragic aspects of life without falling into despair.

It is worth noting how reference to the affective responses that certain types of narratives necessarily or typically prompt has been used, much in Aristotelian fashion, to elucidate the essential nature of some genres, especially in film. As for Aristotle a tragedy aims at fear and pity, so it can be argued, horror aims at some complex of fear and disgust, melodrama at a compound of pity and admiration, comedy at amusement, and a variety of works in what is called the "suspense" genre at the emotion of the same name (see, for example, Carroll 1990).

One of the many issues regarding the relationship between art and emotion is that of the kinds of engagement narrative readers, viewers, or listeners, depending on the medium, entertain with narrative characters and situations, something that the layperson would often describe by mentioning some vague form of "identification." Some thinkers, most notably, Currie (e.g., in Levinson, ed. 1998), Feagin (1996), and Smith (1995), have differently appealed to the notion of mental simulation, developed within the philosophy of mind and cognitive science debates on our capacity to attribute mental states to others, to explain what they consider an important form of engagement with narratives.[11] Roughly, these thinkers emphasize the importance, to a proper understanding and full appreciation of a narrative, of a certain kind of imaginative projection, some form of "getting in the shoes" of characters and more generally of getting oneself into a fictional scenario. Hence, besides the appeal to mental simulation, these approaches, which can synthetically be dubbed the "participant view" (Giovannelli 2008), can be seen as more generally emphasizing an important role for empathy and other forms of projective imagination into fictional situations. Opposed to this general approach is what can be called the "onlooker view," championed especially by Carroll (1990, 1998) and Kieran (in Kieran and Lopes, eds. 2003), who similarly emphasize how projecting oneself into a character's mind or situation is most often unneeded, when not positively a hindrance, to a proper and full engagement with a narrative. Although the debate continues, the distance between the two positions might have been partly reduced by clarifying that there exists a plurality of forms of imaginative engagement with characters and situations (see, for example, Carroll 2010 and Currie's essay in Kieran, ed. 2006; see also Giovannelli 2008).

6. Some dimensions of artistic value

Contemporary aesthetic debate has also addressed questions regarding the kinds of values artworks may have and the possible relationships between such values. The two main issues are the *epistemic* issue, of what, if anything, we can learn from art, and the *art-critical* issue, of whether and how values of an epistemic or a moral sort ever bear on a work's artistic value.

The view that art can have important cognitive, epistemic roles—that it can and perhaps should be a vehicle and instrument for knowledge— was already contained in Horace's (first century BCE) maxim that art ought "to delight and instruct" (see also Chapters 1 and 2, on Plato and Aristotle). Yet, the opposite view, *aestheticism*, which the "art for art's sake" motto of such nineteenth-century figures as Charles Baudelaire and Oscar Wilde epitomizes, also has a long tradition. Aestheticism insists on the necessity for art to be made and judged according to strictly artistic criteria, condemning the attribution of any other duties to art and artists, most notably duties toward truth and moral goodness (see also Chapter 9, on Fry and Bell). Recent analytic aesthetics includes, if greatly revisited, positions that are representatives of both approaches.

Those who believe in art's capacity to convey insights or contribute to knowledge have primarily, though not exclusively, concentrated on insights and knowledge of an ethical kind. Representational artworks, especially of a narrative kind, are claimed to have the ability to contribute to the moral understanding and character of their readers, viewers, or listeners. Among the most notable views are those of such authors as Martha Nussbaum (1990), who, within the articulation of an Aristotelian moral approach, claims literature to be, by its ability to represent the full complexity of moral situations, a necessary component of moral philosophy; Richard Eldridge (1989), who, starting from a Kantian approach, with subtlety and richness of examples sees in some literary works pivotal opportunities for us to develop an adequate understanding of ourselves as moral agents; and Currie (in S. Davies, ed. 1997 and Levinson, ed. 1998), who attributes to fiction, for the way it engages our imagination, a practical role in refining our understanding of others, of ourselves, and of morally relevant situations.[12]

Objections to the possibility for art to convey knowledge have mostly focused on knowledge of a propositional kind (as opposed to knowledge of practical, experiential, or "know-how" kinds), to the effect that art never makes statements about the world (T. J. Diffey in S. Davies, ed. 1997), or that whichever truths an artwork might convey are doomed to be trivial, or that beliefs expressed by works of art, even when true, cannot find in the works themselves the required justification for them to qualify as knowledge (Stolnitz 1992). Several authors have presented arguments against these claims. Budd (1995), for example, with special reference to poetry, emphasizes poems' ability to express beliefs and views of life, which a reader may perceive as true or false, as corresponding or failing to correspond to reality. Carroll (in Levinson, ed. 1998) concentrates on the triviality charge, distinguishing between the acquisition of new knowledge—which, he concedes, is rarely what art contributes—and an improved understanding of knowledge we already have. Gaut (2007) takes up the task of defending the claim that art can be a source of bona fide knowledge by providing the necessary justification, or more generally confirmation, for the claims it conveys. Key to Gaut's reasoning is the role of certain engagements of the imagination: a novel like William Styron's *Sophie's Choice*, he argues, thanks to how it engages the reader's imagination can not just claim but also confirm that moral dilemmas are real.

The art-critical issue, of whether cognitive or moral merits or demerits of a work ever count toward its artistic assessment, has often been discussed with respect to what could be called *transformative* merits/demerits: whether a work improves or confuses one's understanding, whether it is morally educational or corruptive (in addition to the above-mentioned works by Carroll and Gaut, see, for example, Kieran in Bermúdez and Gardner, eds. 2003). That is, the art-critical issue has often been addressed in relation to the epistemic issue. Yet, a work may be flawed or sound, ethically or otherwise, without having, and independently of, any substantial capacity to corrupt or ameliorate those who engage with it. Hence, since the issue has been mostly addressed with respect to moral, rather than more generally epistemic, evaluation, progress in this area could be achieved by specifying the *kind* of ethical judgment that is being addressed. Consider that artworks can be ethically judged in a number of different ways, most notably perhaps (1) for the perspective they embody; (2) for the consequences on those who engage with them; and (3) for the way they were produced (Giovannelli 2007). Hence, the art-critical issue can be raised with respect to a range of evaluations that exceeds the scope suggested by the epistemic issue.

When addressed with respect to ethical evaluation, the art-critical issue amounts to asking whether the art-critical practice known as ethical criticism is legitimate: is it ever appropriate to consider an artwork's ethical merits or demerits as relevant to the overall judgment of the work as art? Specifically, should a work's being in some sense ethically praise- or blame-worthy be considered, respectively, a good- or bad-making feature of the work, at least in some cases? The recent revival of the question of ethical criticism is to be credited mostly to Wayne Booth (1988), who among other things convincingly argued that ethical criticism had disappeared more from theory than from actual literary critical practice. In the past fifteen years or so, a range of positions addressing the ethical criticism of art has been defended. In brief, and somewhat roughly, *autonomist* positions deny the existence of a relation between ethical and artistic value, such that the former can be considered a dimension of or at least somewhat intimately related to the latter. The value of artworks is so to speak shielded from these other sorts of considerations; hence that a work, say, includes some moral insight or is instead potentially corruptive, embodies an ethically praise- or blame-worthy perspective, and so on are all claims that nothing have to do with its artistic value. It should be noted that autonomists need not deny that ethical considerations may enter the process of artistic evaluation: they just need to insist on their artistic irrelevance as such (see, for example, Peter Lamarque in Kieran, ed. 2006 and Anderson and Dean 1998). Further, even a view that allows for the possible bearing of ethical evaluation on artistic evaluation, yet denies that the relation between the two kinds of values is in any way systematic (one work might be artistically better because of an ethical merit, another be artistically worse for the same reason, and yet another work be unaffected by its ethical status), may be argued to be ultimately a form of autonomism (Giovannelli 2007; a paradigmatic example of such a view is Daniel Jacobson's "anti-theoretical" position, in Kieran, ed. 2006).

In contrast to autonomism, *moralist* positions do accept the artistic or aesthetic relevance of ethical evaluation (see, for example, Budd 1995, the essays by Carroll, Karen Hanson, Mary Deveraux, and Gaut in Levinson, ed. 1998, and Gaut 2007). Carroll's defense of the relevance of the ethical dimension is based on the claim that certain works may fail to receive the intended uptake, at least among morally sensitive audiences, because of immorality (e.g., the immorality of a hero for whom the work is attempting to elicit sympathy). Gaut's thesis, which he names *ethicism*, establishes a much more systematic relationship between the two kinds of values than Carroll's view: when aesthetically relevant, moral merits or demerits *are* aesthetic merits or demerits, and quite independently of how audiences in fact respond to the work; what matters for Gaut is not the responses a work receives, but whether the work *merits* the responses it aims at.

Overall, the debate on ethical criticism has suffered from lack of clarity on how best to identify the different kinds of positions—that is, the different strands of autonomism and moralism—though some criteria-driven taxonomies have been offered by Gaut (2007) and Giovannelli (2007). While both of them emphasize, under different terminology, the importance of distinguishing between views that claim for the existence of a systematic relationship between ethical and artistic merits/demerits and views that deny such relationship, Giovannelli also emphasizes the importance of distinguishing between theories that accept the existence of such a systematic relationship across the realm of art (as Gaut's ethicism, or what can also be called "radical moralism," does) and more "moderate" moralist approaches, which maintain the systematic relationship to obtain only within certain artistic genres, but not within all of them.

Notes

1 Sibley's proposals are discussed, in the attempt to also move the debate forward, in Brady and Levinson, eds. 2001.

2 For another view that gives conceptual priority to art over nature, see Chapter 15, on Wollheim.

3 It is here relevant, of course, to look at Chapter 4, on Hume.

4 On the appreciation of nature, see, most notably the work done by Allen Carlson (e.g., 2000) and Malcolm Budd (2002).

5 That is not to suggest that the aesthetic approach has been altogether abandoned by all; Zangwill (2001), for instance, has proposed a sophisticated version of the aesthetic theory.

6 For some recent work on conceptual art, see the essays in (Goldie and Schellekens, eds. 2007).

7 A related issue regarding multiple art forms is the ontological status of the work within them: that is, whether the work is best understood as a class (Goodman 1976), a type (Wollheim 1980), or a kind (Wolterstorff 1980).

8 Though not belonging to the Anglo-American tradition in its dominant, analytic approach, the "death of the author" proposal of Roland Barthes (1915–1980), which goes in the direction of constructivism, is certainly not ignored by contemporary, analytic debate; see Barthes (1977).

9   It should be noted that not every attribution of meaning that was not accessible at the time of work production is to be construed as flat-out anachronistic; indeed, some such attributions may be acceptable even to nonconstructivist views (see Levinson 2011).

10 The role of emotional expression in art has been investigated especially with respect to music (see, for example, Budd 1985, S. Davies 1994, and Levinson 2011).

11 See also Walton (Forthcoming) and Walton's and Currie's essays in (Hjort and Laver, eds. 1997).

12 See also Feagin's contribution (S. Davies, ed. 1997) in which she emphasizes the role literature can play in an *emotional* form of learning, a learning about the emotions as well as through the emotions, and one which is not fully reducible to the acquisition of new beliefs.

References

Anderson, James, and Jeffrey Dean. 1998. "Moderate Autonomism." *British Journal of Aesthetics*, 38, 150–166.

Barthes, Roland. 1977. *Image-Music-Text*. New York: Hill and Wang.

Bermúdez, J. L., and Sebastian Gardner, eds. 2003. *Art and Morality*. London: Routledge.

Booth, Wayne. 1988. *The Company We Keep: An Ethics of Fiction*. Berkeley, CA: University of California Press.

Brady, Emily, and Jerrold Levinson, eds. 2001. *Aesthetic Concepts: Essays after Sibley*. Oxford: Oxford University Press.

Budd, Malcolm. 1985. *Music and the Emotions: The Philosophical Theories*. London: Routledge.

—. 1995. *Values of Art: Pictures, Poetry and Music*. London: Penguin Books.

—. 2002. *The Aesthetic Appreciation of Nature: Essays on the Aesthetics of Nature*. Oxford: Clarendon Press.

Bullough, Edward. 1912. "'Psychical Distance' as a Factor in Art and an Aesthetic Principle." *British Journal of Psychology*, 5, 87–98.

Carlson, Allen. 2000. *Aesthetics and the Environment*. London: Routledge.

Carroll, Noël. 1990. *The Philosophy of Horror: Or Paradoxes of the Heart*. New York: Routledge.

—. 1998. *A Philosophy of Mass Art*. Oxford: Oxford University Press.

—. 2010. *Art in Three Dimensions*. Oxford: Oxford University Press.

Carroll, Noël, ed. 2000. *Theories of Art Today*. Madison: University of Wisconsin Press.

Cohen, Ted. 1973. "Aesthetic/Non-Aesthetic and the Concept of Taste: A Critique of Sibley's Position." *Theoria*, 39, 113–152.

—. 1999. *Jokes: Philosophical Thoughts on Joking Matters.* Chicago: University of Chicago Press.

Currie, Gregory. 1988. *An Ontology of Art.* London: Macmillan.

Dadlez, Eva. 1997. *What's Hecuba to Him? Fictional Events and Actual Emotions.* University Park, PA: Pennsylvania State University Press.

Davies, David. 2004. *Art as Performance.* Malden, MA: Blackwell.

—. 2011. *Philosophy of the Performing Arts.* Oxford: Wiley-Blackwell.

Davies, Stephen. 1991. *Definitions of Art.* Ithaca, NY: Cornell University Press.

—. 1994. *Musical Works and Performances.* Oxford: Oxford University Press.

Davies, Stephen, ed. 1997. *Art and Its Messages: Meaning, Morality, and Society.* University Park, PA: Pennsylvania State University Press.

Dickie, George. 1964. "The Myth of the Aesthetic Attitude." *American Philosophical Quarterly*, 1, 56–65.

—. 1974. *Art and the Aesthetic: An Institutional Analysis.* Ithaca, NY: Cornell University Press.

—. 1984. *The Art Circle.* New York: Haven.

Eaton, Marcia. 1994. "The Intrinsic, Non-Supervenient Nature of Aesthetic Properties." *Journal of Aesthetics and Art Criticism*, 52, 383–397.

Eldridge, Richard. 1989. *On Moral Personhood: Philosophy, Literature, Criticism, and Self-Understanding.* Chicago: University of Chicago Press.

Feagin, Susan. 1983. "The Pleasures of Tragedy." *American Philosophical Quarterly*, 20, 95–104.

—. 1996. *Reading With Feeling: The Aesthetics of Appreciation.* Ithaca, NY: Cornell University Press.

Gaut, Berys. 2007. *Art, Emotion and Ethics.* Oxford: Oxford University Press.

Giovannelli, Alessandro. 2007. "The Ethical Criticism of Art: A New Mapping of the Territory." *Philosophia*, 35, 117–127.

—. 2008. "In and Out: The Dynamics of Imagination in the Engagement with Narratives." *Journal of Aesthetics and Art Criticism*, 66, 11–24.

Goldie, Peter, and Elisabeth Schellekens, eds. 2007. *Philosophy and Conceptual Art.* Oxford: Oxford University Press.

Goldman, Alan. 1995. *Aesthetic Value.* Boulder, CO: Westview Press.

Goodman, Nelson. 1976. *Languages of Art: An Approach to a Theory of Symbols*, 2nd edition. Indianapolis, IN: Hackett.

Gracyk, Thedore. 1996. *Rhythm and Noise: An Aesthetics of Rock Music.* Durham, NC: Duke University Press.

Hirsch, E. D. 1967. *Validity in Interpretation.* New Haven, CT: Yale University Press.

Hjort, Mette, and Sue Laver, eds. 1997. *Emotion and the Arts.* New York: Oxford University Press.

Iseminger, Gary, ed. 1992. *Intention and Interpretation.* Philadelphia, PA: Temple University Press.

Kieran, Matthew. 2005. *Revealing Art.* New York: Routledge.

Kieran, Matthew, ed. 2006. *Contemporary Debates in Aesthetics and the Philosophy of Art*. Oxford: Blackwell.

Kieran, Matthew, and Dominic Lopes, eds. 2003. *Imagination, Philosophy, and the Arts*. London: Routledge.

Kivy, Peter. 1998. *Authenticities: Philosophical Reflections on Musical Performance*. Ithaca, NY: Cornell University Press.

—. 2006. *The Performance of Reading: An Essay in the Philosophy of Literature*. Oxford: Blackwell.

Korsmeyer, Carolyn. 1999. *Making Sense of Taste: Food and Philosophy*. Ithaca, NY: Cornell University Press.

Krausz, Michael, ed. 2002. *Is There a Single Right Interpretation?* University Park, PA: Pennsylvania State University Press.

Lamarque, Peter. 1981. "How Can We Fear and Pity Fictions?" *British Journal of Aesthetics*, 21, 291–304.

Levinson, Jerrold. 1996. *The Pleasure of Aesthetics*. Ithaca, NY: Cornell University Press.

—. 2006. *Contemplating Art*. Oxford: Oxford University Press.

—. 2011. *Music, Art, and Metaphysics*. Reprinted with a new Introduction. Oxford: Oxford University Press.

Levinson, Jerrold, ed. 1998. *Aesthetics and Ethics: Essays at the Intersection*. Cambridge: Cambridge University Press.

Levinson, Jerrold, and Hans Maes, eds. Forthcoming. *Art and Pornography*. Oxford: Oxford University Press.

Livingston, Paisley. 2005. *Art and Intention: A Philosophical Study*. Oxford: Oxford University Press.

Margolis, Joseph. 1995. *Interpretation Radical but Not Unruly: The New Puzzle of the Arts and History*. Berkeley, CA: University of California Press.

Morreall, John, ed. 1987. *The Philosophy of Laughter and Humor*. Albany, NY: State University of New York Press.

Neill, Alex. 1993. "Fiction and the Emotions." *American Philosophical Quarterly*, 30, 1–13.

Nussbaum, Martha. 1990. *Love's Knowledge: Essays on Philosophy and Literature*. New York: Oxford University Press.

Radford, Colin. 1975. "How Can We Be Moved by the Fate of Anna Karenina?" *Proceedings of the Aristotelian Society*, Suppl. Vol. 49, 67–80.

Saito, Yuriko. 2007. *Everyday Aesthetics*. Oxford: Oxford University Press.

Sibley, Frank. 2001. *Approach to Aesthetics: Collected Papers in Philosophical Aesthetics*. J. Benson, B. Redfern, and J. R. Cox (eds.). Oxford: Clarendon Press.

Smith, Murray. 1995. *Engaging Characters: Fiction, Emotion, and the Cinema*. Oxford: Oxford University Press.

Stecker, Robert. 1997. *Artworks: Definition, Meaning, Value*. University Park, PA: Pennsylvania State University Press.

—. 2003. *Interpretation and Construction: Art, Speech, and the Law.* Oxford: Blackwell.

Stolnitz, Jerome. 1960. *Aesthetics and the Philosophy of Art Criticism.* Boston: Riverside.

—. 1992. "On the Cognitive Triviality of Art." *British Journal of Aesthetics,* 32, 191–200.

Walton, Kendall. Forthcoming. *In Other Shoes and Other Essays.* Oxford: Oxford University Press.

Weitz, Morris. 1956. "The Role of Theory in Aesthetics." *Journal of Aesthetics and Art Criticism,* 15, 27–35.

Wollheim, Richard. 1980. *Art and Its Objects,* 2nd edition. Cambridge: Cambridge University Press.

Wolterstorff, Nicholas. 1980. *Works and Worlds of Art.* Cambridge: Cambridge University Press.

Zangwill, Nick. 2001. *The Metaphysics of Beauty.* Ithaca, NY: Cornell University Press.

Index

Bold text indicates thinkers or periods to which a chapter is dedicated, and pages within such chapter.